THE
EXTRAORDINARY
ADMINISTRATOR
CAREER PROGRESSION FOR LAW FIRM MANAGERS

Paul A.C. Malliaté

ASSOCIATION OF LEGAL ADMINISTRATORS

Edited by Jay D. Strother with assistance from John J. Michalik and Susan Umbdenstock.

ISBN 0-9650429-3-6
Printed in Canada

Dedication

Publication of *The Extraordinary Administrator* is made possible through funds contributed to the Foundation of the Association of Legal Administrators in memory of David W. Brezina, 1996-1997 ALA President. His career in legal administration spanned more than 20 years, including a long-time position as Director of Administration at Brownstein Hyatt Farber & Strickland, P.C., in Denver, Colorado. At the time of his death in 1999, Brezina was serving as a FALA Trustee.

Table of Contents

FOREWORD

What career progression is available for legal administrators? How do those in the law firm management profession prepare themselves by education, experience, training and stature to provide greater value to their firms and to advance their personal and professional careers? How do they become extraordinary administrators?

Those were questions that the Trustees of the Foundation of the Association of Legal Administrators (FALA) had on their minds in 2001, as we weighed key issues relevant to legal management. A consensus rapidly emerged that direct answers to those questions were not readily available, and that a need existed for a concise, readable, straightforward, and thought-provoking guide or career development tool. That consensus, in turn, quickly evolved into definition of such a research project as a high FALA priority.

The definition and the priority were clear but an open question remained as to who could undertake the project and provide the perspective that would benefit all legal administrators. Despite the difficulty of the question, the project was well destined. In September 2001, one of the Foundation's Trustees, John Michalik, was a speaker at the annual conference of the Australian Legal Practice Management Association in Queensland, Australia. Another of the program speakers was Paul Malliaté, Regional Executive Officer — Asia Pacific, for Baker & McKenzie. Paul's topic was "Career Progression for Law Firm Managers," and in Paul's presentation John and, thereafter, the entire Board of Trustees saw the basis and the seed of the larger project we had in mind.

Our enthusiasm was matched by Paul's, and the project moved forward on an accelerated basis beginning in the spring of 2002 and culminating with this publication less than a year later. We believe we have met our goals and that *The Extraordinary Administrator* provides a wealth of practical ideas, suggestions and directions to help law firm management professionals unlock their true potential and give their careers solid direction.

It is fitting that the Foundation grant money that has supported the research and the ultimate publication of *The Extraordinary Administrator* came from funds contributed to FALA in memory of David W. Brezina. Dave served as international ALA President in 1996-1997 and was one of the organization's most respected members. His career in legal administration spanned more than 20 years, including a longtime position as Director of Administration at Brownstein Hyatt Farber & Strickland, P.C., in Denver, Colorado. In 1996, Dave was involved in a tragic bicycling accident resulting in paralysis and quadriplegia. Even as he fought this disability, he served his term as President of ALA with courage, distinction and vigor. At the time of his death in 1999 he was serving as a Trustee of FALA. Among his other attributes and qualities, Dave was a mentor and a teacher to many in law firm management and was the personification of the extraordinary administrator.

The Extraordinary Administrator marries the qualities of Dave Brezina with the expertise and insight of Paul Malliaté. It is a product that the Foundation Trustees feel addresses the questions we asked in 2001 and provides the road map for those seeking to advance their careers and become more valuable in their present and future positions. We hope you will find it so and that you will use the roadmap to chart your career and journey.

Michael J. Katos
President, FALA Board of Trustees
Houston, Texas
March 2003

ABOUT THE FOUNDATION OF THE ASSOCIATION OF LEGAL ADMINISTRATORS

The Foundation of the Association of Legal Administrators (FALA) is the educational, charitable and research affiliate of the Association of Legal Administrators (ALA). FALA's purposes and goals extend to the development and presentation of educational programs, research on the changing legal workplace and workforce, and increasing awareness of the value of professional law firm administrators. FALA also strives to promote other activities that advance legal management and that encourage service to the legal profession.

FALA's purposes and goals are met by carrying out the following objectives:

- Sponsor and publish research projects that explore key issues relevant to legal management.
- Provide aid, assistance, and advice to law schools in developing and implementing courses and programs of study related to legal administration;
- Demonstrate the value of professional law office management to the legal community.
- Present lectures, seminars, discussions, and similar endeavors in law office management and administration and related disciplines; and
- Sponsor, present, produce or finance programs to assist ALA members who volunteer their management expertise to assist nonprofit law-related organizations.

These objectives are carried out through a variety of programs and activities. For example, FALA sponsors an annual "Chapter Challenge Program" which makes incentive funding available to encourage ALA's chapters to develop innovative projects and products that benefit ALA members, contribute to the advancement of legal management, or provide needed services to the broader community.

In recent years, Chapter Challenge Program grants have supported projects such as the development of Web sites focusing on careers in law firms and other legal organizations; instructional and training materials for law firm inner-city internship programs; support for diversity enhancement and enrichment initiatives in law firms; prototype materials/modules for ALA chapter-level leadership training; and continuing education programs and symposia on law firm management in conjunction with law schools and local bar associations.

Major FALA research projects and publications include *A Business Skills Curriculum for Law Firm Associates*, which was developed under a two-year grant to the Center for Law Practice Strategy and Management at the George Washington University Law Center. This publication (and its training system) provides managing partners, partners, executive directors and law firm training directors with a comprehensive guide for teaching the 58 business, management and supervisory skills that the research identified as critical to the success and development of associates — and, hence, future partners — in private law firm practice.

FALA is governed by a five-person Board of Trustees and receives administrative support from ALA. It derives financial support from the proceeds of a Silent Auction at ALA's Annual Conference and Exposition; through donations from ALA chapters and other internal ALA groups, such as the organization's Large Firm Administrators' Caucus; by contributions from law firms, ALA members and other individuals; and through the generosity of a number of vendors and suppliers to the legal industry, including Pitney Bowes Management Services, the Xerox Corporation, and Hildebrandt Inc.

INTRODUCTION

Wings are a burden if you never fly.

In the same way that we can choose to be mediocre or average, so too we can choose to be extraordinary. If asked, most law firm managing partners would readily identify extraordinary administrators as the ones who get things done. They make things happen and they play a key role in shaping the firm's business agenda.

In short, they make a difference.

Whatever level of seniority you have and irrespective of the size of your firm, there are many similarities in relation to the key attributes for success. The definition of these essential qualities and, more importantly, the way one acquires and develops them, form the content of this book.

I started my professional services career as finance manager at a small/midsize law firm. Over the years, I moved through a succession of roles including Finance Director, General Manager, CEO, Executive Partner, and more recently National Managing Partner for the Australian offices of Baker & McKenzie. This book reflects, to a large extent, my personal experiences, learned as much by my failures along the way as by my successes. However, I have also included the key learnings from many of my colleagues who are traveling a similar journey.

Not everything contained here will be appropriate for you and there will be much that you may even disagree with. However, I hope that some of it resonates with your own thinking and provides the inspiration to bring out your best.

The ideas and suggestions contained in the following chapters are intended to unlock your potential for professional growth, and to help you take control of your career. Remember that if you don't take control, somebody else will. I hope that some of the thoughts here will help you flap those wings — and soar even higher.

— Paul Malliaté
March 2003

CHAPTER 1
KNOW THE LANDSCAPE

If you can't change the wind, you must adjust your sails.

Prior to joining a law firm, I held various positions in both the government and corporate sectors. I remember during my first interview, the managing partner warned me that law firms were unique environments, with a special culture unlike anything I had previously experienced. I dismissed his concerns with some glib response about being very adaptable. Several months after I started in my new position, I (and no doubt several of the partners as well) was seriously questioning my ability to survive in a law firm environment — which was nothing like what I had expected.

As I look back now, I think that the key to learning is to understand and become comfortable with the law firm culture. Certainly not all law firms are the same, but there are a few special qualities that are prevalent in most firms:

- They are very professional environments with highly intelligent/competent individuals.
- Key decisions are made by consensus.
- Managers and owners have a fairly short-term focus and tend to lack an investment mindset.
- The professionals in firms have a strong client/customer focus.
- Law firms have a highly politicized internal culture.
- The power in most firms is generally based on client/revenue generation.
- Many law firm professionals maintain a competitive and adversarial approach.
- Law firms have flat management hierarchies with few role boundaries.
- Law firm partners, associates and staff are intolerant of mistakes and are trained to detect them.
- Law firms possess few command and control structures — independence is highly prized.

- Law firm principals are generally risk-averse/bound by precedent.
- Partners have a strong bottom-line focus.

In addition to knowing about law firms in general, you also need to understand the defining characteristics of your particular firm, as evidenced by individual partner behavior. Somewhat unusually, your partners are the key production units, frontline sales team, majority shareholders and executive board members (and in any given situation you will never know which hat they are wearing!).

In order to enhance your knowledge about law firms, consider the following suggestions:

- Join appropriate industry groups (ALA, ABA, etc.).
- Read relevant journals and books about law firms (the must-read texts are *Managing the Professional Service Firm* by David Maister and *Aligning the Stars* by Jay Lorsch).
- Network actively with other law firm managers.
- Start your own discussion group and share war stories.
- Go online (the ALA Web site is a great starting point).
- Consider courses on management of professional service firms (Hildebrandt Institute and Harvard Business School run some excellent programs).

Getting to know your firm's culture is invaluable. It will help guide your actions and assist you to adapt your own style and approach. More importantly, it will help you to appreciate why things are the way they are. This is the first step to being able to achieve meaningful progress. I have seen all too many administrators drown by trying to swim against the current instead of working within the system to implement appropriate changes. Invest the time up-front in understanding the law firm environment and your career progression will definitely go more smoothly.

Further Reading

Young, Stephen B., "A Practice of Power Brokers: Lawyers, Staff Could Benefit in Shared-Power Environment." *Legal Management*, May/June 1998.

Duffy DeRaleau, Janet, "Making Changes in a Change Resistant Firm." *Legal Management*, November/December 1995.

McKenna, Patrick J. and Gerald Riskin, *Herding Cats*. Institute for Best Management Practices, 1995.

Haserot, Phyllis Weiss, "Consensus Building in a Law Firm Partnership Culture." *Law Firm Governance*, Autumn 2000.

Maister, David H., *Managing the Professional Services Firm*. The Free Press, 1993.

Bradlaw, David and Murray Silverman, "Managing the Law Firm — Is Democracy Obsolete?" *Legal Economics*, August 1989.

Brashear, Sally, "You Are Not Alone: Experts Offer Guiding Light to Law Office Leadership Problems." *Legal Management*, May/June 1997.

Altman, Mary Ann and Robert I. Weil, *"How to Manage Your Law Office."* Mathew Bender, 1973 (with annual supplementation).

Hildebrandt, Bradford W. and Jack Kaufman, *The Successful Law Firm: New Approaches to Structure and Management*, 2nd edition. Prentice Hall Law & Business, 1988.

Thornlow, Carolyn (editor), *The ABA Guide to Professional Managers in the Law Office*. American Bar Association Section of Law Practice Management, 1996.

Tierney, Thomas and Jay Lorsch, *Aligning the Stars*. HBS, 2002.

The Association of Legal Administrators regularly features articles on the subject of administrator experiences and success. The following article first appeared in *Legal Management*, Volume 16, Number 3 (May/June 1997). It appears here to supplement the ideas in this chapter.

You Are Not Alone: Experts Offer A Guiding Light For Law Office Leadership Problems

By Sally Brashear

When a group of legal administrators gathered for a roundtable discussion of issues facing their firms, they were asked to identify the most difficult leadership issue they faced: Lack of partner leadership was cited by three of the four participants.

"One of the most difficult leadership issues facing my law firm right now is how to get the managing partner motivated to lead the organization, how to get him trained to lead it," one administrator says.

Since these administrators were told they'd remain anonymous, they were especially forthright. "Without leadership, we will just flop along," continues Administrator 1. "We will remain an organization, but not a high-performance organization. We need some goals, discipline, an attorney to take the reins for the organization, to make the difficult decisions."

The reality of reaching a "critical mass"-level need for leadership is especially echoed repeatedly by members of the group. Administrator 4 relays a similar situation in her firm where most partners had a say in all firm decisions. As she describes it, no one would really "step up to the plate and be the leader. We got to a crisis point in 1995 where we were like a rudderless ship and we have changed." She explains how one partner became the managing partner and is now making decisions, running the firm and providing direction. As a result, attorney and staff morale have increased dramatically.

> **Leadership**
>
> Leaders are those who can create a passionate and exciting vision of the future, can align people's minds and efforts to that vision, and, most importantly, can align their personal behaviors with that vision.
>
> *Stephen Pain, Leadership Strategies Inc., Princeton, New Jersey*

These administrators describe a situation that can exist in any organization when it lacks a clear vision or understanding of its values and goals. They recognize that such an organization needs leaders to communicate that vision and make decisions, to move the firm forward, and inspire people to follow.

"When a leadership vacuum exists, and it exists in most law firms," adds Administrator 3,

What is the Cost of Poor, Weak or Undeveloped Leadership?

- Managers with leadership potential that do not receive attention and mentoring leave because of frustration, neglect, or both.
- Managers at almost all levels who try to provide the firm with needed leadership run into an unresponsive bureaucracy or barriers.
- Jobs in lower and middle management often have a large "fire fighting" component to them, which prematurely ages people and does little to prepare them for the strategic and organization-building tasks associated with effective leadership.
- Firms with virtually no depth of management push managers into jobs for which they are not prepared.
- Managers do not get the coaching or support from their bosses that they and their bosses need to develop themselves.

Mark Jacobs, Protential, LLC, Indianapolis, Indiana

"those with the leadership sense and skills should and will step forward to fill the void."

As these Law Firm Experts See It

If these law firm administrators sound like they are distancing themselves from the leadership vacuum at the top, and describing an "us and them" situation, they are not. They see themselves tangled in this leadership dilemma, responsible for it and at the same time affected by it.

While, on the one hand, they point to the managing partner as the person who should step up to the plate and make the hard decisions, they also describe themselves as key facilitators in making it happen. As Administrator 1 says, "... in order to make my organization stronger, ... the managing partner has to be a stronger leader, and I have to teach him how to do that." Although these administrators seem prepared to do this, exactly what should their role be? The idea of someone stepping forward is critical, but should that someone always be the managing partner or can it be the administrator? Some of these experienced administrators would argue that it isn't the law firm administrator who can or should do so.

"In most firms it doesn't happen," Administrator 4 says, "because you have either an autocrat or anarchy," very seldom a happy medium. "The administrator then becomes one of two things, a terrified mouse or the whip associated with that autocrat. It may not be time wasted, but there is an awful lot of time expended on less efficient handling of most issues critical to the firm."

Part of the inefficiency administrators see resulting from such a situation is their inability to be effective in their jobs. All agree that the administrator is challenged by trying to be all things to all people: "One moment, I may be meeting with extremely important individuals or undertaking a broad scope strategic issue," Administrator 3 says, "and the next moment I may be crawling around underneath someone's desk trying to fix cabling or figuring out why a computer or telephone isn't doing its job."

Even under autocratic leadership, there is often no definition or common understanding of the administrator's role. One administrator compared leadership in a law firm to that of the military, where he began his career; "you have clear-cut areas of responsibility in the military. But, [in a law firm] you may find that role not only unstated, but misunderstood or understood differently by different individuals."

Lacking role definition and without consistent directives from the firm, these administrators see themselves and their peers in the untenable position of wondering whether they should lead or follow, facilitate or manage, or just do it all.

When asked to equate their positions to a corporate counterpart, an executive vice president, for example, none of the administrators respond. They can't make the equation. It is impossible. Unlike their corporate cousins, law firm administrators say they work in an environment where the shareholders, or owners — and there are many — get involved in the day-to-day running of the organization. "It is almost like an individual contract with everybody who comes on board, or who departs," one administrator says.

From the Leadership Experts' Perspective

Leadership experts view this dichotomy with varying degrees of empathy. Quality guru Philip Crosby, author of *The Absolutes of Leadership*, thinks administrators like other managers are being naive if they believe their situations are unique: "There are the same problems everywhere," Crosby says. Although he doesn't say it in so many words, Crosby suggests administrators need to get over it and get on with it.

Jim Strutton, president of Fortune Group International, an organizational development training firm in Chicago, says leadership vacuums, lack of mentoring, and unclear roles are "not exclusive to law firms at all."

Still, administrators persist in their view that law firm structures create unique situations and expectations. Stephen Payne, president of Leadership Strategies Inc., in Princeton, NJ, concurs: "Fundamentally, the view of what 'successful functioning' means to a lawyer does not coincide with the same view from an administrator. The more of a 'partnership' the law firm is, the more difficult and diffuse the task of the administrator."

Administrators do have the right to approve policies, to be respected, informed and listened to, adds Crobsy. But, then, he says to administrators, "Ask yourself who is your customer: It's the lawyers. It is the lawyers who generate the money: Administrators can and should run the business but they have to learn how to work with lawyers."

Furthermore, working with lawyers means administrators need to learn how to let the partners know when they're off track, how to "tactfully confront," Strutton says.

Many administrators work in environments that are not ideal incubators for clear leadership. Law firms usually are established by a person or persons with a vision, a leader. As firms grow and prosper, the focus moves from vision to activity, and the leaders, now focused on growth, may lose sight of the original vision, Strutton says. In fact, as the organization changes, the vision may need to be recreated, or revisited. (It is this last situation the administrators describe as a rudderless ship or leadership vacuum.)

Mark Jacobs of Protential, LLC, in Indianapolis, prefers to view a law firm, or any organization, as a "community," a group of different organizations each with its own values and goals that must find a commonality of values. A law firm, especially, has many elements within the community — practice groups, marketing, administration. All these groups possess different goals and values, but there is commonality to be found. The shared values of the community are influenced by its leaders, and, according to Jacobs, these values inevitably are what motivate the community and shape the next layer of leaders.

"If you have an autocrat, you'll get autocratic leaders and a second generation that is timid," Jacobs says. "In an autocratic environment, an administrator might well feel unsupported or fearful to act."

In fact, these experts agree that unclear roles and lack of policies, mentoring, and respect are symptoms of an organization that is probably not functioning at a high level or providing an environment where leadership can flourish. No matter what its values — its leadership style or lack of leadership — if the organization is an impossible environment in which to function, Jacobs believes the administrator has two choices: leave or lead.

Asking the Hard Questions

To establish how leadership and its functions are achieved in your firm, ask yourself these questions:
- What are our firm's values?
- Does it have a shared vision that is clearly understood and communicated?

If operating values are clear but are not ones with which the administrator can align or function, perhaps the environment is not the right one. "Culture is difficult to define much less change," Jacobs says. "Organizationwide values are almost impossible to change." An organization with a clear value system will seek out or attract those whose values align. At the same time, those with incompatible or differing values will not fit. "People who don't fit, need to move on!" emphasizes Jacobs.

On the other hand, if there are divergent or unclear values, or if there is no vision or leadership, it is likely that many members of the firm, including the administrator, will lose heart. Payne describes this as "an absence of a collective sense of direction."

In this environment, the administrator must again ask, Do I leave? or Do I choose to stay and take part in influencing change and leading the firm?

Payne advises administrators "to take on the task of becoming the glue that builds that sense of direction, i.e., get into the vision creating process rather than sounding like a victim."

Furthermore, Crosby suggests getting into the process by taking a broader view of your worth to the firm: "Ask [yourself] what is the value of the administrator to the firm besides serving as a 'caddie' to the lawyers." Articulate what allows administrators to be more useful and reliable: Take responsibility for your performance — this is a key component in leadership.

"Leadership is not mysterious, Jacobs adds, "It is not about charisma or charm or outright manipulation as much as it is about sweat, hard work, and credibility." Choosing to help lead the firm in discovering its values and setting goals is not easy, but working in an environment that does not meet individual needs is even more difficult.

Finding Answers

While some administrators may see their leadership opportunities tied to the managing partner or management committee and wait to be given the opportunity to lead, Payne says leadership opportunities are "waiting to be taken." He wonders if administrators who don't aren't confusing leadership with rank.

"It is wrong to think that leadership must come from the top," concurs David Parks, marketing principal for TPG Learning Systems in Palo Alto, California.

TPG's Jim Kouzes, author of several books on leadership management, says, "While we associate [leadership] with position, it is only 50 percent of the answer," "You don't need to be positioned with top leaders to practice leadership. Leaders have vision and are forward looking. What distinguishes them is the ability to inspire people to follow their vision."

"You have to 'walk your talk' as a leader," concurs Administrator 1 describing his relationship with staff. "You have to know what you're doing ... the technical aspects of what you're doing, the knowledge of being an administrator.... If you 'walk the talk' and exude the confidence and enthusiasm for what you're doing, you are going to be a good leader."

"You need to be excited about what you're doing. And [this excitement] must be seen by the folks you are trying to motivate," adds Administrator 2. "You need to believe in it and communicate it, follow-up and have people become part of a group or team effort. I can't really motivate people without believing that they believe they are part of the group or team and have as much input as I do."

---

5 Point Leadership Model

1. Speak up. **Challenge the process.**

2. **Inspire a shared vision.** Convey your long-term vision.

3. **Enable others to act** by providing information and creating an environment in which to succeed.

4. **Model the way by your actions.** Exhibit integrity and credibility by being consistent in what you say and do.

5. **Encourage the heart** by small wins. You don't have to have appointed authority.

David Parks, TPG Learning Systems, Palo Alto, California

"In other words lead by example," says Crosby. People don't stay motivated for long. Real motivation is internal — the drive a person has to be successful in the organization. You can inspire, not motivate.

There are many ways the leadership experts say administrators and other firm leaders can ensure that they are effectively communicating with and inspiring their staff:

Take Action

"Go where you haven't gone before," advises Parks, "Do something, anything. Take action. Speak up at meetings."

"Start talking about your firm as a business," says Crosby. "Look at service; look at processes. Attorneys' expectations may be wrong. It's not managing a law practice; it's managing a business where attorneys need to do their job."

And while shareholders may involve themselves in firm management between legal matters, administrators are equipped to deal with business issues on a continuing basis.

"Attorneys do not want to be making a decision. What they want to do is hear what your decision was and what the basis for it was." Administrator 2 adds, "Go in and say 'We have a situation and here are the options. I choose A....' I wouldn't say 'Please pick A, B, C or D' or 'Give me your answer.' They don't have time for that and in most cases they don't want to make a decision." To manage business effectively, administrators must place the responsibility of data gathering, measurement, and forward thinking on themselves and communicate it.

Strutton emphasizes the need to "manage up" — to tactfully confront partners and let them know when they are "off track."

"Focus on the problem not the person," advises Strutton. "State what's wrong, how it makes you feel and why. Communication involves both emotion (how it makes you feel) and purpose (why/the results). We tend not to share the why." Relay the purpose, and relate it to something attorneys can understand like client service. Tactful confrontation works best, however, when administrators feel confident in their position and receive recognition, adds Strutton.

LEAD THE PACK

In addition to leadership styles, the following are some ways to move a group toward integration and change:

- Provide clear policies and a consistent environment in line with the values of the group and then "get out of the way!" (Crosby)
- Be accessible. Get out with the people. Move among them. (Crosby)
- Communicate: Listen, provide information, answers and a context, and challenge thinking. (Strutton)
- Influence by example: Be credible, be consistent, have integrity, be forward thinking, and ask what's next. (Kouzes)
- Develop competency and leadership; provide recognition; recognition has to be by one's peers not just selected by upper management. (Crosby)

Push Back

"It's very frustrating," one administrator says, "once a decision is discussed and voted on in a shareholders' meeting and announced by the administrator, that the very attorney who voted for the decision denies responsibility when someone complains. You don't want to be the unpopular person giving the bad news....no one likes to be in that position but you can't waffle.

"Whether you disagree with the decision or not, once it has been decided — you can argue up to that point — but once the decision had been made, it is your decision and you have to present it as though you totally back the decision. If you waffle, you lose credibility." Everyone agrees with this administrator, including the leadership experts. But the time to be tough is during decision making.

"You need to be tough minded, rather than tough," comments Strutton.

"When an administrator gets a directive from a senior partner and doesn't feel strong enough to push back, he takes it to the next level, and someone there pushes and asks 'why?' Then the 'why' turns into a 'who' and you've created a political environment."

To avoid a contentious political environment, organizations need clear policies and a consistent environment, says Crobsy. This frees people to think for themselves and make decisions consistent with their firm's values.

On the other hand, you can lead but not succeed without support from the top," says Parks. You don't have to have appointed authority, although it helps, but you need some "small wins" or achievements that ultimately lead to recognition and encouragement. Feedback is key.

"The reason quality went away," Strutton says, "is because senior management delegated it to a 'quality guru' rather than agree with and take a stand on it. This is a filtering of the message rather than an intensifying of the message."

"Leadership development is linear; it's a journey," says Jacobs. "Leadership is a process."

Learn to Lead and Influence Change

In many ways, administrators are already strong leaders. They earn credibility as a result of their competency as business managers, and their ability to set and carry out policies and manage processes. They work with and inspire co-workers. They identify and eliminate problems.

Some leadership ability is innate, dependent on personality, preferences, and the ability to assess situations and process information. Although some leadership experts say leadership cannot be taught, many trainers and consultants believe leadership skills can be improved or developed.

"Leadership is a skill set. There are specific skills that make up the body of leadership," says Jacobs. "They have to do with the vision, mission, and values of organizations." Jacobs identifies six critical leadership skills:

- **Agreement building** — Bring members of the law firm to the point where they develop, understand, and behave based on a set of defined, shared, actionable values.

- **Networking** — Understand the needs and motivations of the shareholders and employees of the firm and earn their respect.
- **Exercising non-jurisdictional power** — Where there are territories, recognize them politely and learn to influence them through credibility and adherence to the organization's shared values.
- **Institution building** — Focus on evolving the organization, basing the evolution on commonality of purpose, evolution of shared values, and an eye towards building a legacy.
- **Flexibility** — Because things change, manage and predicate change based on the desired institution (as opposed to individual personalities) so that people can understand and embrace productive change.
- **Risk taking** — Learn by taking risks: look ahead, and plan for taking risks that support the development of the firm's legacy.

"Because everyone in an organization can affect these things," Jacob says "everyone can be a leader to some degree. Leadership is learnable. All skills are learnable. The skills of leadership are identifiable and understandable. Successful leadership is an action oriented process that is focused on generating measurable, manageable results." However, just like any skill set, some people have more natural ability than others.

Jacobs, Crosby, and others say leadership cannot be learned just in the classroom: it takes time, knowledge, and experience. Leaders learn on the job by doing. In fact, much of what administrators know about leadership is learned at work. The roundtable administrators agree they learn the leadership techniques that work for their law firms on the job, often by trial and error. They practice their techniques, learn from mistakes, and get better at it.

The administrators also agree that they use a repertoire of leadership behaviors and agree that among these skills understanding the style of the group is key: "I understand how to be a different leader in different situations. I have the style that is suited to the firm.... But you have to be a different kind of leader in each situation," says Administrator 1. "With the executive committee, my leadership style is totally different than with the total partnership, as it is when I'm meeting with associates or secretaries. I have a different way of dealing with those different groups."

Strutton lists four leadership styles that leaders use depending on the group and what the situation calls for:

- autocratic, which draws on "self-strength" by requiring the group to do it "my way;"
- bureaucratic, in which the leader uses policy to guide the group and for this reason tends not to be as strong a style;
- democratic, which asks the group to be part of the decision making process; and
- idiosyncratic, which draws on all of the other three.

Strutton favors the idiosyncratic style. Through this, leaders rely on the context of the situation and can take into consideration what the situation calls for. Idiosyncratic leadership is a flexible style that recognizes that change comes slowly — individuals change first and as they change the group changes. This type of leader understands the group's values and what motivates its members and responds accordingly. Strutton adds that time pressures limit people from using the idiosyncratic style and instead they choose other patterns that take less time and may therefore seem easier.

On the other hand, Administrator 2 says she is consistent with different groups in the firm: the support staff, the executive level, and the associate level.

The leadership experts view situational behaviors differently. Yes, it is necessary to understand the values that motivate a group, and it is possible to adapt one's leadership style to the group while remaining constant to one's own style. But, "future successful functioning will be defined in collaborative ways," aligning the group through "coaching and repetition," according to Payne who identified "integrative leadership" as the ideal.

"Everyone works with several distinct groups," Payne continues. "The 'integrative' leaders recognize their role in helping to create a shared direction — predicting difficulty, anticipating others' needs, and clarifying perspectives."

As the group or organization moves closer to the "same truth," Jacobs maintains, the less it will need situational leadership.

And what about the real world of law firms and other organizations where the ideal has not yet been achieved, where expectations and roles are not clear and where recognition may be lax? This is where administrators can begin to strengthen personal leadership skill: They can know themselves, set and measure their personal organizational goals, and figure out how their value system aligns with the organization.

The administrators in the roundtable have taken this first step by encouraging their firms to recognize and buy into long-term goals for the administrator. Administrator 2, for example, sets goals for herself and looks at this list once a year with the managing partner. Administrator 3 describes his first 90 days with his firm: "They had a lot of hot issues or crises, and they said 'here's what we want to focus on in the first 90 days'.... I [then] gave them a report...here are the changes that have taken place and the efforts that have been put forth." Now Administrator 3 asks constantly where the firm wants to be in five years. Understanding this enables him to adapt his strategies on the daily issues and make decisions that are not isolated or misaligned with organizational goals. "Then I have a benchmark," he says.

"Create an internal dialogue," says Kouzes. "Develop long-term vision. Ask what's next. Remember, you don't have to have appointed authority. Have faith that you can be an effective leader."

CHAPTER 2
ENSURE ALIGNMENT

We are what we do.

Sadly, there are many people who leave their real selves at the office door each morning. To be extraordinary in any vocation, what you do must get reasonably close to your own authenticity — both personally and professionally. Whether working in a law firm or elsewhere, if your work is not aligned with your core values, strengths and personal style, then you will always be achieving less than your full potential. While you may achieve short-term success in the absence of alignment, the real goal of long-term fulfillment will elude you.

In order to ensure alignment, you need to achieve a level of comfort with the firm's culture and values. Start by undertaking a realistic assessment of your personal strengths and natural gifts — and assess weaknesses. Consider this your own personal SWOT (strengths, weaknesses, opportunities and threats) analysis.

List the relevant attributes and then prioritize them. This will help you gain a clear sense of those that are truly important to you. Ideally, do this with the assistance of a close friend or colleague who can provide objective feedback; sometimes others see us better than we see ourselves. Now review your list in light of the environmental factors noted in Chapter 1, together with the requirements of your particular position and the culture/values of your firm. Try to determine whether there is consistency with your professional goals and aspirations. If you need constant self-reinforcement or thrive only if your efforts are truly valued and appreciated, law firms may not be your ideal workplace. Similarly, if you are not highly organized or don't have a strong service ethic, then law firm administration is unlikely to ignite your passion. Indeed, in my experience, the best law firm managers are generally very comfortable with the No. 2 role, being far less concerned about leadership and much more focused on helping others to succeed.

In summary, make sure that who you are is compatible with what you do. We may not always have the luxury of a perfect match, but it is futile to persevere if there is an obvious and significant lack of alignment. Apart from falling well short of being extraordinary, life is way too short to spend it doing something that will never inspire you to be the best you can be.

Further Reading

Anderson, Richard, *Getting Ahead — Career Skills That Work For Everyone.* McGraw-Hill, 1995.

Covey, Steven R., *Seven Habits of Highly Effective People.* Simon & Schuster, 1990.

Keeva, Steven, *Transforming Practices: Finding Joy and Satisfaction in the Legal Life.* Contemporary Books, 1999.

Seligman, Martin E.P., *Authentic Happiness: Using the New Positive Psychology to Realize Your Potential for Lasting Fulfillment.* The Free Press, 2002.

Matthews, Andrew, *Follow your Heart: Finding Purpose In Your Life and Work.* Seashell Books, 1997.

CHAPTER 3
CARE FOR YOUR CLIENTS

No one cares what you know until they know that you care.

As an extraordinary administrator, you must regard the firm's lawyers and staff members as your internal clients and then focus your efforts on serving them to the best of your ability. This requires a marketing-based approach through which you seek to understand the needs of your clients and then develop appropriate strategies to respond accordingly. In order to achieve this, you must first get to know each of your internal clients — especially the important ones who exercise power and influence within the firm.

While you should always demonstrate a fair and unbiased approach in your dealings, it would be foolish not to recognize that some clients are more important than others. Therefore, if you are to use your time and limited resources wisely, you should give special attention to your "strategic" clients:

- direct recipients of your services;
- your team members and subordinates;
- your immediate supervisor;
- your supervisor's boss; and
- the firm's managing partner/chairman.

For each such client, it is helpful to develop a good understanding of their specific needs as well as any personal factors, which can help you to meet or exceed their service expectations and build a worthwhile relationship.

Because the administrator's role is to serve, the key question to ask in many situations is, "What can I do to help you?" This requires you to see things from the client's perspective. Remember that your job is to make the client's life easier. Make an effort to get to know all clients as individuals and communicate with them regularly. Developing good client relationships is more often about the small, everyday things you do, which demonstrate that you care and eventually earns the client's trust. Here are a few suggestions:

- Always respond promptly.
- Agree to and deliver on expectations. (Keep your promises.)
- Show genuine personal interest — birthday greetings, thank-you cards, etc.
- Send articles/clippings on topics of interest.
- Anticipate issues/problems before they arise — be proactive.
- Get to know your client's clients and their priorities.
- Be available/reachable (if you are away, use an absence notification).
- Show respect.
- Be discreet and strictly observe obligations regarding confidentiality.
- Focus on being helpful rather than being right.
- Get among your clients by regularly walking the floors.
- Ask for feedback often: "How can I serve you better?"

One final word of caution: There must be certain limitations to your client-service mindset. Some clients, especially partners, may abuse the "client first" relationship. In such cases, particularly those involving ethical issues, remember that ultimately your most important client is the firm as an institution rather than any individual.

Know who your clients are, understand their needs, deliver outstanding service and being extraordinary will naturally follow.

Further Reading

Berman Fortgang, Laura, *Take Yourself To The Top: The Secrets of America's #1 Career Coach.* Warner Books, 1998.

Alban, Oscar, *"Six Secrets to Successful Customer Service"*

Maister, David H., Charles H. Green, Robert M. Galford, *The Trusted Advisor.* The Free Press, 2000.

Spruill, M. Lynn, "The Delivery of Legal Services in the Future: How is the Role of Professional Management in the Legal Environment Evolving?" *Legal Management*, May/June 2001. (See Appendix I.)

CHAPTER 4
DEVELOP COMMUNICATION SKILLS

If you are not confused, then you don't understand the issues.

The extraordinary administrator must be an expert communicator. In most business environments, effective communication is important — but in a law firm, it is absolutely critical. There are three important elements of communication:
- effective listening skills;
- written communication skills; and
- presentation skills.

Listening

As my wife constantly reminds me, listening is not something I do well. All too often, as soon as someone starts speaking, I am busy thinking about my response rather than giving my full attention to what is being said. For many of us, effective listening needs active, ongoing effort. Nevertheless, it is an important element of skillful communication and certainly plays a key role in delivering outstanding client service. (See Chapter 3.) There are many ways to improve your listening skills:
1. Give the other person your full attention.
2. Minimize distractions (phones, noises, etc.).
3. Don't interrupt the speaker.
4. Practice effective listening by rephrasing and reflecting your understanding of what you have heard.
5. Identify and agree on next steps/outcomes.

Written Communication

In all written communication, attention to detail is essential. Lawyers are particularly well trained to spot any errors. Even a single typo or small grammatical error in a five-page memo will be quickly detected; this will reduce the effectiveness of your overall message as well as your own personal credibility.

E-mail is ubiquitous — 90 percent of daily written communication within law firms is by e-mail. Extraordinary administrators master this tool.

Remember that with e-mail, there is always a danger of informality or responding too quickly. Always think first before going into print. Use the spell check at all times and before hitting that send button; read through your message; double check the address list and confirm that all attachments have been properly appended.

Needless to say, do not write anything that you would regret later or would not want maintained as a permanent record. Even personal or private e-mail messages can be sent in error to unintended recipients or easily forwarded on to a broader distribution list. Additionally, some partners may automatically copy their secretary with all received messages.

With regard to lengthier documents or reports, try to provide a structure using appropriate headings and numbering. This will facilitate the reader's understanding. Given that most lawyers are generally too busy to read beyond page 1, it is often helpful to provide an upfront executive summary that includes the required actions/recommendations. Better still, learn to master the one-page memo/spreadsheet and include everything else as attachments or appendices for the few who want to wade through the detail. Once again, use spell check. And if the document is lengthy or especially important, have someone else proofread it for meaning, effectiveness and accuracy.

Presentation Skills

Most lawyers are very skillful presenters and they certainly expect the firm's key support managers and administrators to be just as proficient. A quick crash course on "Presentation Skills 101" is as follows:

1. Clarify your objective: to inform, to entertain, to reach a decision.
2. Analyze your audience. Knowing the general demographics, seniority, etc., will help you "pitch" your presentation at the right level. This may also help you to anticipate any questions or likely opposition to your proposals/recommendation.
3. Develop the content. A useful structure for your content is opening, body and conclusion:
   (a) Opening — First, provide a strong, attention-grabbing introduction (an anecdote, question, statistic or humorous story). First impressions are important; so make this as powerful as possible. Second, you should identify the overall outcome/objective then briefly outline what you intend to cover in the body of your presentation.

(b) Body — This is the substance of what you want to say. Ideally you should break it down into easily digestible subheadings. In general, a three-part structure works very well: What is the issue? What are the options? What are your recommendations? Or perhaps: Where are we now? Where are we going? How will we get there?

(c) Conclusions — Here you should summarize what you have covered in the body and identify the main "take out" messages and next steps. Essentially, you are saying to the audience that if they remember nothing else, then please remember this. The key messages should therefore be consistent with the initial objective of your presentation. Conclude with a strong rousing finish that challenges your audience and leaves a memorable impression.

4. Prepare visual aids/handouts. If you are using PowerPoint slides, keep them very brief (use bullet points) and limit each slide to a few words. Better still, use pictures or graphs. If you have handouts, think carefully about whether you should distribute these before or after your actual presentation.

5. Rehearse your presentation. Practice as much as possible as this will boost your confidence. Remember to check your timing and never go over time. Concentrate on your body language — eyes, posture, hands — remembering that for most communication, 7 percent of the overall impact comes from the content, 38 percent from inflection/voice and 55 percent from your body language.

6. Review physical layout/equipment. Determine what type of microphone you require (lapel/radio or fixed) and confirm that it is working effectively. Decide where you would like the podium located (or better still, don't use one) and check the lighting. The latter is especially important if you are using overheads or slides. Finally, double-check any presentation equipment. If you will be using a computer, ensure (well beforehand) that your presentation material has been correctly loaded and that you know how to operate the equipment.

Poor communication skills will stifle your personal efficiency and sabotage your career progression. If this is an area of difficulty for you, begin now to develop and implement strategies to improve your performance. Read all you can on the subject. Practice communicating with smaller groups. Write for or volunteer to edit a newsletter. Speak (or introduce a speaker) at educational meetings for your professional association. Attend short courses on public communication. Join Toastmasters.

One final point is a caution against over communicating: More than ever, all of us are suffering from information overload. Review your distribution lists and ensure that your reports, memos and e-mail messages are not only accurate and timely, but also helpful and relevant.

Further Reading

Brashear, Sally, "It is Written: Communicating Effectively Beyond the Age of 'Dear Sir or Madam'." *Legal Management*, January/February 1997.

Daley, Kevin, "Presentation Skills — Sharpen Your Communication Skills to Market your Firm." *Law Practice Management*, September 1997.

Johnston, Karen, "The Communication Gap; or, 'Clearly You Didn't Hear What I Thought I Said in Response to What You Thought You Said'." *Legal Management*, January/February 1997.

Riggs, Bill, "Written Communication: Readability." *People-to-People*, June 1986.

The Association of Legal Administrators regularly features articles on the subject of administrator experiences and success. The following article first appeared in *Legal Management*, Volume 16, Number 1 (January/February 1997). It appears here to supplement the ideas in this chapter.

The Communication Gap
Or 'Clearly You Didn't Hear What I Thought I Said In Response To What You Thought You Said'

By Karen Johnston

In each of the following law firm scenarios there is a common element that, when utilized appropriately, would have prevented the problem. What is that element?

A. As the administrator you have carefully prepared a financial analysis to demonstrate to the six shareholders that they need to increase their marketing activity in order to generate next year's budgeted income. Nearly 15 minutes into the meeting, as you discuss your analysis about where current business is coming from, one of the shareholders notices a client name on the list and announces that he took that individual to Sunday's big football game. The talk then degenerates into how many touchdowns the team should have made, who tackled whom, and how many football games each shareholder has attended this year. Within five minutes of hearing they need to generate more income for next year, the shareholders have decided to buy more season tickets.

B. Your managing partner tells you to look into the cost and complexity of setting up a Web site for your firm, and to have that information by next Monday's meeting. You drop everything, research costs, call administrators and post a message on the Association of Legal Administrators Web site to find out what others have done. You compile a report and bring it to the meeting prepared to answer every question. Before you have a chance to present your information, the managing partner announces that the firm has hired a consultant to help develop the Web site and, since the consultant is the managing partner's brother-in-law, the firm is getting a good deal.

C. As administrator, it is your job to oversee the purchase and installation of computers and the appropriate software for every attorney. Two senior attorneys, who have brought a great deal of business into the firm, have already told you not to bother: They are not planning to start using computers.

D. You have a paralegal who is brilliant technically, but has a problem with "people skills." Your lawyers and staff have complained that he looks bored when you talk to him, stares, and sounds irritated most of the time. When you discuss with other paralegals the importance of getting along with everyone, he looks bored, stares, says very little — you get nowhere!

In all of these frustrating scenarios, a different type of communication may have prevented the problem in the first place, and could possibly solve the problem now that it has occurred. This article addresses why, even though we try hard to communicate as clearly as possible with individuals and in small groups, the message does not get across.

Your employees and executive committees may fancy themselves "people persons," but they don't know how to communicate effectively:

- **Communication is perceived as simple and automatic, when actually it is a complex, energy-intensive skill.** While most people start talking at 18 months, they haven't necessarily been communicating. Communication is a two-way verbal and nonverbal exchange between individuals that creates a mutually understood result. It involves a complicated set of skills that includes listening; asking effective questions; understanding the impact of nonverbal language; understanding learning styles; and paying complete emotional and psychological attention.

- **We don't know what we don't know.** Widely read research by Albert Mehrabain, shows that only 7 percent of our communication comes through verbal content, 38 percent is voice (inflection), and 55 percent is body language. It is ironic that whenever we have a situation that we perceive may be difficult, we tend to focus on the 7 percent. Perhaps our time would be better spent on some of the subtitles that will actually make the communication more effective.

- **Ineffective communication is modeled for us as exemplary communication.** A profession like law that relies so heavily on articulating cognitive expertise to solve technical problems and win cases is destined to view articulating cognitive expertise as the way to solve all problems. The rational goes something like this, *"If I explain it logically, you will change!"* Of course, when we are dealing with peoples' motivations, fears, values, and egos — logic is a weak warrior. (This communication problem is universal.) *"Is there a better way to do this?"* is a question an effective communicator constantly asks.

Poor communication habits can be conquered. Communication can be much more effective when speakers understand the impact individuals' learning styles have on the way they communicate and perceive. Communication in groups continues to improve when we understand the four dynamics through which all groups move.

What is a "Learning Style?"

People process information, or "think" in three different ways: visually, auditorily, kinesthetically. Although we have the ability to think clearly in all three learning styles, we are usually predominantly strong in one style when we take information in and predominantly strong in another or the same style when we retrieve information to give it out. The thinking style that we use has many behavior characteristics attached to it, which is why this information has such a strong impact on communication, especially if our style is different than the style of the person to whom we are talking.

Visuals

When people process information visually (or have a visual learning style), they think in pictures. They create mental movies that consist of images, formulas, pages of documents, financial information, or pages in text books. To protect their need to see these pictures continually in their mind, they want space between themselves and other people when they converse. They like to sit across a table, and if they are standing, they will often backup when asked a question. This way the picture in their mind isn't destroyed by the "real" picture in front of them. "Visuals" think and talk sequentially and, if interrupted, will need to return to the beginning of the sequence in order to get their entire thought or idea out. Visuals need to have time to think before they talk so they can arrange their pictures.

You can identify the learning styles people are using by watching where their eyes move when they think, and by listening to their language. Visual thinkers look up or defocus their eyes so they can see their pictures in their mind. This is a significant observation because the lack of facial expression can be misinterpreted as boredom or disinterest. They use visual words: *"Let's look at how this will work out." "I see what you mean."* They will respond better when you also use visual language.

Think back to Scenario D. That paralegal may not be bored or angry — just visual-oriented. And that ability to organize complex data into a format that is orderly is the very skill that makes him a good paralegal. Instead of talking with him about his behavior, a better approach might be to get the group together to communicate this information about learning styles. This way, everyone can appreciate each other's differences, and the nonproductive dynamic of making this paralegal "odd-man-out" can be stopped.

Auditory

People who are predominantly auditory do not think in pictures at all: They think in words or sounds. Instead of recalling something in writing, they will recall someone or themselves talking. What they have read gets turned into a conversation in their head.

They do not care whether body space is close or distant, but they do care, and are sensitive to the tone of the speaker's voice. They will pick up irritation, impatience, tiredness, and often attach an emotional interpretation to it. Whereas visuals think and then talk, auditories talk to think. The predominantly auditory individual will ask a question and then interrupt the person who is answering. This is because, once they get the answer to their question, they are on to their next idea.

Auditory people like voice mail and are sometimes "phonaholics." They are good at business development and negotiation because they can function effectively in a spontaneous conversation.

Think about Scenario C, the senior attorneys who don't want to use computers. A computer is a visual tool. Clearly there may be other issues here, but if these attorneys are auditory, using a computer will be difficult because it will require them to change their work habits. Perhaps they have dictated all their practice life. Asking them to use the computer is asking them to do important work using their least effective learning style, and to change the work habits that have made them efficient.

Exploring this situation by asking questions would be an important strategy. *"How do your attorneys accomplish their work now?" "What are your concerns about using a computer?"* Try to determine if this is a learning style issue, or about the "right" to do what they want.

People who are primarily auditory tend not to read text, so memos sit in their in-basket or on e-mail while they call somebody for the very information that is in the memo. Their eyes move from side to side when they think, and their language is auditory *"Let's talk this over." "Sounds good to me."*

Kinesthetics

People who process information kinesthetically are the people who are often known as "touchy-feely." They value and respond to their intuition or feelings first. They are people who may not be able to tell you exactly what was said in a discussion, but they can describe in detail how they felt throughout the process. Whereas visuals will sit across the table from you, kinesthetics will sit close to you or even on the same side of the table. When shaking hands they move in close, and touch you with their free hand. (This drives visuals nuts, incidentally.)

Kinesthetic processors are often highly charismatic people. Rainmakers may have a good streak of kinesthetic in them, which is what makes them so personable, helps people trust them quickly, and gives them the intuitive edge to understand what is going on even before it is explained. (Successful kinesthetics and auditories usually have a predominately visual person handy to cleanup the detail, and keep them out of trouble.) Kinesthetics look down to the lower right and say things like *"Let's get a handle on this."* and *"I feel . . ."*

This learning style information should not be used to categorize people. Its value is in understanding why people behave the way they do, and to communicate more effectively because we can alter our learning style to match the person with whom we are talking.

Here are some other suggestions that will help prevent or resolve those scenarios:

Ask process questions.

An administrator is continually asking questions to understand the many issues that are sensitive, political, and/or complicated. The key is to ask both project questions and process questions. A project question gathers information about facts. *"What does the decision involve?"*

"How many computers should we buy?" "When will the project need to be done?"

Process questions are about the *"invisible"* assumptions, values, and motives that created the need for the decision, the computers, or the project. Process questions get at the nonfactual influences. *"How was the decision made?" "What's motivating people to be interested in this?" "What have others determined is the outcome they want from the particular work?"*

A way to have avoided all the Web site research in Scenario B would be to have asked process questions: *"What is prompting the decision about the Web site?" "Why is having a Web site important?" "What did the other shareholders say about it?" "What do you want to accomplish by creating a Web site?"* And most importantly, *"In the framework of the other projects that I have such as (name them), where does research on the Web site fit?"*

Process questions might have saved this administrator volumes of work. The managing partner might have said something like: *"Well, you know, my brother-in-law was over for dinner on Saturday night, and he was talking about this class he is taking on how to setup Web sites. He offered to come in and set ours up for practically nothing so he could practice. I ran this by a couple of the attorneys this morning and they thought it was a good idea."*

Armed with that information, that administrator would have probably approached the Web site problem much differently. Process questions would have not only saved work, but might have helped to avoid a potentially bad decision.

Use reflection to listen effectively.

We have all been exposed to listening techniques such as active listening and paraphrasing. *"What you are really feeling is . . ." "Sounds like you are . . ."* These listening tools are effective but they must be used in a sophisticated manner. (It is easy to sound like we just took a Psychology 101 class.)

Conversely, reflection is a highly sophisticated listening skill whereby the listener absorbs what the other talker is saying and then, once the listener understands the situation, the listener reflects that understanding in his or her own words to the talker. This ensures the talker that the listener indeed understood, and it provides a forum for clarification of any misunderstandings.

Many professionals, especially those who absorb complex information easily, say the reason they don't need to reflect is because they understand everything the other person is telling them. Of course, that communication is only one-way. The talker doesn't know the listener is understanding. So, the reflection technique of absorbing the information, putting it in different words and giving it back to the originator for clarification is a very powerful tool.

Good listeners do not reflect every single thing an individual says. Reflection should be used only when a situation is lengthy, emotional, or complex. In the discussions that would occur to "fix" Scenarios C and D, reflection would be essential. When people "dig in" with a certain perspective, they often want to be understood more than they want to have their way: Reflection demonstrates that understanding.

Handling Small Groups Effectively

Because much of an administrator's time is spent with groups of people and in meetings, let's look at some of the dynamics that make communication in small group interactions work.

Understand and Utilize the "Four Phases of Group Life"

Every group that comes together, whether it meets frequently or is meeting for the first time, moves through three phases before it is productive, effective, and focused on getting the job done. Those phases are: "forming," "storming," and "norming." (Yes, these words are a little "cutesy," but they are the words that are commonly used in the world of facilitation. They also communicate an important meaning.)

A group that is doing the work that it came together to do is in the fourth phase, or the "performing phase" of group dynamics. There are identifying characteristics for this phase: the trust level is high, there is one agreed upon agenda, and everyone is functioning appropriately in their role.

In Scenario A, where the shareholders bought more football tickets, none of these characteristics of the "performing" phase were present. This is because the first three phases of group dynamics did not occur. Here is what the administrator in Scenario A could have done to have a more productive meeting:

Phase One — Forming

The description of a group that is at the forming phase is the opposite of performing. In forming, the trust level is low and there are many agendas. It is the facilitator's (read: administrator's) job in the forming phase to build trust that this meeting will be effective, and to bring these agendas together in a way that the overall goal of the group is accomplished.

One way to begin is to interview people ahead of time to understand their perspectives and the political ramifications of the issues that are on the meeting agenda. The Scenario A administrator may have discovered that there was so much resistance to the idea of developing more business that a better agenda item would be to brainstorm and prioritize the possibilities for generating more income.

Here are some other important forming activities:

- Before the meeting, talk with people who might be disruptive. Give them special attention before the meeting to see if you can prevent problems during the meeting.
- When the meeting begins, seat people around a table so they can see each other — no straight rows like schoolroom days. People simply do not trust people they cannot see.
- Make people comfortable. Have food and coffee if appropriate, and talk with people as they come in. Make sure you include yourself in the pre-meeting banter. This activity helps people relax and begins to establish your role as the facilitator and their roles as the participants.

Phase Two — Storming

In weather, a storm is created from turbulence. In meetings the turbulence occurs when participants are concerned about getting what they want, or having to deal with an issue they would prefer to avoid. The purpose of the second phase, "storming," in small groups is to settle the turbulence by creating an agreed-upon agenda. If participants don't buy in, they will knowingly or subtly sabotage the meeting.

Remember the football discussion? Weave the benefits in by introducing the agenda as if it were an interesting story — *"At our last meeting we were concerned about income for next year, and you asked me to analyze where we could generate more income. I have done that, and would like to present my results here, taking into consideration what you all have told me."*

Yes, it takes more time, but it is going to be much more effective than a topical agenda. *"First we are going to look at the financial reports for the fourth quarter, then we will talk about increasing business development activity."* Let the disagreements occur around the agenda instead of around the issue.

Phase Three — Norming

Norms are the standards by which a group behaves. Norms also include standards for being on time, who talks first, whether people can leave, confidentiality, and commitment to follow-up: Each small group needs to implicitly decide what its norms are.

In Scenario A, there was a norm that it was okay to talk about football at any time, and that it surpassed other conversations. Perhaps, if partners knew how many billable hours were being used up talking about football, they might be convinced that that's a better activity for the social time before.

Most groups, especially those that have met for a long time and are not being as productive as they might be, need to take a look at their norms. Changing norms is not easy because there are usually political- and power-related reasons why meetings are nonproductive. In the practicality of facilitating small groups, norming and storming probably don't occur as sequential steps. That both are dealt with is more important than what is done first.

By utilizing the four phases of group dynamics, most small group problems either diminish or disappear. The skills discussed here regarding individual communication skills are also helpful in small group discussions. During those forming interviews, process questions will help to uncover the real issues. Reflection is crucial during a meeting because every facilitator needs to summarize and clarify complexities for the group. A small group will be made up of people with different predominate learning styles, so a facilitator lists key points for visuals and talks through the points for the auditories.

Practicing these skills and using what is appropriate in your situation will help you achieve understanding and reach a productive flow of communication in your firms.

What are the Key Skills, Personal Attributes and Experience Necessary for a Successful Executive Director?

From ALA's Large Firm Administrators

The extraordinary administrator must truly be an expert communicator. That conclusion was reinforced in a survey of members of ALA's Large Firm Administrators Caucus.[1] The survey was conducted in October 2000 in conjunction with that group's annual Fall Retreat.

Communication skills were, in one form or another, among those most cited in response to the question that forms the title of this Chapter Appendix. What else do administrators in the largest law firms view as the key skills, personal attributes and types of experience necessary to be a successful/extraordinary administrator?

Other responses to the question included:

- *Sufficient experience and maturity to have the respect of partners. At the same time, the ability to control his/her own ego in working with lawyers who frequently have a high opinion of their legal and interpersonal skills. Has to be able to develop relationships of trust and confidence. Has to be willing to work as hard as many lawyers do.*
- *Intelligence. Proactive. Interpersonal skills of the highest order. Respect of lawyers. A macro thinker. Ability to think imaginatively and to be ahead of the firm's strategic objectives.*
- *Initiative. Accessibility. Responsiveness. Candor — polite, but firm.*
- *Financial expertise — budgeting, analysis, inventory management. Administrative experience — supervisory ability, HR skills, selection of effective deputies. Diplomacy — ability to deal with many "bosses."*
- *Integrity, dedication, ability to communicate, financial background.*
- *Pragmatic, results-oriented, good finance background, people person, interest in law (even if no background in law), non-political.*
- *Extensive experience managing a fair-sized organization; extensive knowledge of accounting and finance; ability to relate effectively with subordinates; ability to relate as a peer to partners in the firm; vision for the future and the energy to build consensus on new ideas.*
- *Intelligence, presence, integrity, "public" speaking skills, leadership and management skills, objectivity, decision-making ability, technical skills in all areas of administration, tact, ability to handle pressure, diplomacy.*

---

1 The Caucus is comprised of the principal administrators, generally the Executive Director or Chief Operating Officer, in firms of 100 or more lawyers.

- *The Executive Director must have communication skills that demonstrate maturity, competence and confidence, while at the same time demonstrating a respect and appreciation for the owners/partners. Must have several years of management experience, preferably in a professional environment (law firm or accounting firm). The Executive Director must have enough exposure to other areas of responsibilities (IT, Facilities, HR, etc.) to enable effective management of those areas and their directors.*

A Reader's Exercise: How do your skills, personal attributes and experience measure up against what the large firm administrators see as necessary for success? What "needs work"?

CHAPTER 5
NETWORK EFFECTIVELY

It's not what you know, but who you know.

Actually, it's not even who you know but rather who knows you — both within and outside the firm. The international 2001 survey of the Association of Career Management Professionals identified networking as responsible for approximately 70 percent of all job placements. The survey also found that 80 percent of vacancies are never even advertised.

As one of the most effective career-advancement and professional-development strategies, networking is a vital skill set for the extraordinary administrator to cultivate. Networking is essentially about acquiring and sustaining meaningful relationships. This is so important that you cannot simply leave it up to chance. It must be approached in a systematic way with a specific plan of action. The goal is to manage your social capital with a view to maintaining effective ongoing relationships.

This strategy involves a general approach combined with a more focused targeted action plan. The general approach emphasizes building your personal profile so that the right people know you (See Chapters 8 and 18). The law is very community based, so word of mouth is important. Write articles, and wherever possible let people see you in action. Use industry groups such as the Association of Legal Administrators and ensure that you attend appropriate conferences and events at least once a month. Once you are there and among the right people, you to need to schmooze effectively:

- Use eye contact.
- Look for people who are by themselves.
- Have a good opening line (or several of them).
- Find a point of connection. Genuine compliments work well.
- Always remember people's names.
- Be self-confident and enthusiastic.

- Work the room. Go for volume and don't get stuck for too long in one conversation.
- Always keep your business cards handy.

In short, build your visibility and position yourself strategically by getting out and about. This applies both within and outside the firm.

The targeted strategy starts with an understanding of your past, existing and future contacts. Make a list of all the key people (those who you once knew, those who you know now, those who you would like to know and those who know you). Review this list carefully and identify the key contacts that you should convert into strategic relationships. Focus in particular on centers of influence (other professionals, recruitment consultants, influential partners, rising star lawyers, etc.). Also take into account the likelihood for commonality of interest, as this will greatly facilitate the relationship-building process. Remember that your time is limited so cull the list regularly to avoid duplication (people from the same industry group or same social circle).

The next step is to meaningfully categorize these critical relationships (1 - maintain; 2 - build; and 3 - establish) and then develop appropriate action plans for each relationship. In general, maintaining relationships will involve a pattern of regular communication. This can be formal (quarterly get-togethers) or informal (phone calls, e-mails or office visits), but regularity is important. It is also vital to progressively establish a base of shared experiences to underpin and sustain the relationship. Building or establishing new relationships requires a much more proactive approach to identify ways where you can be of genuine assistance — introducing others, sending articles, etc. As with any relationship, building trust through genuine personal interest will nurture its development.

Networking assists your career progression and builds your knowledge base. Plus, the social dimension can inject an element of fun into your working life. Those who network best often do it without conscious thought or planning. However, if you feel that this is an area where your performance needs improvement, you need to take deliberate action and persevere until it becomes second nature.

Further Reading

Hart, Rupert, Nigel Scott, *Effective Networking Skills for Professional Success: Making the Most of Your Personal Contacts.* Kogan Page Ltd., 1996.

Henderson, Robin, *"People Want to Work with Someone They Know, Like and Trust"*

Saxon, Bret, Steve Stein, *The Art of the Shmooze.* SPI Books, 1998.

Susman, Karen, *102 Top Dog Networking Secrets: Follow up, Keep in Touch and Turn Contacts into Customers.* Top Dog Guidebooks, [n.d.].

Smith, Michael M., "Making Contact: The Importance of Networking in a Changing Business Environment." *ALA News*, June/July 1994.

The Association of Legal Administrators regularly features articles on the subject of administrator experiences and success. The following article first appeared in *ALA News*, Volume 13, Number 3 (June/July 1994). It appears here to supplement the ideas in this chapter.

Making Contact: The Importance of Networking In a Changing Business Environment

By Michael M. Smith

During the past decade law firms have experienced significant change. Things just aren't the way they used to be. During better times, business was easier to acquire and maintain. Client fee sensitivity, competition, specialization, and poor public image have made the practice of law much more difficult. It requires much more effort to manage and sustain a successful law practice.

What constitutes the basic requirements for developing and sustaining a successful law practice in today's business environment? One thing is for certain: What used to work may only suffice in the future. Attorneys and firm managers who recognize this fact and adjust early are likely to be ahead of the game.

Two basic objectives of business remain unchanged:

• Maintain existing clients and expand business to better meet their needs.
• Acquire new clients to replenish lost clients.

While this basic focus to develop and sustain a successful practice does not change, the ways in which these objectives are accomplished have changed dramatically. The strategies and tactics used by attorneys change as the market makes it difficult to retain and acquire clients.

There is one common denominator to sustaining a successful practice: acquiring and sustaining meaningful relationships. While the answer may seem obvious, it must not be dismissed. Networking develops and maintains meaningful relationships.

The word "networking" causes some people to shrink in disdain. Networking is an important part of business, but few really know how to go about it.

What is Networking?

Networking is at the very foundation of all business development activities. As a business development tool, it requires some understanding: You can't expect to attend an occasional cocktail party and consider that networking.

Networking is maintaining regular contact people for the ultimate purpose of developing business. It is the sincere and constant effort to help others, anticipating that you will, in turn, be helped.

Effective networking involves defining possible contacts, determining your networking purpose, developing a plan of action and committing the time and energy necessary to produce meaningful results.

Why is Networking Important?

Networking works! Most practices know that business is generated through sustained networking activity. They know the nuances and benefits of networking:

- Quality relationships take time to build and get stronger over time. They cannot be maintained without regular communication.
- People tend to feel most comfortable with others in their age group. Typically, a range of five to seven years on either side of a person's age creates an atmosphere of compatibility.
- People who share common interests (religion, political affiliation, physical exercise, children of the same age) transcend most age barriers.
- People are attracted to others who are most like them, or to those who offer unique perspectives.
- People appreciate and remember when you show personal interest in them or others important in their lives (family, employees, charitable activities).
- People do business with people they like, trust, confide in and feel comfortable around.

How Can I Network Effectively?

Networking concerns two key issues: how you establish new relationships and how you maintain effective and ongoing relationships.

Building new relationships is difficult. Firms must clearly define who they would like to have as new clients and then develop a complete listing of their current and future network of contacts. A firm's network is a group of people who may, over time, refer business to the firm or become clients themselves. By taking the time to define its network, it is better able to utilize the network. Keep the many facets of any successful network in mind:

- **All the people you used to know** – former neighbors, old friends, former clients, fellow employees, school acquaintances
- **All the people you now know** – church members, family, current clients, social contacts, charitable affiliations
- **All of the people who know you** – former students, attendees at your speeches, newsletter recipients
- **All of the people you would like to know** – prospective clients (by person or company name), influential people, leaders of trade/business associations

Decide which people on your networking list are strong possibilities for a sustained business relationship. Make these the firm's priority contacts.

Obviously, the stronger the relationship becomes the easier it is to maintain. It is important to remember that all business relationships, no matter how solid, require time and attention. Older relationships can more effectively be maintained by introducing new and creative ways of staying in touch.

Many people may balk at developing a networking list. They believe they already know their business contact. Administrators should view this as a red flag which indicates employees are more interested in perpetuating old habits that produce familiar results. Prove that developing a network list can be illuminating.

Formerly strong client relationships that weaken over time are indicators of poor networking. If a firm does not communicate with its good clients, the door is open for other attorneys to develop relationships that could replace your firm.

Now that the networking list is clearly defined, the firm may proceed. Keep these hints in mind to ensure success:

- Establish a strong relationship so that networking contacts recognize you even from among a large group.
- Maintain one-on-one name recognition.
- Invite the person to an office luncheon and exchange business information.
- Establish a mutual point of interest — search for something you have in common.
- Send informal notes to confirm meetings.
- Follow-up with a breakfast meeting to stay in touch.
- Express interest in finding out more about the person's business — extend a desire to visit the person's place of business.
- Forward articles of interest.
- Invite business contacts to social events attended by other friends and associates.
- Make some type of ongoing contact every four to six weeks until you feel comfortable that this individual is a viable part of your network.

Maintain Your Network

Consider yourself the "gardener" in maintaining business relationships. Gardeners know strong growth requires constant care. Only through long-term commitment and vision will a beautiful garden flourish.

Business relationships will prosper with diligent care and nurturing. If unattended, they too will wither away. Attorneys who recognize the value of relationships will take the time to manage and nurture those relationships and ensure a successful practice.

Firms can never stop managing their network. Even well developed networks can deteriorate within a year if they are not properly maintained. Keeping the network viable can be relatively simple:

- Make regular telephone calls to prospective clients.
- Invite people to quarterly or semi-annual luncheons or holiday parties.
- Send copies of firm newsletters with personal notes. Also send birthday and anniversary cards.
- Plan annual meetings with clients to review satisfaction level.
- Occasionally stop by clients' offices.

To manage effective networking systems, firms must define the strategic focus of their efforts; define their existing and future contacts; and develop a specific plan of action for managing networking efforts.

An effective business network is the foundation of all successful business development efforts. Attorneys and administrators must be focused and deliberate about how they maintain current clients and generate new business.

CHAPTER 6
EDUCATE CONTINUOUSLY

"The future ain't what it used to be." — *Yogi Berra*

It is hardly surprising that good educational qualifications are highly regarded within law firm environments. However, in addition to reinforcing your personal credibility, it is also clear that the knowledge requirement for the professional administrator is becoming increasingly more onerous. Consequently, there is a need to implement a life-long education program in order to maintain effective performance.

There are benefits of continuous education:
- increased skills/expertise;
- improved credibility;
- broader career options;
- improved self-esteem; and
- additional networking opportunities.

The Association of Legal Administrators conducted a knowledge, skills and abilities assessment in 1995 and again in 2000. The analysis that followed identified the key learning areas for law firm administrators. (See Appendix II.) Paramount in that list were communication (See Chapter 4.), interpersonal relations and accounting. Technology and, depending on seniority, strategy development also made the top 10.

In many law firms, there is a baseline expectation that the firm administrator has very good financial skills. If these financial skills are not an existing strength, my advice would be to first focus your attention in this area. You don't necessarily need to be an accountant or financial guru, but given the strong bottom-line focus prevalent in most law firms, it is difficult to be an effective administrator without having a sound grasp of the key economic drivers.

Remember that continuing education need not be just about multiple degrees or other qualifications. It also includes short courses, seminars and conferences; books/articles; tapes; and even informal discussion with other professionals. You should also not disregard the benefits of education through experience by debriefing after major projects or using feedback/evaluation reports.

In addition to the traditional key learning areas, it is important to include general industry knowledge such as key trends, future developments and competitor activity. Consider also enhancing your knowledge about your own firm by reading relevant documents such as strategic plans, and annual reports. Review key client information as well.

Many law firms create sophisticated professional development programs for the lawyers while the administrators and managers are left to fend for themselves. It is therefore easy to lose sight of this issue and then suddenly find that your skills are out of date. Consequently, you need to make a special effort to take personal responsibility for your professional development. Failure to educate continuously will result in your career prospects stagnating or — even worse — going backward. In today's business environment, change is occurring at a rapid pace and to be extraordinary requires a life-long commitment to knowledge development.

Further Reading

Boldt, Jenny, "From Secretary to Administrator: A Personal Voyage." *People-to-People*, August 1988.

Capozzi, John, *Why Climb The Corporate Ladder When You Can Take The Elevator?* 500 Secrets For Success In Business. JMC Industries, Inc., 2001.

ALA Survey Report, "Jacks of all Trades." *Legal Management*, May/June 2001. (See Appendix II.)

Spruill, M. Lynn, "The Delivery of Legal Services in the Future" *Legal Management*, May/June 2001. (See Appendix I.)

Change and Education March Hand-in-Hand

What do you envision the primary responsibilities of the Executive Director will be in your firm five years from now?

What will be the Executive Director's authority and span of control in your firm five years from now?

Those were two related questions posed in an October 2000 survey of members of ALA's Large Firm Administrators Caucus.[1] Some of the answers to these questions, reflecting the changing face of the practice of law and the evolution of management responsibilities in law firms, indicate new skill sets, new responsibilities and new challenges, which the extraordinary administrator will meet only by continuous education.

What sort of future do these large firm administrators see?

- *Technology responsibility will grow in complexity and importance, and require a higher portion of resources and attention.*

- *Manage and direct all business activities of the firm, including areas beyond the practice of law.*

- *Responsibilities about the same but will probably have more delegates (i.e. people with delegated responsibilities and special skills) reporting to him/her.*

- *Higher internal profile in performance appraisal and career counseling of lawyers (including partners) and in practice management.*

- *The administrator will truly be the Chief Business Officer; responsible for all administrative staff; ex-officio non-voting member of the Operating Committee and governing body; business advisor to the Managing Partner.*

- *Responsibility for the operations of the firm in all areas for all offices — planning, accounting and finance, human resources, technology, recruiting, marketing, facilities, purchasing, library services…and as more pressure is put on lawyers to bill time (as opposed to "managing"), more responsibility and authority will need to be given to the Executive Director.*

---

1 The Large Firm Administrators Caucus is comprised of the principal administrators, generally the Executive Director or Chief Operating Officer, in firms of 100 or more lawyers. The survey in question was conducted in conjunction with the group's annual Fall Retreat.

- *The Executive Director is (in five years) authorized to make most all decisions that are a function of the areas and personnel that report to the Executive Director, and are within the established firm operating and/or capital budget.*

And then there was this comment about the position of a firm legal administrator in five years that, in the context of the discussion of the survey at the Large Firm Administrators 2002 Retreat, drew general agreement:

The position will be defined by the talent of the individual, more than by the job description.

CHAPTER 7
MAINTAIN BALANCE

Success and fulfillment are not synonymous.

One day, years from now, you will look back on this period in your life and wonder whether you had everything in balance. Did you make the right choices in your commitment to work, leisure, family, social circle, spiritual growth, health, community, learning and the other important dimensions of your life? Do you have any regrets? Have you left behind the desired legacy?

No doubt, years from now, the answers will probably be clearer than they are now. Hindsight has a way of improving our perspective. Right now though, many of us are paddling as fast as we can just to keep up. The continuing challenge is to periodically pull our canoes onto shore and ask the key questions now, while we can still influence the outcome.

Maintaining balance has become a catch-cry of 21st-century living. And despite the rhetoric, many people are living proof that you can have it all. Law firm environments are very demanding and they reflect a very high work ethic, so it is easy to lose one's balance. However, to be an extraordinary or even highly effective administrator, requires that you are comfortable with the lifestyle choices you make. Doing otherwise inevitably leads to unhappiness and regret, which over time, adversely impacts performance.

In that regard, the important issue to emphasize is that having a balanced life is a matter of personal judgment, which cannot be defined by others. Your definition of balance will also change over time, so accept that there will be tradeoffs or compromises and do not become too obsessed with having it all right now.

The important ingredient is to take time out and periodically reflect on all aspects of your life, to make sure you are comfortable with the choices you are making. Do not wait for the crisis to manifest itself or the life-changing wake-up call to occur. You can benefit from the unfortunate experience of so many others who waited until it was too late. Review and re-evaluate your priorities: Do it now!

Further Reading

Kaufman, George W., *Lawyers' Guide to Balancing Life and Work - Taking the Stress Out of Success*. American Bar Association Section of Law Practice Management, 1999.

Lang, John, *Re: Life — Find Your Balance and Master Work, Change, Career, Family, Nutrition, Exercise, Sleep*. John Lang & Associates, [n.d.].

Lurie, Sylvia, "The Quality of Life Among Legal Administrators." *Legal Management*, September/October 1994.

Andelt, Deborah K., "Get a Life!" *Legal Management*, July/August 1998.

Diehl, Linda, "Empowerment: Reducing Stress Among Support Staff." *Law Practice Management*, May/June 1997.

Daniels, Dianna K., *Get a Life Without Sacrificing Your Career: How to Make More Time for What's Really Important*. McGraw-Hill, 1999.

Smith, Jeffrey D., *Stress-Free Success: How to Really Achieve All Your Goals Without Giving Up Your Life*. Center for Personal Excellence, 1997.

Sher, Barbara, *It's Only Too Late If You Don't Start Now: How To Create Your Second Life At Any Age*. Delacorte Press, 1999.

McDargh, Eileen, *Work for a Living and Still Be Free to Live*. Bookpartners Inc., 1997.

The Association of Legal Administrators regularly features articles on the subject of administrator experiences and success. The following article first appeared in *Legal Management*, Volume 17, Number 4 (July/August 1998). It appears here to supplement the ideas in this chapter.

Get a Life!
(It'll Be Good for You and Your Job.)

By Deborah K. Andelt

Time is money. The cliché is so pervasive that no one questions its truth. In a law firm environment, where most firms measure value by the "billable hour," time is the commodity. As an administrator in that environment, it's easy to believe that the more time you put into your job, the more value you have. But at what cost?

To have a personal life and still accomplish our professional goals we need a shift in perspective. If time is money, then time is an asset — something to invest wisely. What can we invest in for the greatest growth, return and value?

Stephan Rechtschaffen, M.D., suggests in *Time Shifting* that we change our view from thinking overwork is important and necessary, to thinking overwork is wasting time and "play" is valuable. Work is only part of our lives. Studies show that people with more activities outside of work are healthier than people with no activities. People who exercise regularly report increased energy and creativity. Vigorous exercise can improve memory, relieve stress, and even make intelligent people smarter. Taking time to do things away from work actually makes us more productive at work.

Get Active

Lois Nafziger, administrator and practicing attorney at High, Swartz, Roberts & Seidell in Norristown, Pennsylvania, knows first hand that an active lifestyle outside the office helps her at work.

"Exercise is very important. At 47 I learned to [in-line skate]; at 48 I learned to ski; and at 49 I started golfing," she boasts. Nafziger learned to skate by practicing in the dark on her driveway. Now she keeps her Rollerblades handy in her trunk for impromptu travels.

Nafziger explains that earlier in her career she didn't have an active life outside of work. Then she noticed an attorney in her firm who regularly took off one of every 10 weeks. That attorney was by far the most productive. Nafziger says she learned from that example that it's important to have weekly activities as well as at least two one-week vacations annually. "Investing time in outside activities leads to greater creativity, focus and generally being more effective at work," she says.

Setting boundaries for personal time during the week is critical. This time must be scheduled and not pushed aside. One of the things Nafziger does each week is sing in her church choir.

"My church is a beautiful building built in 1863. Part of the positive effect of my involvement in choir is being in that building and letting the beauty soak in. It's an important time for me, and really puts the week in perspective," she says. Nafziger notes that spiritual experiences like those are an important part of anyone's quality of life.

What nurtures and inspires us is as diverse as we are. In the legal services culture, it's easy to get caught up in the workaholism syndrome and not even know what to do outside of work. To identify what you can do for yourself, put some things in writing:

- Write a list of activities that nurture you. Include anything you think of — watching the sunrise, dancing, having a massage, or reading for pleasure.
- Next, make a list of things you would do if you didn't have to do them perfectly.
- Make another list of things you would do if you didn't mind seeming silly.

Let these lists be your starting point for creating a fulfilling life for yourself. Identify one activity you'll pursue this month; and one for this year. Then do it. Block out the time and don't let anything interfere with your self-nurturing.

Balance Your Life

To find out how balanced your life is now, take two pieces of paper and draw a large circle on each one. Divide each circle into eight pie-wedges. Label the sections: work, play/relaxation, self-nurturing, family, health/physical wellness, spirituality, romance, and friends. On one page, fill in the sections based on how "filled" your days are with time or activity is for each area of your life. Post these in a visible place as a reminder. Then make new circles every three months to chart your progress. Most of us spend large amounts of time at often un-fulfilling work. By the time we get home, we have very little time for the more fulfilling activities — ourselves, loved ones, physical health, play and spirituality. To find balance, aim for a full circle of fulfilling areas, and whatever your comfort zone is for time commitments.

Work pace continues to accelerate. In the 1990s, 60- 70- and 80-hour workweeks were no longer the exception. Long working hours were commonplace across professional services industries — bankers, lawyers, accountants — according to Juliet B. Schor in *The Overworked American.*

Achieving Equilibrium

Take These Steps toward a Balanced Life
Here are some life management ideas — these aren't in any magical order. For each of us, what we do needs to reflect what we want and need at any particular time.

- Set boundaries for your personal time.
- Identify your personal priorities.
- Create support systems.
- Spend time alone.
- Plan. Plan. Plan.
- Simplify your life.
- Do what you love.
- Experience nature.
- Develop rich personal relationships.
- Exercise — move your body.
- Enjoy a spiritual practice.
- Spread joy.

Economic competition, innovative business management, and efforts to reduce expenses combined to raise the number of hours we work. Schor notes that working mothers averaged 65 hours a week of total working time. The average employed person today works an extra month each year compared to 20 years ago.

As our pace quickens we try to do more in less time and we often feel a time squeeze. Time management and calendaring systems may help schedule the time we have, but they don't do much to expand our time. To do that we need to identify our priorities and eliminate things and people that really aren't necessary.

Bianca Moreiras, executive administrator at Bedzow, Korn, Brown, Wolfe & Lipto in Miami, Florida, says, "The key is to plan, plan plan." Two years ago she and her husband found themselves new parents — with one week's notice — when they adopted their first child. Two years later with her second child, Moreiras says her priorities have definitely changed. "The first thing to go was [extensive volunteer work with] ALA. I was on about six committees and had been active for 13 years," she says.

Moreiras recently restructured her job to a four-day workweek to allow even more time with her family. "I have a policy of not working from home on the fifth day," she notes. She's accomplishing this change by letting go of even more. Projects she used to do at work are now delegated to the staff. By carefully choosing people and projects, she found her staff welcomes the additional responsibilities.

Even more important than delegating is planning to avoid ongoing problems. "Staff attendance used to be a big issue. Attorneys would complain about secretaries being late. Then I built attendance into the bonus system. The problem self-corrected," Moreiras says. She holds weekly meetings with the managing partners. This is her time and her agenda. "That way I plan my tasks and identify priorities," she explains.

"I've also learned that most things really aren't a crisis. Now when I get a request for a project, I tell the attorneys when it will be done. But, the key is that I meet my deadline. They know they'll have what they need when I say it will be done," she adds. Investing time in planning actually reduces time spent in crisis management or unimportant projects.

Create Positive Change

For some people, changes we experience naturally allow us to identify our priorities. Making changes is relatively easy. For others, there may just be a feeling that "something" needs to change, but we're not sure what our priorities are — much less how to make changes. Try this exercise: Take another sheet of paper and write about your fantasy perfect day. From the time you get up, perhaps even before, until you go to sleep. Where are you? Who are you with? What are you doing?

This doesn't need to reflect reality as you know it. Perhaps you enjoy waking to the sound of the rhythm of ocean waves — but you live in Kansas. Write about what you hear and how you feel when you wake up by the ocean. Continue with your day. If you don't have children, but want to spend time with children, write about what you do, what the children are like, and how you feel. The reverse could also be true. A day away from your four children could seem heavenly. Be detailed in your descriptions.

Review the elements of your perfect day and find ways to incorporate elements of what you want into your present life. If you're in Kansas longing to be on a beach, buy a CD of wave music, or an alarm clock that lets you wake to the sound of the ocean. If you don't have children, borrow some — offer to spend time with nieces, nephews, or neighborhood kids. Find a volunteer program that works with children. If you want time away, enlist the aid of family and friends to watch your children while you create time for yourself. Keep it simple. Find ways to create your perfect day that fits where you are now.

One woman I know realized she had let an interest in live musical performances slip away. With a busy family and limited budget, she wasn't sure what she could do to experience that again. Soon after this discovery, she was thrilled to learn about concerts at a local community college. They fit her budget for both time and money. Expand your thinking to look for things that are possible, rather than focusing on what won't work. Frequently we discover we can have the essence of what we want.

Maybe part of your perfect day is tending a beautiful garden. Then you hear voices in your head saying there's not room or you don't have time. Start small. Put a flower box in your window. Or plant a small herb garden and share the harvest with friends.

You may also have discovered some things you want that require bigger shifts. I met a woman once who realized she liked working — that was part of her perfect day — but she needed to have a window. In her existing office situation there were no windows. She needed a job shift to create this change. Perhaps your perfect job or working environment evolved as a result of this writing exercise. Some people discover they really need a change of geographic location. Continue making small, simple changes to let you experience the essence of what you want as you plan and work toward the ultimate goal. For example, if part of your perfect day was photographing nature, start on the weekend. Take an advanced photography class. Take yourself on a weeklong photography vacation.

Four years ago, Sharon Abrahams, director of education/training at Greenberg Traurig Hoffman Lipoff Rosen & Quentel in Miami, Florida, realized she needed a change. After 18 years in the training field, she thought she needed either a law degree or something else to gain credibility in the legal field. She also wanted to do something personally beneficial. She enjoys teaching and learning, so she decided to pursue her doctorate. This spring she got her Ph.D.

She travels for her job and has an active family life with her daughter and husband. These things stayed in place as she found a degree program that offered Saturday classes. "One of the keys is to re-prioritize." Abrahams says, echoing Moreiras. Relaxing with her family became more important to Abrahams than doing the dishes.

Abrahams also has terrific support systems. As a facilitator in stress management, she knew that was important.

"My mother read every paper I wrote. She was my copy editor for four years. My husband was the biggest support, both emotionally and sharing the physical demands of running a household," she says. And Abrahams also credits the firm. "The firm let me use the library for research, the associates were my subjects for my research dissertation, and they gave me time off when I needed it," she adds.

Abrahams notes that she invested her time into her Ph.D. for herself, but in the end the firm benefited. "I'm better at my job in helping lawyers be more human, and the firm now has tuition reimbursement program," she says. Two people in her department have returned to school to complete their degrees.

A supportive firm environment can be a factor in individuals being able to have a thriving personal life. When Nafziger switched firms, she looked for a firm that supported outside activities. She explains that in 1914 the founding partners believed that service to the community and family were important. Those values have continued. "When prospective lawyers are interviewed, we actually ask what they do outside of work. We want people working here who have balanced lives," she says.

"In a law firm, clients come to fix things that are broken — by definition they are under stress. The best way to deal with their stress is to deal effectively with our own stress," Nafziger explains. She recently started a staff meeting with a big sign "Stay Inspired" and invited the staff to take a big breath and keep the big picture in focus. "It had an amazing calming effect," she says.

Moreiras notes that there can be resistance to making changes in a firm, like moving to a four-day workweek or flexible hours. "The problem is that the attorneys fear the job won't get done," she says. The key to overcoming the fear is credibility. "If you don't have credibility, don't ask," she adds.

"Do what you love," Abrahams says. "Build toward your end goal by taking small steps. Work up to your ultimate goal, rather than trying to take a big leap," Moreiras adds.

CHAPTER 8
DEVELOP YOUR IMAGE

Above all be sincere. If you can fake that, you've got it made.

Being extraordinary is largely defined by the perception others (especially your key clients) have of you. Consequently, you need to devote appropriate time and energy to developing and maintaining the right image. Image, in this context, should not be regarded as merely an illusion or facade. Rather, it is about ensuring that your real capabilities are presented in the best possible light. This is not a substitute for substance nor is it an attempt to manipulate or deceive. There are numerous dimensions to creating a winning "image," but three areas stand out: behavior, appearance and environment.

Behavior

Your behavior and, more importantly, how you spend your time, will communicate the strongest message about your image. Start by ensuring that you have a meaningful job title that conveys as much seniority and breadth of scope as you can negotiate. Law firms are very status-driven so this is not an unimportant issue. Also ensure that, when you are first appointed to a position, the announcement to all partners/staff is well drafted to emphasize your qualifications and experience for the new role. Personal credibility, especially in the early stages, is vital to your image perception.

Finally, pay particular attention to how you determine your priorities as these, more than anything else, will probably be the ultimate guide to how others see you. Make sure that you attend the right meetings and that your name is added to the distribution list for key firm reports or newsletters. Wherever possible, avoid the "back-office" tag and try to position yourself on equal terms with the lawyers or the more senior managers. I see many administrators who continue to perpetuate the "us and them" mindset when referring to the lawyers or partners: This is definitely not consistent with the desired image profile.

Appearance

Your appearance is another key image factor. How you dress, your personal hygiene and your grooming all reinforce a certain image perception. This image should be consistent with your next career move. A good guide is to "look the part" by reference to your supervisor or senior partner. Despite the increasing popularity of "casual days," remember that law firms are still highly professional environments and select your wardrobe accordingly.

Related to your appearance is your body language, so make sure that your posture, handshake, eye contact, etc., reinforce the desired image. Personal impressions are generally formed within the first 30 seconds; once made they are slow to change. It is important therefore to get it right the first time. If you are unsure about the image your appearance is conveying, ask a close friend or colleague for honest feedback.

Environment

The final area for attention is your environment. One of the non-negotiable qualities that the firm will look for in its administrator is good organizational skills. Despite what you see in most lawyers' offices, your work area should reflect order and neatness rather than chaos and clutter. Also, use the latest technology tools to reinforce your high standards of personal efficiency.

Your image identifies your strongest attributes and creates a mental picture that others will recognize, remember and to which they will respond. It is your brand and you want it to be a positive force in promoting career advancement.

There's more to image than acting the part, looking good and being neat: You should also have a healthy self-image and positive attitude. (See Chapter 12.) If you need to change or reposition your image, make sure the changes are genuine and try to make them gradually rather than all at once.

Further Reading

Cummens, John, "Success Factors for the Legal Administrator." Management & Administration, February 1986.

Gray, James Jr., *The Winning Image: Present Yourself With Confidence and Style for Career Success*. AMACOM, 1993.

CHAPTER 9
BUILD YOUR TEAM

"None of us is as good as all of us."
— Ray Kroc, Founder of McDonald's

There is an old Chinese proverb: If you want one year of prosperity, grow grain; if you want 10 years of prosperity, grow trees; and if you want 100 years of prosperity, grow people.

More than ever before, achieving success requires a strong team effort. Therefore, if you want to advance your career, you must focus on your own personal achievements and — equally if not more importantly — build an outstanding team. This will involve selecting the right people and then inspiring them to find their passion. Good managers (extraordinary administrators) motivate team members to achieve their full potential.

Choosing your team members is obviously a key prerequisite. Indeed, many would suggest that if your people are outstanding, everything else follows. Your goal therefore is to learn how to recognize talented individuals and then create an environment that will encourage them to join your team.

Remember that most skills and competencies can be learned through training. So as part of your selection criteria, focus in particular on inherent character traits and attitudes. Always hire the best people your budget can afford and never be threatened by individuals who have the capacity to be more competent than you. Their success will always reflect well on you and help your progress. In addition to recruiting well, you will need to constantly "scrape the barnacles" from the bottom of your ship. Weeding out the poor performers is a necessary part of maintaining a high-performance team.

Having selected the right team members, your goal is to motivate them. This involves providing good training as well as ensuring that everyone has the right tools and resources. Your team members must be inspired to perform. Set appropriate goals and provide suitable incentives and rewards.

Goal setting is an important task. In addition to ensuring that goals are specific, measurable and realistically achievable, it is essential to review them regularly with each team member. In setting goals, remember to delegate as much as possible (See Chapter 10.) and also harness the diversity of your team members by playing to each individual's strengths. Obviously this requires that you get to know each of your team members as individuals. This will also help you determine suitable reward mechanisms.

Many managers assume that the key performance incentives relate to financial remuneration, career progression and job security (in that order). However, most surveys confirm that employees actually value respect, personal growth and freedom even more highly. Remember that law firm support staff members have particular needs because they generally have limited career paths and, in contrast to lawyers, there are no prospects of equity ownership. You therefore have to work hard at removing the obstacles and empowering these important team members by providing a sense of autonomy in carrying out their duties.

The performance expectations within a law firm are very high and at times extremely demanding. Mistakes are not easily tolerated. So in addition to being the captain and coach, a big part of your role as an extraordinary administrator will be to act as cheerleader, even when things don't go according to plan.

In addition to the usual rewards, think about the small things such as a thank-you note, congratulatory dinner, or few encouraging words of praise. These acts can often be very effective in demonstrating your genuine appreciation. Also ensure that you are constantly communicating with your team members to provide feedback and help them develop a big-picture "context" for their day-to-day activities. Above all, try to make it fun!

To be an extraordinary administrator will require the support of an extraordinary team. This involves finding talented individuals and then inspiring them to produce outstanding results.

Further Reading

Carnegie, Dale, *How to Win Friends and Influence People*. Pocket Books, 1994 (reprint).

Colbert, John R., Jr., Silvia L. Coulter, "Making Your Team Work." *Marketing for Lawyers*, May 1999.

Conti, Al, "The Administrator As Coach: Developing a Winning Team." *Legal Management*, May/June 1997.

Dodd, Carol Vodra, "Making Them Part of the Team: Motivate Your Support Staff." *ALA News*, June/July 1995.

Luebke, Robert, "Designing the Effective Team in a Law Firm Environment." *Legal Management*, September/October 1995.

Ryan, Mary Claire, "Team Building in the Law Office." *Legal Administrator*, September/October 1988.

"What's the Hallmark of a Good Administrator? It's Good Stuff." *Law Office Administrator*, September 2001.

Collins, James, *Good to Great: Why Some Companies Make the Leap*. Harper Collins, 2001.

CHAPTER 10
DELEGATE

"There is no limit to what a man can achieve if he doesn't care who gets the credit." — Robert Woodruff, Coca-Cola

Once you build a well functioning team, it is even more important to your role as a successful administrator that you delegate effectively. Failure to delegate will hinder your efforts at team building, and it will thwart your ability to devote personal attention to the firm's more demanding, value-adding tasks. Instead of focusing on looking forward and working toward your next career move, you will be forever caught up with the day-to-day burdens of your current (and sometimes even previous) position.

Many obstacles keep administrators from delegating:

- fear of losing control;
- a lack of trust in the performance/competence of others;
- concern at the loss of power/influence with partners; and
- the lack of time to properly explain to someone else what is required.

Effective administrators transcend each of these obstacles. A good starting point to do this is to list all your current duties and then review each one to determine the appropriateness of delegation. In general, unless it is absolutely essential that you personally carry out the activity, you should consider delegating all or selected parts of the particular task to a subordinate.

The law firm culture is not sympathetic to mistakes or learning as you go. Consequently, there is a tendency for many administrators to hold on tightly to mundane, routine tasks that should be delegated. Surprisingly, some administrators continue to carry out their previous tasks even after being promoted to a new position. Resisting such tendencies requires deliberate and proactive effort.

Once you have decided to delegate a particular task, clearly communicate the requirements to your subordinate. In outlining the objectives, provide some contextual information so that the subordinate can see the "big picture" and fully appreciate the project's importance. Provide the necessary training/resources and, where possible, allow flexibility in how the objective is to be achieved. This will enhance the sense of ownership and empower the subordinate. Your charge may even surprise you by doing the job better than you expected.

Never delegate responsibility without also providing sufficient authority to carry out the delegated task. The next step is to confirm the subordinate's understanding of your requirements and to address any problems or concerns. Once the task is underway, regularly monitor performance and provide appropriate feedback. The final step is to acknowledge the effort made and show your appreciation for the contribution.

To move forward, you must be willing to let go. This is not easy to do (and it may be uncomfortable at first) but you will soon appreciate the freedom and opportunities that it brings. Delegation will not only boost your career advancement, it will also help you to contribute to the development of others.

Further Reading

"The Art of Giving a Work Assignment So the Work Gets Done." *Law Office Administrator*, April 2002.

Krylowski, Kathy and Madelyn Yucht, "Strategies for Success." *Management & Administration*, Fall 1988.

What to Delegate...

If the need to delegate effectively is a key attribute for success as a legal administrator, including the very willingness to "let go" and to effectively communicate the requirements of the delegation, what is it that you can delegate? More specifically, beyond the obvious tasks, what sorts of tasks or functions that principal administrators generally handle could or should be delegated to others? What do you perhaps "hold on to" too long and to your own detriment?

One twist on this issue was explored in a survey of members of ALA's Large Firm Administrators Caucus in October 2000.[1] Though the survey respondents operate in organizations of significant size, many of their responses raise possibilities in the context of firms of all sizes — particularly in terms of repetitive tasks that, once mastered, may not require or involve the best use of an administrator's time. The specific survey question posed was:

If you could delegate or eliminate one task/function related to your job, what would it be and why?

By far the most frequent response had to do with the administrator's role as a minute-taker or recorder at executive committee and partnership meetings. While recognizing that this role ensures the administrator's presence at these meetings and that minutes are accurately and concisely prepared, survey respondents found the clerical nature of the role and, most importantly, its interference with full participation in the meeting as the firm's chief operating officer, to be significant drawbacks to their role, influence and ability to provide advice. Among specific comments and responses were the following:

- *Taking minutes of Executive Committee meetings is a terrible waste of an Executive Director's time and the value they can add to substantive discussions. In my case, unfortunately no other member of the Committee will do it and they do not want a secretary doing it. Ergo, I am stuck.*
- *I would eliminate taking minutes at Board of Directors, Management Committee and Stockholders' meetings. I believe that my secretary can take minutes at the first two for me to review, revise, and distill in draft before going to the Chairman for approval. I believe the Secretary of our professional corporation should take the minutes of Stockholder meetings. I know this may be a dream as the Board and Management Committee members are uncomfortable with the suggestion of discussing the usual topics with any staff member present. This is their view regardless of the fact that my secretary has been with the firm for 20 years, has worked for me for 11 years, and has access to all my personal, financial and other confidential*

---

1 The Large Firm Administrators Caucus is comprised of the principal administrators, generally the Executive Director or Chief Operating Officer, in firms of 100 or more lawyers. The survey in question was conducted in conjunction with the group's annual Fall Retreat.

material...I believe taking notes/minutes limits my participation in discussion. I find myself trying to focus on the accuracy of what was said for the record rather than formulating a better approach to a problem or add a different perspective to a topic.

The last two sentences of the second excerpt above suggest some facts and approaches that might be used in any firm to achieve delegation of this function and enhance the role and value of the administrator in these meetings.

In addition to some traditional items, the following also made the "I would like to find a way to delegate" wish lists of survey participants:

- Being responsible for the minutiae of firm financial reports. In one survey participant's words: *I would prefer to spend less time in this area and more time with the "troops" mentoring and coaching them. I believe this would add more value to the firm.*

- Spending less time in day-to-day HR issues. Some noted that this would insulate the administrator from easily resolvable issues, while saving his/her "clout" or perspective for the difficult problems. As one participant put it: *In order to do this, you need a good HR Director, and you need a firm culture that does not tolerate game playing mumbo jumbo from partners, associates and staff.*

- Operations issues. *I would (and shortly will),* responded one participant, *delegate operations issues to an Operations Director. She will be responsible for cost management, cash flow and other operational issues at the office level.*

- Being the "flow through" for everything. In one person's words: *Firm members seem to call me about any little thing and despite educating them continuously on who does what, I would like firm members to contact the responsible person, not me.* The issue, paraphrasing another response, is that of delegating a task or function and then communicating that delegation to others, without abrogating final responsibility for subordinates actions, responses and duties.

A Reader's Exercise: In terms of *your* career and *your* situation in *your* firm what obvious and not so obvious tasks can you delegate without abrogating responsibility? What can you realistically and psychologically let go of? If you need to justify or make the case for delegating something, what is the benefit — in terms of value, better use of your time, new areas you can tackle, etc. — that this brings to the firm (and you in your career)?

CHAPTER 11
BE DECISIVE

"Nothing will ever be achieved if every obstacle must first be overcome." — attributed to Samuel Johnson

It may be true that prevalent law firm culture is one averse to risk. An unfortunate consequence of this culture, combined with the emphasis on "always being right," is a predisposition to avoid making decisions. Consider this scenario: The "extraordinary administrator to be" is well credentialed and joins the firm full of promise. The expectations are high. Almost immediately, the administrator sees opportunities for change and numerous areas for improvement. However, the new manager quickly realizes that some members of the firm resist almost any decision or recommendation put forward. Indeed, some lawyers seem to enjoy taking a contrary position, just for the hell of it. And in a law firm, even a small minority of disaffected partners can make life very difficult. Over time, and faced with such opposition, the manager starts to make fewer and fewer decisions, rationalizing that it's just all too hard. Eventually, the manager slips into "maintenance mode" carefully avoiding doing anything that may upset anyone in the firm. Instead of becoming extraordinary, the administrator achieves mediocrity.

Lawyers are trained to get it right the first time, which is in part why the culture is so risk-averse and intolerant of mistakes. There is always a tendency to get more facts before making a decision; and this sometimes leads to paralysis through analysis. In addition, the egalitarian partnership structure often means that there are numerous key stakeholders on any issue — no matter how trivial.

To be an extraordinary administrator, therefore, requires courage. Your goal is to be an agent for change. This requires decisiveness and boldness. Indeed, many successful law firm managers would suggest that if in doubt, you err on the side of asking for forgiveness rather than seeking permission.

Successful administrators educate the partners that management is not about being right the first time or even every time. Unlike law, if managerial/administrative decisions are running at a 60 percent success rate, you are probably doing very well. If a few firm members do not agree with your decision, explain that, while you will try to accommodate their concerns, your primary responsibility is to the firm at large and not to selected individuals.

It is easy to just say, "have courage and be decisive." In reality however, we probably all know of very competent and hard-working law firm managers who have fallen from favor due to a few bad decisions. Sadly, some of these administrators never recover. The following suggestions may help you improve the quality of your decision making:

1. Determine at the outset how significant the decision is. Use this to guide your approach and to determine the extent of information gathering, consultation, and consensus building as well as the willingness for compromise.
2. Be well informed. This generally involves constantly moving around the firm, talking to key stakeholders and reading background material carefully.
3. Consider those who may be affected or have an interest in the outcome of your decision. Anticipate their concerns.
4. Review all your options carefully and have a well-reasoned basis for your chosen alternative. Demonstrate that you have properly thought through the issue.
5. Identify one or two key influencers and get their support before publicizing your decision.
6. Communicate, communicate, communicate.
7. If you make a wrong decision, admit it, learn from it and move on. In most cases, a wrong decision is better than no decision at all.

Making decisions is a high-risk activity within any law firm. And in certain situations you don't even get the luxury of three strikes. Do what you can to improve your batting average. However, also remember that in order to score any home runs, you must first swing the bat.

Further Reading

Spencer, Margaret S., "Overcoming Procrastination: How to Get Things Done — Despite Yourself." *Law Practice Management*, April 1997.

CHAPTER 12
MAINTAIN A POSITIVE ATTITUDE

"The most important decision you make is to be in a good mood." — attributed to Voltaire

As the lens through which you view the world, attitude is the little thing that makes a big difference. Although a positive attitude is no guarantee of success, the wrong attitude will almost certainly lead to failure. Having a negative perspective limits self-confidence and alienates you from others.

In contrast, an enthusiastic, positive attitude is infectious to all around you and it reflects the overall strength of your commitment. Your personal passion provides the fuel to ignite and inspire others that, as noted in Chapter 9, is an essential ingredient to building your team.

Moreover, you will feel better and be a happier person: Act happy and eventually you will be.

Notwithstanding all the obvious benefits, maintaining a positive attitude is not an easy task. The working life of a law firm manager is full of problems and setbacks. In addition, the constant pressure to perform can be highly stressful. So who has the time or inclination to smile and be positive?

Well, once again, this requires deliberate choice on your part and a genuine proactive effort. It's certainly more than just putting on a happy face. This requires self-awareness to understand your own emotional state, combined with a disciplined tactical approach that will modify your behavior as required. Here are a few suggestions to help you along:

- Start each day doing something you enjoy. This will get you off to a good start.
- Exercise and maintain a healthy diet.
- Know your trigger points and manage stress. If necessary take time out and try to control your anger.
- Surround yourself with optimistic people.
- Do not whine.

- Find the positive in others and praise them for it.
- Greet people warmly and with enthusiasm.
- Take yourself a little less seriously and cultivate a sense of humor.
- Focus on solutions rather than problems.
- Keep your negative comments to a minimum.
- Have a set of genuine up-beat responses to the question, "How are things going?"
- Look to the future rather than dwell on the past.
- Play to your strengths (and those of others).
- Keep your happiness in perspective to the situation: Be sincere and realistic.
- Be thankful and show your appreciation.
- Develop a basic understanding of conflict resolution and mediation skills.
- Focus on what happens if things work rather than why they won't work.
- Use creative visualizations to engender positive thoughts.
- Be a calming influence, especially in the midst of a crisis.
- Read motivational books.
- Create a happy workspace that is personalized to your tastes (photos, music, plants, etc.).
- Distance yourself from those who continually whine and complain.
- Display a sense of cheerfulness — even when you don't feel cheerful.
- Make work fun and enjoyable.
- Celebrate successes — even small ones.
- Smile.

Contrary to what certain law firm partners may convey, being surly and grumpy is not an indicator of "Gosh, I'm working so hard," nor is being busy an appropriate excuse. Your goal is to be happy. The place to be happy is here. And the time to be happy is now.

Further Reading

"Negativity Busters: What to Do with Chronic Naysayers." *Law Office Management & Administration Report,* August 1999.

Taksa, Patti S., "Creating an Environment of Positive Change." *ALA News,* April/May 1992.

Warner, Mark J., "Enhancing the Self-Esteem of Your Employees." *Legal Management*, July/August 1995.

Scott, Michael, "Beating the Blues (Without Beating Yourself Up): How to Tackle Depression, Aggression and Burnout — for You, Your Attorneys and Staff." *Legal Management*, November/December 2000.

Andersen, Richard, *Getting Ahead: Career Skills That Work for Everyone*. McGraw-Hill, 1994.

Stone, W. Clement and Napoleon Hill, *Success Through a Positive Mental Attitude*. Simon & Schuster, 1992 (reissue).

Will, Kriss, "Put on a Happy Face (and Mean It): Ponder These Points to Make Your Firm a More Pleasant Place to Work." *Legal Management*, January/February 2001.

Ziglar, Zig See You at the Top. Pelican, 1982 (reprint).

Rowland, Michael Domeyko, *Absolute Happiness: The Way To a Life of Complete Fulfillment*. Hay House, 1995.

Robbins, Anthony, Frederick L. CoVan, *Awaken the Giant Within*. Fireside Books, 1993 (reprint).

The Association of Legal Administrators regularly features articles on the subject of administrator experiences and success. The following article first appeared in *Legal Management*, Volume 20, Issue 4 (January/February 2001). It appears here to supplement the ideas in this chapter.

Put On a Happy Face (and Mean It)
Ponder these Points to Make Your Firm a More Pleasant Place to Work

By Kriss Will

Last year, I spoke at a national law firm marketers' conference on the topic "How to be an effective manager in a partnership structure." To begin my presentation, I posed a few inquiries to my audience:

- "Hands up if you think as a general rule lawyers have no idea about marketing."
- "Hands up if you think lawyers do not understand their clients."
- "Hands up if you think lawyers lack respect for their clients."
- "Hands up if you think lawyers lack respect for you as a professional."
- "Hands up if you think most lawyers just get in the way of the marketing department."
- "Hands up if your lawyers can be arrogant and really difficult to work with."
- "And hands up if you think work would be a whole lot more fun if the lawyers were not there."

As I suspected, the majority of people put their hands up in the air in response to these questions, almost whooping with agreement in relation to the last question posed. They were among peers. It was all right for them to vent their frustrations and anger toward lawyers. Finally, they thought, a presenter who understood how terrible it was to work with lawyers.

I then posed the final question: "As a law firm manager who are your clients? Do you respect them?" The mood of the conference theater changed abruptly. There was silence.

I then posed the concept that to be effective working in a partnership, you actually need to consider yourself in partnership with your clients and colleagues, and not in competition with them. I challenged the notion of professional respect and bemoaned the increasingly popular manager sport of lawyer bashing.

As a management professional, I explained how tired I was of people claiming that lawyers are notoriously difficult to work with. And I suggested that whining and groaning managers are not that much fun to be around.

The message I wanted these delegates to take home was that they have some control over how they feel at work. Especially as management professionals, they can influence the culture of an organization. People who moan and groan all the time at work are no fun to be around.

It's as your mother used to tell you: If you cannot say something nice, say nothing at all. But work life as a manager is even more than that. Those of us who work as law firm managers chose to do so. No one forced us into our positions. We affect the work environment of our employees and the attorneys for whom we work.

Why then do some otherwise excellent firm administrators and executive directors seem intent on having a bad time at work? Why is it that some people who work in law firms have the perception that they work in the most difficult employment environment conceivable? (Interestingly, most managers you speak to from other fields find their work challenging and at times frustrating. I believe that fundamentally it is the nature of management, as opposed to the nature of law firms, that creates these challenges.)

I am not claiming that working as a manager in a law firm is just one big barrel of fun. Things do not always run smoothly and change is a continual companion. If everything did always run smoothly, and nothing changed, I do not think law firms would need management skills as much, and the management roles that did exist could be rather boring. And how many managers are interested in boring jobs?

I do not believe, however, that management is always serious and staid. There is no rule against having fun whilst managing. The two can occur simultaneously. In fact, your effectiveness may even improve.

You will find many books about personal motivation, work motivation and organizational culture. Here are a few thoughts for you to consider in light of your own work situation in a legal practice management position.

- If you do not like working with lawyers, find a new profession in which to work.
- If you like the intellectual rigor of working with lawyers, then enjoy the developmental opportunities this work environment provides. Set personal goals to maximize what it is that you want to learn.
- Check if you view the glass as half empty or half full. Or, as a law firm HR colleague of mine said "Are half the lawyers mad, or half of them sane?"
- Identify what frustrates you at work and develop plans for overcoming these frustrations. Tackle it as you would any other project, and aim to reduce frustrations and increase effectiveness.
- A common complaint about the law firm environment is the decision making process. With everyone wanting to have input, it can be ineffective, inefficient, and for managers, down right annoying. The partnership structure has a lot to answer for here. One strategy that I recommend is to understand which people in your firm actually make the decisions and what and who influences these decision-makers. You can get results far more quickly if you take the time to learn about these aspects of your firm's operation.

- Realize that if you get up in the morning thinking you are going to have a bad day, you will have a bad day. Self-fulfilling prophecies cannot be underestimated. Start the day thinking about what will go well.

- Identify your GOOB factor: your "Get Out Of Bed" factor. What is it that makes you want to go to work? Think of ways to work with your team to increase the interesting, exciting and challenging parts of your work. Ask your team for ideas on how to make the less exciting factors at least more fun. Maybe you could institute a "silly hat day" in the accounts department at month end. This might lighten things up a little.

- Very few managers relish giving staff negative feedback. Many managers tell me that they worry about this for quite a period before actually handling the issue. Consider undertaking a staff management refresher course, one with a practical focus. Maybe run one in-house where you can learn from each other. Minimizing the stress involved with people management can only be good for everyone.

- Take your work seriously — but do not take yourself too seriously. A friend of mine is a senior partner in an Australian law firm and is often ridiculously busy. He has a series of sayings that indicate to his colleagues and subordinates whether he is able to make time for amusing diversions at work. Here's the one I like best: "Sorry, don't have a lot of time today because I am wearing my serious pants." He has said that he is busy, but has done so in a light-hearted manner.

- "Grinners are winners." Work to build a little joy in your team. Maybe just smiling each day and greeting your co-workers could be a start. There is nothing like the smile to put a spring in your step. And do not be a "status smiler" — you know, the one who only smiles at associates and higher.

- When the going gets tough (a partner has lost his cool and considers throwing files around his office an adult response to the fact that the photocopier has run out of paper), the tough respond in a positive manner. Remember that people in distressed states generally respond well to positive, calm responses.

- A de-stress tool that I often recommend when training managers and lawyers is to "walk the block before you do your block." Just getting out of the office and clearing your head can greatly assist when dealing with challenging situations. It is amazing what a breath of fresh air does for the mind. And if you are up to it, try to see the funny side of the situation. There usually is one.

- Do not become a slave to work. While I think work should be fun, it should not be the only fun in your life. Work/life balance is a juggle but not one that we managers should shy away from. It will be hard to have fun at work if you are constantly begrudging the amount of time you need to spend there.

- If your partners' meetings are bordering on repulsive, add a few agenda items to get a more positive focus: "Things we have done well in the past week;" "Great service we have received;" "People who deserve special thanks;" or even "The latest lawyer joke competition."

- Many people — and managers are people — really dislike conflict. Again, any manager must master conflict resolution skills. These are even more important in a workplace where a litigious outlook dominates. I always said that one of my greatest challenges was giving negative feedback to litigation lawyers because they seemed to love the fight, not deal with the issues. Consider attending a conflict-management course and then put your skills into practice. Do not be afraid to learn from your mistakes, and do reward yourself for your successes.

- Consider encouraging your partners to attend a workplace conflict-resolution workshop. The difference between a courtroom battle and office debate is at times lost on our colleagues the lawyers, and training in this area can be enlightening.

Be an effective manager. Go and create more opportunities for people to enjoy their work and have a little fun along the way.

And if after reading this article, you still do not think that work should be fun, then consider the alternative approach to work. The Microsoft Word thesaurus provides the following antonyms for fun: misery, melancholy, sadness and woe.

The choice is yours.

CHAPTER 13
MAKE YOURSELF INDISPENSABLE

If you walk in another person's footsteps,
you will leave no footprints.

Many law firms actively promote the "up-or-out" philosophy. I have attended numerous partner meetings to consider the admission of new partners, and one thing is very clear: To be truly regarded as a key member of the firm, your contribution must be so demonstrably valuable as to make you indispensable.

In reality, we all know that no one is indispensable. But ask any firm blessed with an extraordinary law firm manager, and the sentiment expressed by most partners will always be, "We would be lost without him/her," or, "He/she makes a real difference to the firm's success."

The ideas and suggestions in the other chapters will help to make you indispensable. In many cases, longevity in the job will of itself be of assistance, as you progressively become more experienced in firm affairs. However, the key challenge is to be a genuine agent for change.

Focus therefore on being proactive and try to champion causes that make a tangible difference. Concentrate your efforts on projects, not on routine tasks that are often time-consuming but far less meaningful. Identifying the worthwhile projects will require that you maintain a keen awareness of all the big-picture issues and stay abreast of key industry trends.

If you run out of ideas, talk to others, both within and outside the firm. What firm issues keep the partners awake at night? Consider a feedback meeting or innovation summit. Anything that enhances efficiencies or otherwise improves the bottom line will generally get the partners' attention. Many firms are awash with fantastic ideas but there is no one to implement them or willing to champion the particular cause. If you have too many to choose from, focus initially on the quick wins or low hanging fruit before looking to expand your horizons.

In addition to developing your project-management skills, become known and acknowledged as the expert in a particular field that you can claim as your own. For many administrators, their expertise is in the area of finance but your talent could be key client programs, associate morale, partner compensation, technology or anything else that is key on the firm's agenda. Research your chosen area thoroughly and develop your expertise to world-class standards. In short, make it known that you stand for something and that your contribution is uniquely valuable to the firm's ongoing success.

Further Reading

Peters, Tom., Dean LeBaron, *The Circle of Innovation: You Can't Shrink Your Way To Greatness*. Knopf, 1997.

Peters, Tom, *The Pursuit of Wow! Every Person's Guide to Topsy-Turvy Times!* Vintage Books, 1994.

Bringing Value to Your Firm...Making Your Own Footprints

As Paul Malliaté notes in Chapter 13, if you make a real difference to your firm's success, you will help to make yourself "indispensable" and, derivatively, respected, successful and a real contributor to the organization and to the lives of those who work there.

In addition to the suggestions noted in the text of Chapter 13, what other ideas are there for making your own footprints and bringing your own independent value to the firm? That question was explored in an October 2000 survey of members of ALA's Large Firm Administrators Caucus.[1] Caucus members were asked:

What is the most significant thing you have done outside of your expected duties to bring value to your present or past firms?

Many of the responses raise possibilities for administrators in firms of all sizes. For example, the very real influence an administrator can have on a firm's culture:

* *I think that I have had a material impact on the culture of the firm which, when all is said and done, is critical to how people feel about the enterprise and how loyal they remain. I've done some good things in terms of saving money, developing strategic plans, implementing policies, developing branch offices, managing firm finances, etc., etc. but having a positive effect on how folks feel about where they work and with whom they work is probably, dollar-for-dollar, the most valuable legacy I can leave this firm.*

* *So far, it has been humanizing the firm some and engendering more firm unity. I have focused on a number of staff welfare issues that have been effective; also, I have successfully brought a fresh view of the firm's business practices.*

* *If you were to ask lawyers and staff that question about me, I think they would say that I made this a more compassionate, respectful and enjoyable place to work.*

* *Changed the perception of how much an Administrator can positively influence the morale of individuals at all levels of the organization by being accessible and supportive, and by making a personal effort to communicate and connect with as many people as possible. That's not easy in a firm of 350 lawyers and 400 paralegals and staff — but the effort is changing the face of the firm.*

---

1 The Large Firm Administrators Caucus is comprised of the principal administrators, generally the Executive Director or Chief Operating Officer, in firms of 100 or more lawyers. The survey in question was conducted in conjunction with the group's annual Fall Retreat.

Sometimes it's doing what legal administrators should do but which a firm may not have witnessed in the position:

- *In general, reducing the amount of lawyer time spent on administrative functions. In both my current and previous firms, this had to be the number one priority. In both cases we eliminated unnecessary committees and reduced firm management time on administrative issues. Also, providing rational, objective and business-minded observations on firm management issues.*

- *This firm has historically had very little senior level administrative direction and leadership. I have spent a great deal of time establishing the credibility and value of the position, making it something more than simply a coordinator of internal administrative and financial functions.*

In other cases, it's bringing to bear the resources of the administrator's professional network and the impact that can have:

- *Involvement in professional organizations, including both ALA and the ABA Law Practice Management Section. Also, locally and nationally published articles, as well as speaking engagements, have added value.*

- *The network I have established with other Executive Directors at respected law firms… This brings incredible value to my role and a wealth of information that makes me very credible when I recommend a certain course of action, practice or policy to be adopted, or a product to be selected.*

- *My leadership involvement in ALA has opened many new doors; it has brought value to me and therefore to the firm…presentation skills, networks within our profession and networks beyond our profession.*

And often it's something very specific, very needed and very important in the firm. Some examples:

- *I became plan manager for our firm's retirement plan about a year ago. During the year, with my leadership, we have added a significant number of options for lawyers and staff, to an accompanying level of satisfaction. If anyone had suggested such a role to me when I came to the firm, I would have scoffed.*

- *Direct involvement in billing rates. My firm was not used to that, and it needed a fresh look…which I provided.*

- *I have managed to get practice managers to adopt a profitability enhancement model and use it as a tool to manage their respective practices.*

- *Recognized the need to commence our space search long before the lawyer-leaders thought it necessary. Recommended working with an outside tenant representative to thoroughly search the market and work through the firm's internal politics.*

- *Significantly improved the due diligence process for lateral partners, and particularly lateral groups joining (the firm). In addition to the expected interviews and checking references and conflicts, we spend considerably more effort in understanding their client relationships, historical billing practices and practice economics.*

- *One "dumb" thing I do that you won't find in any legal administrator's job description is management education for partners; sometimes by sending articles from the Harvard Business Review or other publications, sometimes by writing "white papers" on management, once by just getting everyone on the Management Committee to read Who Moved My Cheese?, which they thoroughly enjoyed, although some were loath to admit it. Sounds corny, but these people just aren't exposed to good business writing or writing on topics such as leadership.*

- *Identified new clients, wrote responses to RFPs, negotiated fee arrangements with clients, sit on client/law firm "Executive Committee" to continually improve provision of service and manage legal services.*

Regardless of the specifics, it often boils down to simple propositions, including being the agent of change and the one who actually takes responsibility and gets things done. As one administrator put it, the "new" value he added was that he took the firm beyond *the endless talking stage* and actually *implemented the strategic plan. Implemented a sophisticated client intake system. Implemented lawyer management programs.*

CHAPTER 14
BE FLEXIBLE

"Those are my principles, and if you don't like them I have others." — *Groucho Marx*

At first glance, this may appear to be contradictory. On one hand, you have been encouraged in Chapter 11 to be bold and decisive. But now the advice is to be flexible. The overriding message is to exercise appropriate judgment in any given situation.

The role of law firm manager or administrator is extremely diverse. One day, you are expected to play a key leadership role in pushing through with merger discussions, and the next day you are being questioned about the shortage of marker pens in the stationery cupboard. To some extent, this goes with the territory and you need to be comfortable with the contradictions and diversity in focus.

Moving expertly and effortlessly between the different levels, while demonstrating your ability to be both a very-hands-on-when-called-on or a strategic/big picture manager, is certainly a hallmark of the extraordinary administrator.

There must, of course, be certain limits to your flexibility. As noted in Chapter 13, it is important that you stand for something. Trying to please everyone or accepting whatever tasks come your way is not desirable. However, being able to operate across different functions and being comfortable with the lack of absolutes in the decision-making process are prerequisites.

Very few law firm issues are "black or white" and almost everything exists in "shades of gray." Even decisions made with confidence and unanimously endorsed by the firm's management committee can quickly be reversed in light of opposition or resistance from a few influential partners. The extent of your flexibility will be tested in such situations, especially if — as is often the case — you are the one charged with implementing the initial decision. Any law firm manager who has had to discipline a partner's secretary or some other "protected individual" within the firm, will readily identify with this challenge.

Another important area is a hallmark of flexibility: the need to be both task driven and highly people focused. Many administrators who have a strong financial background are very comfortable with the former but struggle with their interpersonal skills, which (as noted in Chapter 9) are so essential. Push yourself to be equally competent in both areas.

One of my colleagues summed up this trait very well: He commented that, in order to survive as a law firm manager, you need to be a chameleon.

Further Reading

Scheele, Adele, "Skills for Success." *Legal Management*, September/October 1989.

CHAPTER 15
PICK YOUR BATTLES

"Don't teach a pig to sing. It wastes your time and it annoys the pig." — sometimes attributed to Mark Twain

Law firms are highly political environments. This is especially the case in small/midsize firms. As a consequence, there is always plenty of potential for conflict. Even very small, insignificant issues such as the color of the new waste paper bins, can become emotionally charged deal-breaker issues.

The required skill for extraordinary administrators is to know when to make a stand and when to compromise or let go. This is related to the flexibility issues covered in Chapter 14. Ultimately there are very few things that are worth going to the barricades.

In general, lawyers are intelligent, adversarial, articulate and they always enjoy a friendly, or even not-so-friendly, joust. They prize their independence and are very protective of their autonomy, which will often put them into direct conflict with the manager who is charged with acting in the firm's collective interest.

Compounding the issue, is the fact that it is often the administrator who is responsible for implementing decisions made by central management. Inevitably conflicts will arise and you need the right skills to deal with these effectively and professionally.

The first point to remember is that your role is to serve others. Remember that the firm's members, especially the partners, are your clients. (See Chapter 3.) It is not about being right or wrong, but rather whether you are meeting the needs of your clients. Hard as it may be, you must appreciate that your ideas will not always be accepted, even if they are based on sound business principles. Communicating your point of view effectively and convincingly is essential but, if after having done so your view does not prevail, then it's time to move on.

If you find yourself in a situation of direct conflict, here are few helpful suggestions:

- Focus on the issues, not the individual.
- Try to resolve it privately on a one-to-one basis.
- Find the common ground and move forward from there.
- Demonstrate your understanding of the other person's point-of-view.
- Don't retaliate and never write nasty memos.
- Attempt to forge a compromise.
- Be patient and, if necessary, take time out.
- Emphasize the firm's collective interest as the ultimate touchstone.
- If all else fails, seek assistance from others.

Due to the nature of the administrator's role, the management professional may sometimes feel like a pawn in the partners' chess game or power struggle. Recognize the warning signs early and prevent this from happening.

On any issue, you should emphasize your objectivity and avoid playing favorites. Treat all members of your firm with respect, remembering that today's junior trainee associate may be tomorrow's managing partner.

In summary, exercise good judgment in deciding which issues to champion. Other than ethical considerations and situations where the firm's interest is clearly being threatened, most issues lend themselves to compromise. Always keep your eye on the big picture and remember that sometimes the dragon wins!

Further Reading

Carlson, Richard, *Don't Sweat the Small Stuff... and It's All Small Stuff: Simple Ways to Keep the Little Things from Taking Over Your Life*. Hyperion, 1997.

CHAPTER 16
PROMOTE YOUR ACHIEVEMENTS

"Never expect any recognition here—the system prohibits it. The cross is not affixed to the genius, no, the genius is affixed to the cross." — Franz Grillparzer, Austrian author

There are many outstanding law firm administrators who work incredibly hard and make a fabulous contribution to their firm's success — and yet are never acknowledged or fully appreciated. Put bluntly: To be extraordinary you must be perceived as such by others.

Law firms are notorious for constantly making their managers and administrators feel the need to keep justifying their existence. This is partly due to the lack of value that many lawyers attribute to any activity that is not directly client related. Also, in contrast to the support staff, the firm's fee earners have an obvious tangible performance measure through their billable hours and billing/collection results.

Your contribution as a manager or administrator is far less tangible and, even when something amazingly brilliant does happen, there is never a shortage of people stepping forward to take the credit. As the saying goes: Success has many fathers; failure is an orphan.

The challenge is to proactively market your achievements: You should not rely on anyone else to do this for you. Start by clarifying the expectations of your role and, where possible, translate your objectives into measurable performance indicators: timeframes; cost savings; staffing ratios; satisfaction survey scores; and industry benchmarks. This will allow your achievements to be readily recognized, especially if you report regularly on the progress you have made.

Consider issuing a brief e-mail update or newsletter and ensure that your projects/initiatives are on the agenda at appropriate firm meetings. Celebrate your successes and make sure that the right people are aware of them. A good track record will induce credibility and fuel further success. Be particularly wary of those who consistently take credit for your efforts without appropriately acknowledging your contribution.

In additional to internal promotion, focus on the external marketplace. Becoming known as an expert in your particular industry or function can be assisted through active participation in industry bodies, attending/speaking at seminars, writing articles or establishing links with key journalists and magazine editors. Your newly acquired networking skills (See Chapter 5.) will also prove invaluable.

Further Reading

Ryan, Petrice and Diane Marx, "Blow Your Own Horn: Let Management Know Your Accomplishments." *ALA News*, October/November 1994.

"Marketing Yourself" Chapter 18 *The Lawyer's Handbook* 3rd Ed. American Bar Association. 1992.

CHAPTER 17
BE RELIABLE/RESPONSIVE

"Just do it." — *Nike slogan*

Being reliable and responsive may be regarded as obvious aspects of good-quality service — but these facets of greatness are important enough that they justify a dedicated chapter.

Law firms are overflowing with very talented individuals. The quality of discussion at most partner meetings is generally first-rate and few organizations have more comprehensive strategic/business plans. The problem, however, is that after all is said and done, more is said than done. Maybe it's the consensus-driven culture or maybe there is a leadership vacuum — but whatever the reason, the inability to implement effectively is almost always a major stumbling block. And this is precisely where the extraordinary administrator can show value: by being the one "who gets it done," on time and on budget — every time.

If you are able to consistently display reliability and responsiveness, your skills will be sought — by your own firm and by many others. Ability is important, but reliability is essential. Many lawyers will interpret your responsiveness as a tangible measure of the extent to which you care about their needs. If you are unreliable or unresponsive, the message you communicate is that you consider your clients to be unimportant.

To reinforce your responsiveness objective, focus initially on the small day-to-day things and commit to doing these more promptly. Voicemails, e-mails and phone messages are a great place to start. In general, I would consider no response within 24 hours to be unacceptable. And if the query or request is from one of your key clients, then the timeframe is probably even tighter. If you are absent or likely to be tied up in lengthy back-to-back meetings, you should advise your secretary and also use an absence notification on your e-mail or voicemail so that each client's expectations are managed. If the caller's message will take some time to deal with or you need to get additional information or you are waiting on someone else, then send a quick reply to that effect.

Law firm managers spend a large part of their working life attending meetings. Despite what the lawyers do, as the administrator you must arrive promptly. Some firm members have a habit of always arriving late to meetings because somehow this conveys a sense of importance or busyness on their part. Do not be misled by this. If the administrator arrives late, all it communicates is a lack of professionalism, disorganization or, even worse, a feeling that the other attendees (your clients) are less important.

With regard to the more significant projects or tasks, always obtain an upfront agreement on timing as this will avoid any confusion regarding expectations. Obviously, do not commit to a timeframe you cannot meet. There always seems to be a sense of urgency within law firms but in general you can negotiate some flexibility, especially if you explain your other priorities.

The key is to ensure that there is a common understanding as to your client's expectations. The next step, of course, is to deliver on those expectations — and to do so consistently. If for some reason you cannot meet a deadline, let this be known as soon as possible and renegotiate a revised timeframe. The goal is to manage the expectations of your clients.

Further Reading

Schorr, Morris E., "Climbing the Law Firm Ladder." *People-to-People*, June 1988.

CHAPTER 18
FIND A MENTOR/COACH

*"The ultimate responsibility of a leader is to facilitate
other people's development."* — *Fred Pryor*

At this point, you may be wondering whether this is all worth the effort — or
even whether it is humanly possible to harness all these qualities and skill sets.
It can certainly seem overwhelming. This feeling is also exacerbated by the
loneliness and isolation many law firm managers experience. You are not a
partner and (in most cases) not even a lawyer, so you are not part of the "fee
earner's club." Similarly though, you are not really a member of the support staff.
These employees generally regard you as someone representing the partners' or
firm's interests. So in whom do you confide? With whom do you share your
frustrations? And who guides you through the difficult issues? The answer is to
find either a mentor from within the firm or an external coach.

A mentor or coach can help you maximize your potential and provide a
tremendous boost to your progression, particularly in the early stages of your
career. These professional helpers can offer you guidance:

- They can teach you through their successes and failures.
- They will help you set goals.
- They will get you motivated.
- They will help you increase accountability.
- They will help you to work through the options.
- They will provide effective feedback.
- They can ease the isolation and loneliness administrators feel by just being
  there when it is time to unload.

Despite the obvious benefits, the major obstacle is finding the right person to
be your mentor/coach. For some very fortunate administrators, this happens by
chance. But for most, it needs careful planning and orchestration. In general, the

qualities you seek are fairly subjective because there needs to be a strong personal connection and recognition of the individual as an appropriate role model.

What makes a good mentor?

- a passion to help others;
- good judgment;
- strong personal connection;
- willingness to devote time; and
- an inspirational quality.

Someone with these qualities who also has law firm management or similar experience would be ideal. Choose someone more senior than yourself so you can benefit from experience or, alternatively, attach yourself to a rising star. Once you have found someone, the ideal way to start the relationship is simply by asking for help and going from there. Remember that your relationship need not be formal and, in fact, the informal ones probably work best. The key is in maintaining contact. Regular meetings, e-mail messages or phone conversations can assist this process.

If you already have a coach or mentor, then you should count your blessings. Certainly acknowledge the assistance you are given and let your mentor know the positive difference in your job satisfaction.

Finally, depending on your seniority, consider being a mentor/coach to someone else. In addition to enhancing your own leadership and team-building skills, you will find it immensely satisfying to be contributing to the growth and development of others.

Further Reading

Clifford, Deb, "Coaching from Within: Tips from an Executive Coach." *ALA News*, December 2001/January 2002.

Olmstead, John W., Jr., "Technology Tech University: Coach Your Firm Staff Members for Better Performance." *Legal Management*, March/April 2001.

Tyler, Kathryn, "Employee Development: Mentoring Programs Link Employees and Experienced Execs." *HR Magazine*, April 1998.

Zey, Michael G., *"The Mentor Connection"* 1997.

David, Mark, *"When to Call in the Coach"* Consulting to Management, 12(1) p16-19.

The Association of Legal Administrators regularly features articles on the subject of administrator experiences and success. The following article first appeared in *ALA News*, Volume 20, Issue 6 (December 2001/January 2002). It appears here to supplement the ideas in this chapter.

Coaching from Within: Tips from an Executive Coach

By Deb Clifford

As a leadership consultant, I have the good fortune to work with a lot of dynamic, committed and talented business people. Most of these people aspire to be the best at what they do in their organizations. As successful, motivated employees, these men and women possess similar characteristics. They do many things very well. But the one area in which they often fall short, is one that many of us can relate to as the pace of work continues to increase: We don't take the time to look at ourselves.

Self-reflection is a critical skill for anyone who wants to be a better employee or manager, whether they work in the legal field or any other industry. Before you can work at your highest level, you must know enough about yourself to be fulfilling your own purpose in your life and work. If the work you do is not aligned with your genuine interests, values, strengths and personal style, then you, the work, and the people you work with - will all suffer.

Think for a moment about the best boss you ever had. What made that person so effective? Chances are he or she was an inspiration to those around them. Inspired employees are people who achieve a deep sense of purpose and meaning in their lives through their work and encourage those around them to do the same.

Executive coaches can hold a mirror in front of clients to teach them how to be more reflective and, in many cases, help them find the alignment mentioned above. The practices for better self-reflection are simple and can be adopted by anyone on their own, but most of us live such busy lives that we don't take the time to look at ourselves on a regular basis. In fact, working with an executive coach is a little like hiring a personal trainer. Meeting the trainer at the gym on Monday morning is the only way some people can stick to an exercise program.

Developing into an inspirational employee requires the same kind of commitment and repetition it takes to get in shape. One of the most important practices you can adopt is to ask the right questions of yourself and really listen to the answers. Let's say you just had a confrontation with a colleague that didn't go as well as it should have. Set aside a little time at the end of the day to use this as a learning opportunity by asking yourself the following questions:

• Why did I react that way?

• Do I see any patterns in my reaction or behavior?

- What has worked well for me in the past in similar situations?
- What could I have done differently?

The answers to these types of questions will give you more insight into what makes you "tick" and foster continuous personal improvement. You may say, "Maybe I'm so upset because I hate conflict and take it personally."

There are a variety of other tools and exercises that can help you get in touch with who you really are, including assessment tools, journaling, and awareness raising exercises such as creating an "activity pie." Here's how that works: Draw a circle and place inside it all your life's roles, such as work, family, church choir, volunteering, etc. How is your time divided at the moment? Now, how would you like your time to be divided? Another helpful exercise is to write a press release. It's the year 2004 and a writer is doing a story about you. What does the article say about you?

These types of writing exercises help them focus on where they want to go. Based on these findings, they can set goals to accomplish that vision. Sometimes the goals are basic, such as spending more time with the family or getting along better with a colleague. The most common problems aspiring business people wrestle with are:

- Improving interpersonal relationship skills;
- Maintaining a balance between work and home/personal life;
- Confronting problem employees and colleagues; and
- Discerning the appropriate way to communicate in certain situations: in person, by telephone or via e-mail.

Regardless of the problem or situation, the foundation for being a better employee and leader, lies with regularly holding that mirror up, and reflecting on what and whom you see.

CHAPTER 19
JOIN THE RIGHT FIRM

"Skate where the game will be." — *Wayne Gretsky*

Managing your career progression requires that you actively seek out opportunities for growth. If your current firm cannot provide you with adequate scope for future development, then it may be time to look elsewhere. It can be very tempting to coast along within the comfort zone of your current position — even though it is clear that the opportunities for career progression have evaporated. This can be because there is no more room at the top or maybe the firm itself is going nowhere. In any case, you certainly owe it to yourself to regularly evaluate your options — including the possibility of a lateral move.

One of the most effective career-advancement strategies is to preserve your options and ensure that you are marketable to other firms. This can be done without being unduly disloyal to your current employer. Indeed, many associates knocking on the door to partnership use this strategy very effectively in order to secure their progression. In addition to boosting your own self-confidence, having realistic options will provide you with added control and avoid any sense of feeling trapped. It is also worth noting that many law firm managers inevitably accumulate some unwanted baggage, especially if they are decisive and bold as suggested in Chapter 11. Consequently, there may come a time when it is desirable to establish a new base from which to move forward.

If you are contemplating such a move, there are a few factors to look out for, as indicators of potential for career advancement:

- The firm is growing (no one shrinks to greatness!).
- There is strong leadership.
- Management is valued by the partners.
- The firm has clear reporting lines and role definition.
- You witness good decision-making processes.
- The support team is the appropriate size and is a quality group.

- There is a breadth of operations — branch/overseas offices.
- Firm owners show agreement and respect for your role.

It is difficult to soar with the eagles if you find yourself working with turkeys. Choose your firm carefully and keep your options open.

Further Reading

Coburn, John F., "The Administrator of the 1990s — A New Breed?" *Legal Administrator*, May/June 1988.

Kanofsky, Florence, "Legal Administrators Today: Success Strategies for a Changing Profession." *Legal Management*, September/October 1995.

The Association of Legal Administrators regularly features articles on the subject of administrator experiences and success. The following article first appeared in *Legal Management*, Volume 14, Number 5 (September/October 1995). It appears here to supplement the ideas in this chapter.

Legal Administrators Today: Success Strategies for a Changing Profession

By Florence Kanofsky

It's been an eventful decade for legal administrators. With the availability of new technology, the increase in mergers and acquisitions of firms and, most importantly, the greater financial pressures on operations, today's legal administrator has greater and more varied responsibilities than ever. What led to these changes and how have successful administrators adapted to this new environment?

Growing Status

In the wake of the past recession, many firms downsized their staffs, and some were forced to make adjustments after significant partner departures or acquisitions necessitated consolidation or reallocation of resources. As a result, attorneys became more acutely aware of the need to run the firm "as a business."

This climate created a pressure to make the entire office more cost-efficient and led firms to seek legal administrators with strong financial experience. If there is one reason that the status and responsibility of legal administrators has grown, it is this new reality.

In addition, staffing experiments by some firms have taught them the value of legal administrators. When some of these firms tried eliminating the position as a cost-cutting measure, they soon realized how vital the administrator had been to the smooth day-to-day operations of the office. This realization has also contributed to the increased status that legal administrators now hold.

The Association of Legal Administrators (ALA) has been a key force for change too. Through national conferences, local seminars and other networking events, the organization has enhanced the reputation of the profession.

A New Role

Legal administrators have always been the link between attorneys and support personnel, but now that many firms operate with leaner staffs, their efforts at keeping everyone working efficiently have become critical to the firm's effectiveness and profitability.

- **More Hands-On Experience:** While some firms are looking outside the legal field for candidates who previously held key management positions in other industries, most are now hiring exclusively from within the legal community. Attorneys seek seasoned professionals with law-firm experience, and they are willing to invest the time it takes to find people with this background.

- **More Responsibilities:** Traditionally, the legal administrator primarily managed operations such as purchasing equipment, supervising the office staff and providing basic bookkeeping. With today's demands, however, administrators are often asked to resolve more complex problems due to their expanded duties.

More often than in the past, legal administrators participate in partnership meetings and play a vital role in strategic planning. They are privy to important financial information and have greater autonomy in decision-making. They are expected to be able to examine a profit and loss statement and implement long-term plans. There are many areas where this increased responsibility is apparent:

- Apart from the financial accountability, legal administrators often play a key role in guiding the firm's decision on technology purchases, setting up leasing programs, and relocating or re-configuring an office.
- Opportunities for marketing law firms have expanded greatly and the legal administrator may be expected to develop promotional materials campaigns.
- A decade ago, an administrator could manage the office by using good "people skills." Today's administrator must understand and comply with a range of complex employment law issues.

- **More Education:** Once, the legal administrator could enter the field with a general education and garner skills on the job. While this still accounts for many of the administrators entering the field, the legal profession is also drawing more people with advanced educational backgrounds. Even those already within the field are seeking additional training. Far more administrators today have at least a college degree and many have master's degrees, usually in business administration.

Strategically Assessing Where You Stand

How can you stay challenged and successful as a legal administrator? The first step is to evaluate your current position and firm. Does the firm offer challenging opportunities for you? Will it be expanding in directions that interest you? If you think the office could benefit from something like a computerized library, you can suggest the changes to a partner and add new and exciting possibilities to your job.

What kind of advances have you made in your current job? Have you streamlined the operations to a point where another person can administer the new systems? Have you found ways to "elevate" your own role and make yourself "indispensable?"

Are you where you want to be professionally? Consider doing a career "audit" to assess what skills you have now and what skills you can develop that will be valuable to your firm. To conduct this "audit," gather and review as much information about yourself as possible in a manner that's strategic, focused and well detailed. What skills do you possess and which of these do you most enjoy utilizing?

To determine this, revisit three projects where you felt proud of your achievements. Then look at the components that gave you the most satisfaction and consider how the skills you used can be applied more fully in your current work.

Long-Range Thinking

Now is the time to think about projects you would like to work on — not just immediately, but one, two, five and ten years ahead. Examine what new skills or credentials you might need to advance in the firm. As more law firms rely on new technology products, it may be necessary to learn more about hardware and software applications tailored to the law profession.

If, for example, your firm relies heavily on topical research on recent cases, you may want to take a course on navigating the Internet. Magazines such as *NetGuide*, *PC World*, and *Information Week* can give you a jump on the newest technology tools to bring to the firm. In addition, you might want to volunteer to test new software within the firm. Serving as a role model for change can counter the resistance of your staff to new technologies. Then, as a user of the technology, you can give feedback on security and training issues.

By assessing your career and your work from many angles, you should have a broader sense of what you have accomplished and what factors contribute to your success. Honest self-evaluation using a career audit strategy will help you formulate strategies for succeeding in your profession.

Increasing Your Visibility as a Decision-Maker

As a legal administrator, you face the challenge of how to increase your role as a decision-maker. Increasing your credibility will undoubtedly allow you to play a bigger role in strategic decisions.

Like many legal administrators, Mimi Shore, Director of Adminstration for California-based Frandzel & Share, started out twenty years ago as an office manager in a law firm. The turning point in her career came when she switched to a new law firm, where she says "not one system worked." She identified and concentrated on the areas in which she could make a difference, such as organizing the billing and creating a personnel manual. After she streamlined the operations of the

Strategies That Work

If you want to play a larger role in strategic decisions, you may want to incorporate some of these strategies:

1. **Be proactive:** Partners hire top administrators to be innovators and the best way to increase your visibility is to approach a decision-making partner with a creative idea. Provide information on the kinds of resources that will be required to make it happen (such as people, money and time), what the timing is expected to be and what kind of results can be anticipated.

2. **Take on more:** Always look for ways to broaden your skills on the job by offering to undertake additional assignments that may not be part of your normal responsibilities. (One caveat: be sure to choose significant tasks appropriate to your position.)

3. **Leverage smaller projects:** Start out with one small project, such as matching one secretary with one mentor, and build it to a larger program after it has had a chance be successful.

4. **Communicate with the partners:** The best way to gain authority is to be a good communicator. Don't stay in your office. Get out and move around to observe what is going on. If possible, go to lunch with the partners and ask their advice.

5. **Develop the agenda for management meetings:** Volunteer to collect items for the agenda. That way, you may have the option of adding your projects to the list so that the group can discuss them.

6. **Become a techno-whiz:** Technological expertise can be a powerful asset as you seek to move forward in the firm. You'll increase your visibility if you can help attorneys and staff choose and utilize appropriate technological tools to make them more efficient.

7. **Talk to the partners about their numbers:** Make sure that you have thorough knowledge of the figures that concern the partners most. Show expertise in explaining revenues and expenses, and offer suggestions on how to improve or change them.

8. **Start a legal executive team:** Many firms have developed a legal executive team, which you may consider suggesting to your firm. Generally composed of managing partners, executive committee members and administrators, this team is responsible for providing leadership and establishing goals, objectives and strategies concerning law firm operations.

9. **Stay adaptable:** Don't ally yourself with only one partner. In today's legal environment, partners may move to another firm and you could find yourself with no close allies if your mentor departs.

10. **Move on:** Sometimes, the best strategy for getting more authority can be going to a new firm. In a new position, you may be better able to redefine your role, and may find greater receptivity to your ideas.

office, she had the confidence to move to a larger firm where she took on broader responsibilities.

Now she manages operations for a 60-attorney firm, where she is responsible for "everything that isn't lawyering." The human resource, technology, facilities and controller areas report directly to her.

For Shore, the interaction with the partners has increased over the years as they became more interested in how much could be gained from the staff. She noticed her visibility increasing when she began attending monthly department meetings as a contributor rather than a note-taker.

Shore recognized that the power at these meetings is held by the person who makes the agenda. When she volunteered to create it, she could add her action items and accomplishment reports to the list.

In the '90s law firm, communication and management skills are highly valued. Mimi has initiated a team system so that paralegals, secretaries and partners all work on projects from the beginning of the case. This way, everyone who comes in contact with the client can be up-to-speed on a project.

She launched the program with a small group and instituted it firmwide when the rest of the office recognized that this team system was effective.

In addition, many legal administrators are heading back to college to get additional business, financial, and computer training. Mimi moved from a career as a CPA for a multinational corporation to the legal administration field, yet she has subsequently gone back to school to learn different computer skills and specific software applications. She continues to learn strategies and skills through taking management courses at a local college and attending seminars offered by ALA.

Take On New Responsibilities

Marcia Rocker, now Director of Administration at Winston & Strawn in Washington, D.C., has been at her firm for sixteen years. She started out as a legal secretary and attended night school. After five years, she was promoted to Personnel Manager, then Director of Personnel and Training. When her firm merged with another, she was named Director of Administration, overseeing the branch office of a 450-attorney firm.

She supervises the managers of the library services, accounting, human resources, secretarial, information systems and office support areas. In addition, she works with department heads at the attorney level to ensure they meet budget figures on both the expense and revenue sides.

Rocker made her first transition from secretary to manager because she volunteered to help set up a temporary office out-of-state. She garnered experience on a small-scale project that showcased her capabilities.

Sometimes it is difficult to rise out of the pre-conceived role of your last position in the firm. Rocker believes that the key to increasing your credibility in a firm is to project authority. Her strategy for dealing with requests for something that she no longer handles is to answer, "Let me give that to John who does that now."

Rocker also set up a mentoring program for new secretaries to make them feel valued and help them to continue learning about the field. She identified a receptive attorney at the firm who had been a mentor before and who was willing to propose the mentoring program to the other partners.

Communicate with the Partners

Jim Fairchild, Chief Administrative and Financial Officer of Richards, Watson & Gershon in Los Angeles, entered the profession fifteen years ago with an undergraduate degree from West Point and a master's degree in economics from the University of Michigan.

When he began his career, Fairchild was primarily responsible for personnel and day-to-day operations. Now, he supervises all administrative areas of the 65-attorney firm, including long-range planning and marketing. He manages 55 administrative employees.

A part of Fairchild's strategy for success has been to approach one partner with a detailed plan for a new idea, describing what it will cost, what personnel it will require and how much time it will take to put into place. That way, he helps the partner "sell" the idea to the rest of the decision-makers at the firm. He believes it's important to gather all the facts before making any recommendation, so that you can present all of the advantages and the projected results to the partners.

Fairchild solidifies his role as a decision-maker by initiating and implementing long-range planning for the firm. He starts by issuing questionnaires to the partners and devises a plan from their collective direction. An ad hoc committee works with him to refine the plan, which goes back to the partners for approval. Jim is then responsible for implementing the plan. When the project is non-attorney-related, such as opening a new office, he also directs the logistics.

Another technique he uses to garner high visibility in the firm is to keep the partners informed of what is going on behind the scenes. He suggested that he give an Administrator's Update at the monthly shareholder meetings and now he has established a direct link to the partners through these status reports.

Psychological Challenges

Law firms are unique. Where else do you find such a group of strong personalities — highly educated, accomplished professionals, each one potentially capable of being CEO of a company — all under one roof? The task of managing a firm with that mix of personalities is an undertaking that administrators have long recognized as a special challenge psychologically.

To thrive in this setting, legal administrators need to be excellent communicators, as well as think clearly, have a high level of self-esteem, and be extremely empathetic. In addition, they must have a good understanding of the environment of the firm and the approaches to take with partners. They also need to:

- Recognize that every firm has its own personality, and that you'll be most successful if you can identify and understand the subtleties of how things work at your office. Where and how are decisions made? Are meetings only a forum for discussion, with the real decisions made later by several partners behind closed doors? Is there usually closure on a decision following a one-on-one meeting with a particular partner?
- Observe the partners and determine which approach is appropriate for each one. Recognize that they cannot all be treated identically. One may prefer to communicate via electronic mail; another may prefer face-to-face meetings.
- Identify the factors that are important to each person's success in the firm and help them achieve their goals. Does one lawyer want daily updates on the firm's revenues, while another cares more about the status of the client database? At the same time, how can you make your staff feel appreciated for working late to finish a closing for a client or to complete a filing?
- The key is to try to treat everyone with equal respect. We all know that today's first year associate may be the managing partner of the future — and in any case, needs your support now.

Networking Is Vital

Within a law firm, there are multiple attorneys and multiple secretaries who can talk over problems and strategies but for the sole legal administrator, trade conferences and meetings may be the only place to exchange ideas and concerns with his or her peers.

Membership in the ALA can be invaluable for learning how your colleagues solve similar problems in their firms. At a recent conference, seminar topics ranged from "Managing a PC Network Without a LAN Specialist" to "Intervention in the Workplace" to "Are You Sick or Is It Your Building?" to "Redefining the Relationship Between In-House Counsel and Law Firms." Many also find it extremely valuable to become involved in association committee work.

For Jim Fairchild, one of the greatest benefits of membership in the ALA is the opportunity to talk with other people in the profession. Networking at meetings and conferences can provide contacts for a career move and give you emotional support.

Interaction with her peers is vital to Mimi Shore. She is currently guiding her firm through a conversion from a 10-year-old WANG system to a PC network, and has received valuable advice from her contacts in the industry. As a result of networking, she also decided to upgrade the firm's library by putting it on an inter-office network and adding CD-ROM.

"Every good administrator is a juggler," says one professional who manages an office with 110 attorneys. The legal administrator of the '90s has to tackle far more than juggling to succeed in this demanding field. By identifying and focusing on your own set of success strategies, you can stay challenged and become a greater asset to your firm.

CHAPTER 20
MANAGE YOUR TIME

The most urgent things are generally not the most important.

It is no accident that this is the final chapter: As one of the key value indicators, there are few things more prized within a law firm than time itself. And how effectively you manage your time will be one of the most important determinants of career success.

Certainly your ability to respond to the challenges in the preceding chapters will depend to a large measure on your time-management skills. It always amazes me how some people are forever busy and rushing around and yet achieve so little, while others make quantum progress and get results with seemingly no effort. The answer often comes down to time management.

Effective time management starts with a clear vision of what you want to achieve. Many law firm managers are very focused on educating partners about the need for strategic thinking/planning. Yet, these managers often fail to apply the same good business disciplines to their own lives.

You need a personal strategic plan, complete with vision statement, long-term goals and related priorities/action lists. Nothing is more crucial to good time management than having a proper understanding of your own priorities. This will ensure that your efforts are well directed toward achieving agreed upon goals. It will also give you added focus and minimize any unnecessary distractions.

In determining your priorities, think carefully about all aspects of your life (See Chapter 7.) and make sure that you are genuinely committed to directing personal effort and energy to these items. Your goals should not be merely wish lists. Make them specific, measurable, realistic and, where appropriate, attach a targeted timeframe. Use daily "to-do" lists and categorize your tasks by reference to your agreed priorities.

Here are a few ideas to help you create more hours in your day:

- Use the appropriate technology and latest software tools.
- Master an excellent diary/planner (consider an electronic organizer or PDA).

- Be highly organized and eliminate clutter (this can be a big time waster).
- Learn to say no.
- Secure the services of an outstanding secretary or personal assistant.
- Do not procrastinate. If the task seems overwhelming, break it down into manageable portions.
- Eliminate time wasters: interruptions, phone calls, spam e-mails, etc.
- Avoid irrelevant/unnecessary meetings.
- Have agendas for all meetings and run them efficiently.
- Use conference calls and video/Web-conferencing in place of face-to-face meetings.
- Make good use of dead/wasted time (traveling, commuting, waiting for meetings to start, etc.).
- Don't let the urgent things push out the important things.
- Plan ahead. (Proper Prior Planning Prevents Poor Performance)
- Hire a great support team and delegate wherever possible. (See Chapter 10.)

How you spend your time will provide one of the strongest communications to others of what is important to you. Therefore, focus your efforts on those initiatives that truly reflect your priorities and will advance your career prospects. If you have no idea where your valuable time is disappearing, keep a daily log and use this as the basis for improvement.

Finally, remember to take time to reflect and plan ahead. A regular period of creative silence with no interruptions or distractions is absolutely essential to being effective. Time is one of your most important assets: Invest it wisely.

Further Reading

Grussman, Eric, *"Time Tactics for Successful People"*

Smith, Hyrum W., *"The 10 Natural Laws of Successful Time and Life Management: Proven Strategies for Increased Productivity and Inner Peace"*

CONCLUSION

"It's not the strongest nor the fastest nor the most intelligent which ultimately survive, but those most capable of adapting to change." — Charles Darwin

At whatever stage you are in your law firm management career, you owe it to yourself to fully realize your maximum potential. The ideas here will help you to achieve this, but only if you commit to make the necessary changes. This means taking action — now!

Start by thinking about what skill sets you most need to develop: What areas need improvement? What are the things that may be holding back your career progression? Consider also your natural strengths, available resources and driving passions.

Next, review the recommended strategies outlined here and seek those that resonate with your thinking. Use these as the foundation from which to construct your own wisdom. Prioritize them into specific goals and action plans. Attach measurable indicators or timeframes to each task and display the resulting plan in a prominent place as a source of inspiration. The final step is to implement your plan. Regularly review progress and remember to celebrate your achievements — even the small ones.

Your career progression is a vital aspect of your overall life plan. It needs personal attention and dedicated effort. The challenge to change begins with you and it cannot be left to chance. As with life itself, career management is not so much about being dealt a good hand, but more importantly it means playing your best — even with a poor hand.

Best wishes for a fabulous journey.

An ALA White Paper

THE DELIVERY OF LEGAL SERVICES IN THE FUTURE: HOW IS THE ROLE OF PROFESSIONAL MANAGEMENT IN THE LEGAL ENVIRONMENT EVOLVING?

Introduction
A Message from 2000-2001 ALA President M. Lynn Spruill, Stoel Rives, LLP, Portland, Oregon

Those who have been legal administrators for some time regularly reflect on the changes in the profession over the years. They note with pride the growing professionalism among their colleagues and the growing respect paid in many organizations to those who play the role of legal administrator, whatever the title.

Nonetheless, many in the profession believe we are at critical juncture — a moment when the legal profession is changing in profound ways and when the legal administration profession is maturing. The White Paper that follows, the second in the history of the Association of Legal Administrators, asks, and provides answers to, some very simple questions:

- *What role do you want to play in your legal organization?*
- *How can you prepare yourself to play that role?*

During the 2000 year a group of legal administrators representing all elements of our profession and all sizes of organizations began to work with their colleagues to answer these questions. We asked these individuals (Betty Greene, Brenda Barnes, Jim Allen, Gary Dodman and Marianna Beem) to help us describe the origins of our profession, to predict what the profession would be like in years to come, and to tell us how to best position ourselves, as administrators, to be most successful in our chosen profession.

I assembled the materials provided by these volunteers and prepared a first draft of the White Paper. Then Mike Palmer, Char Coulbert and Patti Lane took their turn. What evolved is a concise statement of what we believe the profession can become and a road map to help it become what it wishes to be.

We are challenged by the conclusions of this Paper to take risks, to be aggressive in advocating for our own interests, and to take responsibility for our own educational growth so that we can continue to gain respect from those for whom we work.

The Paper is meant to be provocative. It includes sketches of individuals who we believe are on the track toward great success — the same track most of us would choose. And, at the end, the creation of the Paper will be a useful exercise if it leads to consistent and continuing efforts toward growth in the profession and respect in the legal arena by and for all who read it.

— Lynn Spruill

The past decade brought some breathtaking changes to law firms. The strong economy and the conditions it creates — competition for young lawyers, the attendant upward spiraling of compensation, the movement of senior partners among firms, and the possibility of multidisciplinary practices — present leaders of law firms with new challenges. The evolution and growth of legal organizations bring similar changes in governance structures. Likewise, corporate and government legal departments have changed dramatically. Mergers and acquisitions of corporations lead to mergers and acquisitions of legal departments, along with the requisite turmoil. Within the government, regardless of the level or branch, dockets are full and competition is fierce for lawyers and leaders willing to enter public service.

As with all organizations in rapidly changing economies, adaptability, responsiveness, timeliness and efficiency are increasingly becoming essential to the success of legal organizations. Who will lead these changing legal organizations as they strive for new levels of economic performance while continuing to deliver high-quality legal services?

This White Paper will answer this question— and many others. It

- reviews the development of professional management in legal organizations;
- compares roles of professional managers in legal organizations of various sizes and structures;
- suggests ways in which lawyer leaders in legal organizations would be better served by using professional managers more effectively; and
- describes an ideal set of characteristics, skills, and qualities a professional manager should have in order to be an effective leader in a legal organization.

HISTORICAL DEVELOPMENT

Before the 1980s, most legal administrators (an all-inclusive term for a group usually, but not always, composed of non-lawyers) held narrowly defined roles. Their positions were largely administrative, with limited management discretion and little decision-making authority. In an article from PLI's 1978 *Course Handbook Lawyer's Assistant: Administrator*, Bradford W. Hildebrandt said an administrator of a larger firm (considered at that time to be more than 12 attorneys) needed "skills in financial management, systems and procedures, word processing, data processing and, most of all, the ability to act as father confessor and resident psychologist." These have been duties historically associated with the role of an office manager, as contrasted with a true business leader.

During the 1980s, the administrator's influence in many law offices began to grow. Administrators were no longer limited to the traditional duties of an office manager. New responsibilities included an expanded role in the development of firm policies and procedures, and planning and oversight of the firm's information systems. These professionals began providing advice and analysis in more strategic decisions, such as geographic or practice diversification, pricing of services, productivity analysis, and leverage of both staff and billable personnel. As business development and client relations took on new importance, many administrators also became more active in external matters such as marketing and lawyer recruiting.

It is difficult to assess whether the growth in the administrator's role was due more to enlightened hiring and utilization practices of firm leaders or the efforts of administrators themselves to improve business practices and expand the range of their contributions. However, it is clear that firms increasingly recognized the need for, and began to value, more sophisticated management expertise. More firms began to hire professional managers from outside the legal industry. Accounting firms provided new talent for the evolving legal management field, as initially there was a bias toward those with a financial background. Over time, more and more firms gravitated toward generalist managers, assisted, when the size of the firm permitted, by technical specialists or managers in areas such as human resources, finance, technology and office services.

Jim Lantonio, former ALA Board Member, now Executive Director of Milbank Tweed Hadley & McCloy, said in a 1989 discussion with section directors of the Association of Legal Administrators: "Legal administrator duties have changed from administrative to managerial to leadership in nature. Not too long ago, they were administering billing and collections, data processing and bookkeeping. In the next decade, they will be more involved in practice development, lawyer evaluation and quality control. What's more, there will be a blurring of the we/they mindset as legal executives with influence and authority see themselves and lawyers as peers."

The 1990s, driven by a rapidly changing economic climate, saw increasing levels of responsibility for many administrators. For the first time, firms began to look to their administrators for assistance with practice management and mergers and acquisitions. Many firm owners consulted their administrators regarding individual partner compensation and lawyer evaluations, and charged them with ensuring quality control within their firms. Administrators also became involved in developing responses to the threat/opportunity of multidisciplinary practices. Those in corporate or government legal departments had to deal with mergers, acquisitions, changes in government policy and the pressures of alternative employment opportunities.

CURRENT SCOPE OF AUTHORITY

What is the present role of legal administrators? What probable changes will affect this role in the future? This Paper examines the roles of legal administrators in firms of different sizes and in corporate and government legal departments. To be consistent throughout, and noting the wide variation of titles used within different firms and organizations, the title "principal administrator" will be used for all those with primary responsibility for the business and administrative operations of a legal organization. Similarly, the term "law firm" will be used to include both private law firms and corporate and government law departments.

SMALL LAW FIRMS (1 TO 29 LAWYERS)

In small law firms, principal administrators are the front, and sometimes only, line of management. Most staff members report directly to the principal administrator. This person is often engaged in all aspects of the firm's business (strategic planning and implementation, business development, recruiting, practice management, finance, technology, human resources and facilities), in addition to managing the day-to-day business operations. In very small firms, the day-to-day responsibilities are all consuming and tend to make the "big picture" issues more difficult for the principal administrator to address. Professionals in these positions typically report to an executive committee or managing partner/shareholder.

Smaller firms are not significantly less sophisticated than larger firms. As organizational structures, however, they tend to be less complex and choices are more limited. While the nature of smaller firms is not always conducive to substantial growth in responsibility for a principal administrator, this fact neither relieves this person from striving to become more effective and involved in leadership of the firm, nor excuses the lawyer managers from learning to delegate appropriate responsibility to the principal administrator.

MID-SIZED FIRMS (30 TO 99 LAWYERS)

The principal administrator's scope of authority in mid-sized organizations varies from firm to firm, often in relation to the level of confidence lawyer leadership has in the individual filling the role and the willingness of that person to test the role's limits. As in smaller firms, principal administrators of mid-sized firms typically exercise no direct oversight of lawyers. However, they are often "managers of managers," supervising a team of functional specialists and branch managers. Given the limited resources of mid-sized firms, it is common for the principal administrator to continue to have primary responsibility for one or more management functions requiring hands-on involvement in day-to-day operations.

LARGE FIRMS (100+ LAWYERS)

As part of the research for this study, the Association of Legal Administrators queried managing partners of 125 large firms about the present and future role of the principal administrator. Respondents revealed little inclination to change principal administrator responsibilities beyond the traditional business and administrative functions that already define the position in most large firms. While many respondents said they expect the principal administrator's role to grow during the next five years, most expect it to do so in the functional areas currently within the position's realm.

Although a minority view, others were supportive of the integration of the principal administrator into practice management. One managing partner said, "This is an area where we would like to see the role of our principal administrator expanded. We would like to see him complement and serve as more of a resource to our practice group leaders in terms of their role in more effective utilization of resources. In order to do this, there needs to be some reduction of time requirements associated with the principal administrator's role in the management of other directors and their responsibilities. In a growing law firm, this likely means an elevation of the role and performance of some of the director positions in the firm."

CORPORATE/GOVERNMENT LEGAL DEPARTMENTS

Principal administrators in corporate/government legal departments are involved in most of the roles and functions as their counterparts in private law firms. They, too, tackle technology, human resources, facilities and equipment management, research, budgeting and financial management, strategic planning and general administration. However, they probably do not supervise an HR department or a finance department, but rather interact closely with the departments that support the entire corporation or government agency. The corporate/government principal administrator may also have responsibility for functions such as compliance, corporate secretary or government affairs that do not exist within a law firm setting.

In the future, the expected changes for the role of the corporate/government principal administrator include a generally increased involvement in, and accountability for, all functions. Primarily though, the principal administrator will need to become more involved in strategic planning, with significant focus on mergers and acquisitions and the attendant blending of legal departments, and on internal and external customer service.

PROFILE OF SUCCESS: KNOWLEDGE, SKILLS, AND ATTRIBUTES OF A LEGAL ADMINISTRATOR

In 1995 and again in 2000, the Association of Legal Administrators conducted surveys of managing partners and administrators to document the desired knowledge, skills and abilities for administrators. These surveys' findings confirm that a successful principal administrator has knowledge sets that center on finance, communication, organization and management in general, as well as an ability to delegate and recognize the appropriate level for decision-making. Principal administrators must understand and implement a business approach to a professional-services organization. Training or experience outside of a law firm environment is helpful in adding perspective as well as knowledge. To be truly effective, principal administrators must have an understanding of the practice of law.

Of course, the required skills of successful principal administrators vary from firm to firm and depend on the firm's philosophy and organizational structure and, to some extent, on the size of the firm. Nonetheless, many skills are basic:

- The principal administrator needs to be highly organized and able to prioritize.
- The principal administrator needs the ability to work with individuals at all levels of the organization, build interpersonal relationships and manage conflict resolution, thus helping staff and attorneys to work together toward a common goal.

- The principal administrator needs excellent communication skills, both written and oral, with superb negotiation skills.
- The principal administrator must also be technologically savvy.

Among the attributes needed by the principal administrator, the most important is high personal integrity. Principal administrators must also be able to recognize which leadership, management and work styles are critical to the persons with whom they interact. No personality or leadership style should prevail. Instead, the principal administrator's approach must be flexible in order to succeed in the dynamic environment of a legal organization:

- Principal administrators must be able to command respect and be confident in their actions.
- Principal administrators must be able to determine and be responsive to the key players in the firm, while managing for the best interests of the firm and not just those few individuals.
- Successful principal administrators are those who are creative and can think "outside the box," considering alternatives that might seem to deviate from the norm.
- Finally, successful principal administrators will have two very highly active senses: common sense and a sense of humor. The former facilitates the making of good decisions and the latter helps preserve a semblance of sanity.

FUTURE ROLE OF THE PRINCIPAL ADMINISTRATOR

It is clear that broader utilization of principal administrators in significant leadership and authority roles will require major changes in firm philosophy. It is logical to assume that greater reliance on experienced senior-level professionals with business backgrounds will allow attorneys to focus on the practice of law. It is also logical to believe that law firms, especially the largest organizations, will eventually look like traditional corporations with chief financial officers, chief information officers and chief operating officers, with the managing partners being the chief executive officers. But any shift from lawyer responsibility and authority would, in most law organizations, represent enormous change.

What is necessary for these changes in legal management philosophy to occur? Two areas must be affected: the legal organization and the legal management profession. Both the organization and the profession are at critical points in their evolution. The organization is adapting to major changes in the external environment, and the profession has matured to a point where seasoned leaders are available from within the legal industry. Perhaps the changes are occurring at an opportune time for both the organizations and the profession, a time when law firms and legal departments can take advantage of seasoned professionals to solve leadership and management issues.

THE LEGAL ORGANIZATION

In the March/April 2000 issue of *Legal Management* (Volume 19, Number 2), Carl Leonard, the former chairman of Morrison & Foerster and founder of The Hildebrandt Institute, predicted that managing partners would gravitate to a role approximating that of corporate chief executive officer. Even as Leonard makes a case for a different business/leadership role for the managing partner, he also forges a compelling argument for why most lawyers do not make effective CEOs. This is important because the personality traits and training described by Leonard make it difficult for lawyers to serve as leaders in a corporate sense, and also make it difficult for them to vest the leadership of their firm in a professional manager. Yet, without changes in the philosophy of senior lawyer leadership, how much significant change can be expected in principal administrators' roles?

Leonard asserts that, by reason of their training, most lawyers are risk-averse and ultraconservative, with the very thoroughness that makes them successful in the practice of law making it difficult for them to make decisions as quickly as are necessary in a corporate setting. The practice of law is often directed toward recommending solutions, not implementing them. Since those who counsel are generally not charged with implementation, their accountability to owners is less than what would be expected of a true CEO.

The foregoing, coupled with the reluctance of lawyers to accept decisions by professional managers that directly impact either them or the strategic direction of their firm, poses a dilemma that has plagued the legal administration profession for years. If lawyers are unlikely to give principal administrators a significant leadership role, but they are unprepared to provide the leadership required by their changing organizations, there is an obvious gap. Even if qualified and capable of serving as a leader, the lawyer-manager's highest and best use lies in the area of dealing with ownership issues, developing business, and strategic planning regarding practice areas and the practice of law. Everything else, including implementation and organization of the same, is better served by principal administrators.

Any question concerning an expanded role for principal administrators must be considered in conjunction with the future role of the managing partners of these same organizations. Generally speaking, principal administrators' functions and responsibilities will increase only if authorized and supported by the lawyer leadership of the legal organization. This might occur under two likely scenarios:

- In one, the managing partner position is not filled, for whatever reason, and the principal administrator assumes many, if not all, of the managing partner responsibilities, including lawyer leadership.
- In the other, the managing partner's role moves to a higher level as CEO, making it imperative to delegate to or share with the principal administrator certain traditional managing-partner functions and responsibilities, such as strategic planning and practice management.

As multidisciplinary practices become a reality, their leadership and management almost certainly will take on a corporate look. It is in this environment that Leonard's prediction of a corporate CEO will probably come true out of necessity. The manner in which most legal organizations make decisions today will change to meet the faster-paced demands of an increasingly competitive environment. Corporate legal departments are already facing the faster pace. With the evolution of the managing partner to a true CEO (whether in a multidisciplinary practice, a mega-firm, or in an enlightened firm of any size) will come the opportunity for the principal administrator to assume not only new responsibilities but also to fill a much-needed role.

If firms begin acting more corporate-like in their business operations and to some extent in their practice of law, and if managing partners begin, as suggested by Leonard, to function as CEOs, then principal administrators need similarly to operate at a higher level in the manner in which they build and lead their teams. This will require the hiring and development of a new kind of departmental director — one who demonstrates not merely a high degree of technical expertise and competence along with strong management skills, but one who possesses strong leadership skills as well. For just as the corporate COO strengthens his/her corporation by building a strong leadership team, tomorrow's principal administrator needs similarly to upgrade the quality and credentials of those who will help lead tomorrow's law firm. In order for the principal administrator successfully to accomplish expanded responsibilities and fill a larger role in the firm, it is essential to have a more competent, committed and leadership-oriented support team.

Competition from nontraditional sources — CPAs, Web lawyers, corporate counsel in other companies, outsourcing and privatization in government — will all blur the traditional borders between the old style legal organization and the new style. The speed required to turn work around and the near commoditization of the work product, often being driven by access to the Internet and an information retrieval capability only imagined several years ago, are daunting. Law firms are asked to invest in their clients, a largely unheard of concept until recently. In this changing environment, legal administrators in firms of all sizes must seek ways to lead their organizations through these changes and add value beyond their present roles.

THE LEGAL MANAGEMENT PROFESSION

Those who have been in the legal management profession for more than a decade have witnessed a gradual but recognizable shift in lawyer perceptions concerning professional management and leadership. Today's principal administrators assume a more pronounced role in law firm and legal department management than did their counterparts 15 to 20 years ago. While the redefining of the position and growth in responsibility can be expected to continue, albeit slowly, it will not in and of itself be the reason or catalyst for major change. That catalyst will come from outside the law firm in the form of competing professional service firms. As noted by Mike Katos and Ed Wesemann in the September/October 1999 issue of *Legal Management* (Volume 18, Number 5), if law firms become part and party to multidisciplinary partnerships, then "the complexity of a multidisciplinary firm promotes the need for sophisticated professional management." Who better to address that need than the qualified principal administrator?

Ultimately, the continued growth of the principal administrator position must involve awareness and opportunism on the part of the professional in that position. Historically, an individual principal administrator's initiative and an inherent drive to improve the business practices of the organization have done more to advance the position than the foresight of those to whom they report.

Leadership, by definition and in practice, requires the identification of opportunities and the taking of considered risks. Principal administrators who seek greater roles in law firm leadership and management must create more value by asserting themselves appropriately into the future of their firms. They cannot wait for lawyer management to expand their present roles. Principal administrators must be at the forefront of change and be willing to exercise leadership via their actions and recommendations. Each demonstrated success builds credibility with lawyer-owners, adds value to the principal administrator position, and leads to a more responsible and rewarding role within the organization. The responsibility for creating this role change lies squarely with these administration professionals. Ultimately it will be principal administrators, not lawyer management, who can and will make this happen.

The relevant question remains: How does the principal administrator achieve success and gain credibility? In addition to filling voids and taking considered risks, there is a further step — a movement toward higher, recognized levels of educational achievement, credibility and possible certification, perhaps choosing from among several existing types of certification — that will give administrators greater stature.

Lawyers are highly educated professionals who value academic achievements. Their hiring practices have usually demonstrated the value they attach to the credentials of principal administrators and others who manage important aspects of their business. The message is inescapable: Those who aspire to assume more responsibility in legal organizations will benefit from strong educational and professional credentials. These credentials are no substitute for the leadership and management skills and other strengths required to actually do the job. They provide a base on which to build the credibility required to succeed. Principal administrators who have advanced degrees or professional certificates will benefit from increased credibility not easily gained by those without such credentials.

No one career path qualifies someone to manage a firm or law department. However, the Association of Legal Administrators' research into the knowledge, skills and abilities (collectively referred to as "competencies") required of successful administrators provides the framework for assessing one's strengths and weaknesses and for mapping a path toward self-improvement. That same research provided the basis for requirements in the Association's Certified Legal Manager (CLM)[SM] program, the only certification of legal administrators now available. It remains to be seen whether the CLM[SM] designation affords an advantage to candidates in a job search or secures them additional respect upon hiring. However, the program was not developed solely for those purposes: Certification is a way to ensure that the Association's education is relevant to the demands of the legal management profession. From an individual standpoint, whether or not a legal-administration professional pursues certification, the program provides direction for personal and professional development in areas that both lawyer managers and other administrators consider pertinent to the job. In the final analysis, it is the way administrators apply education on the job that demonstrates its usefulness and worth.

CONCLUSION

Change is occurring in the legal community, and those organizations that do not adapt to change will fail or, at the very least, not prosper. It is unlikely that lawyers will yield authority and responsibility absent the significant belief that professional managers can, in fact, lead firms and legal departments. However, it is up to principal administrators themselves to create the competency, demonstrate the capability and seize the opportunity. They must arm themselves with appropriate tools, such as advanced degrees, continuing education and the CLM^{SM} program, which demonstrates knowledge and commitment to the profession. Principal administrators must earn the trust and respect of the lawyers: Do what you say you'll do. And lastly, principal administrators should take charge and make things happen.

It is better to ask for their forgiveness, than wait for their permission. It is up to you!

CASE STUDIES

CASE STUDY: Small Firm Administrator
Judy A. Anderson, Director of Client Service and Firm Administration
Managing Partner: Richard W. "Rick" Riddle
Firm: Riddle & Wimbish, P.C. (Tulsa, Oklahoma)
Firm size: 2 lawyers

From the firm's beginning, Anderson has been a leader in the firm, has been treated as a partner and has been given a partner's authority. In fact, Riddle is and has been the sole shareholder since inception. Riddle formed an ancillary business — a title insurance company — a number of years ago and, because of her value to the business, Anderson was made a shareholder. In addition to her vested authority, her stature as a shareholder of the title insurance company plus her participation in attorney interviews provided staff and lawyers with recognition that Riddle sees her as a valuable contributor to the firm. Prior to that, she spent a lot of time proving herself, which was both frustrating and time-consuming. Anderson and Riddle feel her title now could be changed to Chief Operating Officer because society is at a point where sophisticated clients have a grasp of the COO concept.

Anderson's role gives Riddle the time he needs to practice law and develop business. Strategic planning and visioning have been shared responsibilities over the firm's history; while she serves as facilitator for strategic planning sessions, in Anderson's opinion, it is clearly Riddle's vision they follow, her vision having more to do with implementation and infrastructure. Anderson believes it is important for legal administrators to be committed, enthused, and excited about their role because even with strong management support and leadership, it is not always a smooth ride.

Riddle believes the legal industry is years behind other industries in coming to the realization that theirs is a business that must be run as such, preferably by a professional non-lawyer. He feels law firms are missing the boat by not recognizing the bottom-line significance of business issues such as lawyers dealing fairly with staff, marketplace awareness and close monitoring of the firm's economic health.

CASE STUDY: Midsize Firm Administrator
Kelli A. Kohout, Chief Operating Officer
Managing Partner: Roger A. Myklebust
Firm: Ryan Swanson & Cleveland, PLLC (Seattle, Washington)
Firm size: 45 lawyers

As a result of the vision created by former Managing Partner Jerry Kindinger, it was decided at the 2000 partners retreat to turn over substantially more authority to the firm's executive committee and Kohout. Many of the partners simply said, "Let Kelli run the business," and they've proceeded to do just that. Her title was changed to COO, and Myklebust's directive to Kohout was, "If you can do it, go do it — so I don't have to."

Although she has been at the firm for seven years, Kohout took sufficient time to build relationships with the partners. This gave them an opportunity to become comfortable with her dedication to the best interests of the firm, as well as her communication and diplomacy skills. Although Myklebust receives an occasional complaint or "appeal" about one of Kohout's decisions, he refuses to do more than hear the person out and encourage them to talk with Kohout.

According to Myklebust, law firms have to start with their rules of governance. If the managing partner or executive committee has fairly broad authority, these entities can delegate authority however and to whomever they wish—like to the COO. Then it is up to the managing partner or executive committee to support and stay out of the COO's way.

In Myklebust's opinion, the firm's lawyers should practice law on a daily basis while managing their practice with Kohout's assistance. They work with COO Kohout in activities such as the pricing of legal services, coordination of practice management responsibilities, and supporting efforts at business generation through marketing — particularly enhanced name recognition. Although both Kohout and Myklebust participate in strategic planning, Myklebust's role is primarily that of a strategic thinker in the areas of size, space, and practice issues. He relies on data fed to him by Kohout. He then turns his ideas over to Kohout for implementation. Kohout's future goal is to spend 50 percent of her time on strategic and business planning regarding market forces and firm direction.

CASE STUDY: Large Firm Administrator

John R. Gerhard, Managing Director
Co-Managing Partners: Harry P. Trueheart III, Nestor Nicholas
Firm: Nixon Peabody LLP (Rochester, New York)
Firm Size: 512 lawyers

As a result of the much-publicized 1999 merger of Nixon Hargrave Devans & Doyle and Peabody & Brown, Nixon Peabody LLP currently has 11 offices in the New York, New England and Washington, D.C., areas. With a background in regional, national, and international business, Gerhard is well suited to the complexities of modern-day large firm administration. At Nixon Peabody, his primary focus is on broad-based aspects of building and strengthening the firm, such as mergers and acquisitions (M&A) opportunities; risk-sharing pricing strategies; lateral (partner-level) hiring; marketing and branding; strategic planning; budgets and reporting; and overall technology strategy (including capturing intellectual capital into the knowledge management system of the merged firm). Of these major areas of responsibility, M&A opportunities are particularly time consuming for Gerhard.

By surrounding himself with an excellent support staff, Gerhard has delegated most of the day-to-day aspects of running the firm. There are six functional specialists reporting directly to him: Operations Director, HR Manager, Finance Director, Marketing Director, Information Systems Director, and Information Services Director. Ten of the firm's 11 offices have office administrators, all of whom report directly to the Operations Director. Gerhard believes one of the biggest mistakes made by principal administrators and law firms is hiring people who won't pose a threat to their leadership. To the contrary, Gerhard feels strongly that only the best people should be hired and that they should be paid well, given direction, and then left alone to do their jobs.

The firm employs quality management principles that provide a focus on internal- and external-client satisfaction and employee satisfaction. The firm receives regular feedback regarding satisfaction levels in all three areas. In addition, all partners have ready access to Gerhard, especially through e-mail. As a result of the regular feedback processes, Gerhard deals with few partner complaints or attempts to override his decisions. Also, because of the thorough intake process for lateral partners in which Gerhard is involved, there are few surprises for either lateral partners or the firm in terms of learning to work with one another. Both staff members and the staff-management function are highly respected throughout the firm.

An ALA Study

Jacks of All Trades: Study of Administrators' Knowledge, Skills and Abilities Reveals Diverse Skills

Law firm managers and administrators need to know a lot about a lot of things. And ALA has the scientific evidence to prove it.

In 2000, the Association of Legal Administrators recently conducted a Job/Needs Analysis survey of administrator-practitioners and law firm managing partners. This was a follow-up to the 1995 Job Analysis. (See the previous results in *Legal Management*, November/December 1996.) The 2000 survey's scope included legal management professionals in Canada and the United States — the 1995 study was U.S.-based only.

The survey revisited the previous study to identify the critical tasks performed by principal administrators and, more importantly, the knowledges, skills and abilities (competencies) needed to perform those tasks. Few jobs or occupations remain the same over time. Therefore, it is necessary to periodically reassess job requirements. The frequency of required job analysis updates varies by occupation, with the rule of thumb being every four or five years. The purpose of the 2000 study, then, was to collect more recent information about principal administrator job requirements and their professional development needs.

The latest report reveals that there are 55 fundamental competencies that administrators need to master to be successful in their jobs. The list appears to be expanding: The 1995 survey identified 47. Differing degrees of knowledge in these areas will help legal administration professionals — and their employers — succeed.

The survey consisted of statements about knowledge areas that pertain to an administrator's functions. Survey respondents rated these statements and professional human resources research consultants tabulated and reported the data. The final report (and the knowledge areas it highlights), plays a major role in how the Association approaches its educational offerings for members. In fact, the identified competencies are the foundation on which everything from articles to sessions during ALA's Annual Educational Conference is based. And, it serves as the foundation for ALA's Certified Legal Manager (CLM)^{SM}* certification program.

Not only did this study shed light on what principal administrators do (and what they need to know to do it), it offered insight into educational preferences — how they want to learn. It delved into what factors contributed to their decision to participate in professional development activities, and about their opinions/reactions to the CLM certification examination.

This information helps ALA help its members. When legal management professionals are busy doing their jobs, it may be difficult for them to look ahead. They may be too attentive to today's work to predict what they'll need to know tomorrow. With this study, ALA can ensure its members will be exposed to the information they need to succeed in the future.

Survey Development

Separate surveys were developed for legal administrators and managing partners. The managing partner survey was shorter in hopes of making it easier to complete and increasing the response from this group. Focus groups were held with experienced principal administrators and interviews were conducted of managing partners to gather input regarding the survey content.

The ALA Certification Committee was also asked to review the task and competency lists and assist in the development of other items for the surveys (e.g., items related to respondents' perceptions of the CLM program). The 1995 study asked legal administrators about their thoughts on the prospect of a certification program. Now that the CLM program exists, the new study asked respondents how they felt the CLM program has benefited them and the legal administrator profession.

Survey Distribution and Sample Obtained

Surveys went to 1,188 principal administrators (1,100 in the United States and 88 in Canada) and to 322 managing partners (296 in the United States and 26 in Canada). Respondents were asked to provide employment and demographic information, such as their firm size and ALA region, so that survey tabulators could describe the sample obtained and assess whether it was sufficiently representative of ALA's total membership.

Results of Competency Analysis

Information Obtained

The survey revealed shifts from the 1995 study. Many of the top-ranked competencies for legal administrators remain high in the rankings. Others moved down or were combined with another competency listing because of changes in the workplace (i.e. technology changes). Here is a comparison of the results.

Competency[1]	Rank in 2000	Rank in 1995
Written communication skills (e.g., writing memos, policy manuals, proposals, job descriptions)	1	2
Interpersonal relations skills (e.g., performance counseling, client contacts)	2	5
Oral communication skills (e.g., presentations to staff and attorneys, interactions with clients and vendors)	3	3

Knowledge of general accounting procedures, systems, terms, concepts and policies, including familiarity with general ledger, general journal entries, cost accounting, fixed asset accounting, accounts receivable, and accounts payable	4	1
Knowledge of budgeting, financial reporting, cash flow analysis, and variance analysis	5	n/a
Knowledge of time management strategies (e g., setting priorities, delegating)	6	6
Skill in using computer systems (e.g., word processing, accessing informational databases)	7	2
Knowledge of leadership styles and techniques	8	8
Knowledge of the features and capabilities of desktop computer and network hardware and software systems, including general purpose packages (e.g., spreadsheets, database programs, and word processing applications)	9	19 and 33
Knowledge of compensation, employee benefits, and reward systems	10	7
Knowledge of procedures and tools for recruiting, selecting, and retaining employees	11 (tie)	11
Knowledge of the features and capabilities of the Internet, web-based technology, and hardware and software systems, including security and confidentiality	11 (tie)	n/a
Knowledge and skill in conflict management techniques	13	27
Knowledge of changes/trends in the legal industry	14	18
Knowledge of stress management techniques	15	25
Knowledge of methods of financial analysis, including reading and interpreting financial statements, calculating and interpreting various financial ratios, and analyzing comparative financial information across fiscal years	16	14
Knowledge of employee motivational techniques	17	16
Knowledge of performance management systems (e.g., appraisal procedures, disciplinary procedures)	18	10
Knowledge of special issues in accounting for law firm operations, including time and billing systems, alternative billing methods, collection procedures, and cost-recovery guidelines	19	4 and 22
Knowledge of team development and management principles (e.g., self-directed teams)	20	n/a
Knowledge and skill in negotiation techniques	21	24
Knowledge of organizational development techniques (e.g., change management)	22	31
Knowledge of US federal employment laws (e.g., Civil Rights Act of 1991, Americans with Disabilities Act, Fair Labor Standards Act)	23	21

Knowledge of planning techniques (e.g., strategic, disaster, and business planning)	24	29
Knowledge and expertise in personnel training methods	25	15
Knowledge of financial controls (e.g., division of responsibilities)	26	n/a
Knowledge of US employee benefit laws (e g., Consolidated Omnibus Budget Reconciliation Act [COBRA], Family and Medical Leave Act [FMLA], Health Insurance Portability and Accountability Act [HIPAA])	27 (tie)	37
Knowledge of computer-based tools for financial analysis and management	27 (tie)	n/a
Knowledge of space assessment, design, and development strategies	29	32
Knowledge of filing systems, records management, and retention requirements	30	36
Knowledge of project management	31	39
Knowledge of facilities management procedures and techniques	32	n/a
Knowledge of lease/contract agreements	32 (tie)	35
Knowledge of payroll and employee benefit procedures, and tax and reporting requirements (e.g., Internal Revenue Service Code, Canadian Customs and Revenue Agency [formerly Revenue Canada] regulations)	32 (tie)	9
Knowledge of the features and capabilities of automated financial management systems	35	12
Knowledge of professional liability issues	36	18
Knowledge of trust accounting procedures and regulations	37	17
Knowledge of workforce demographics and trends	38	n/a
Knowledge of work product quality control procedures and techniques	39	41
Knowledge of the features and capabilities of document assembly and management systems	40	45
Knowledge of research techniques (e.g., locating and analyzing information)	41	43
Knowledge of banking/investment policies and procedures and types of accounts	42	13
Knowledge of the features and capabilities of practice support systems (e.g., LEXIS/NEXIS, QUICKLAW, research, document management, litigation support, case management)	43	46
Knowledge of the American Bar Association Code of Professional Responsibility (e.g., conflict of interest issues, advertising rules, client file management)	44	38
Knowledge of financing methods and investments	45	n/a
Knowledge of legal organization structures and the laws and regulations regarding accounting procedures for each structure, including tax reporting requirements	46 (tie)	30

Knowledge of laws and regulations regarding business insurance coverages	46 (tie)	34
Knowledge of Request for Proposal procedures	48	40
Knowledge of marketing techniques, including market analysis and marketing tools	49	44
Knowledge of survey methodology (e.g., sampling, survey design)	50	47
Knowledge of general tax regulations	51	28
Knowledge of client service strategies (e.g., cross selling, value pricing, serve/product packaging, business process re-engineering)	52	42
Knowledge of Canadian federal and provincial/territorial employment laws	53	n/a
Knowledge of Canadian Bar Association and/or provincial law society codes of professional conduct	54 (tie)	n/a
Knowledge of Canadian benefit laws (e.g., Canada/Quebec Pension Plan, employment insurance, workers compensation)	54 (tie)	n/a
Knowledge of the features and capabilities of telecommunications systems	n/a	12

[1] Most statements received some minor wording changes for the 2000 survey.

It is interesting to note that seven of the top 10 competencies are the same for administrator-practitioners and employers, indicating agreement between the two groups. The statistical correlation between the mean ratings of administrators and employers was .95, indicating highly consistent ratings across the two samples.

The differences: Whereas the administrator respondents ranked time management, computer skills and knowledge of leadership styles near the top, their employers highly ranked specific knowledge of accounting issues (time and billing, alternative billing), employee motivational techniques and knowledge of financial controls.

Likewise, few differences appear when comparing results for Canadian and U.S. respondents. Canadian respondents replaced three of the U.S. top 10: These professionals viewed knowledge of financial analysis methods, knowledge of special issues in accounting for law firms and knowledge of the Internet/Web-based technology as priorities.

* CLM is a service mark of the Association of Legal Administrators.

What Qualities, Skills and Personal Characteristics Lead to Being a Great vs. a Good Administrator?

Views From the "Top of the Mountain"

In an October 2000 survey, members of ALA's Large Firm Administrators Caucus[1] were asked to describe the qualities, skills and personal characteristics that distinguish the great or extraordinary administrator from the administrator who, while competent at his or her task, might be a rung or two below the top of the ladder.

Those responding to the survey are among the professionals who many would consider to be at the top of the profession. They operate in the context of the largest and most complicated law firms. They are often possessed of decades of management experience in law firms, other professional service firms, government, the corporate sector and/or the non-profit community. Many have advanced degrees and professional certifications. Their career progression, while varied in the details and representing many paths to the "top of the mountain," provides a perspective that can be instructive to their colleagues in any size law firm or at any stage of their careers.

This Appendix reprints a number of the responses by members of the Large Firm Administrators Caucus to the survey question "What Qualities, Skills and Personal Characteristics Lead to Being a Great vs. a Good Executive Director?" Each numbered list shares the thoughts of a unique respondent.

1. Excellent people and communication skills (not just good)
2. Strong sense of confidence/self-worth (thus enabling the Executive Director to provide honest views rather than what he or she thinks is politically correct at the moment)
3. Excellent team-building skills (Executive Directors don't have to be experts at anything but they must know how to develop an outstanding team of experts to handle the various phases of the administration of the firm and they must be able to develop a sense of teamwork between administrative staff and lawyers.)
4. Excellent analytical skills so as to see beyond the obvious
5. Great sense of humor and thick skin
6. Excellent presence (the "look" that enables partners to see the Executive Director as an equal)

---

1 The members of the Large Firm Administrators Caucus are the principal administrators, generally carrying the title of Executive Director or Chief Operating Officer, in firms of 100 or more lawyers. The survey in question was conducted in conjunction with the group's annual Fall Retreat.

1. Sense of proportion (what's merely important vs. what's critical and what's worth falling on your side over)
2. Cleverness (you don't have to be smarter than the lawyers, but you have to be clever, flexible and nimble enough to stay with or in front of them, and sometimes out of their way)
3. A sense of humor (or you won't last a year)
4. The ability to stay between the lawyers and the staff and not be viewed as an agent of either (and to keep key staff motivated after lawyers treat them badly)
5. Working harder than you've ever before worked

---

1. Great Executive Directors are master team-builders. They have a clear sense of the organization's vision and strategy (and if there isn't a clear vision/strategy, they are instrumental in creating one).
2. They are smart enough to share credit for the successes of the organization that they're responsible for; and they know that a good idea can come from anywhere.
3. They are secure enough to speak their mind (and wise enough to choose their battles).
4. They are consistently fair.
5. The really good ones invariably have a good sense of humor.

---

1. Vision
2. Courage (to "take a stand")
3. Deal with partners/associates on really tough issues
4. Mental toughness
5. Ability to lead (and have the lawyers follow)
6. Anticipate practice/industry trends
7. Work ethic that rivals the lawyers
8. Ability to remain impartial and untainted in the midst of lawyer leadership changes

---

1. Ability to keep the big picture in view and keep pushing toward it
2. Good communicator, persuader, self-starter, thick skin, optimistic
3. Jack-of-all-trades in regards to your functional direct reports (knowing enough to be dangerous about technology, marketing, HR, etc.)

4. Strong financial grasp
5. Open mind, flexible about means but not about ends (goals)

—————•·•—————

Must keep pushing yourself to stay current and keep your eye on what needs to be done to enhance the firm. If we look at our role next year like we did this year, given all the changes that are constantly taking place in the profession, we are less than great. Firms that fail to see the light of what is going on around them and who have Executive Directors or Chief Operating Officers who are content to say "the lawyers just don't get it" and blame them, are less than great. Our role is to figure out how to get their attention on the critical issues and push for action. If we cannot do that over time, we are less than great.

—————•·•—————

1. The ability to listen
2. The ability to juggle 400,000 balls in the air at one time
3. The ability to remain flexible in outlook and approach
4. The ability to tailor one's approach to one's audience
5. The ability to make people feel heard and feel that they matter and that their concerns matter (even when you want to tear your hair out or laugh yourself silly at yet anther outrageous request or action)
6. A really good sense of humor
7. Tons of patience
8. A sense of urgency that makes people feel that taking care of their needs is truly important to you
9. The ability to be a strong cheerleader
10. Excellent leadership skills
11. A reputation for fair dealing and honesty

—————•·•—————

Good Executive Directors would have all of the qualities listed in any ALA publication for administrators: leadership, organized, management skills, communication skills, analytical skills...

Great Executive Directors need, in addition to the others: ability to deal with every type of personality and professional level (client, partner, associate, staff); humility (at least a controlled ego); and [extreme perseverance and personal strength]. You should also have all qualities necessary to be a partner in your firm (with, of course, the exception of practicing law).

Act as if you are an owner/partner of the firm. Every day focus on how you can make it a better firm.

———•◦•———

1. The ability to get your point across with as few words as possible
2. Strong analytical abilities
3. Incredible people skills
4. Tremendous common sense

———•◦•———

1. Trustworthiness
2. Compassion for people and passion for the firm and the job
3. Positive outlook
4. Quiet determination and unlimited patience
5. Unquestioning support of and loyalty to staff and partners
6. Sense of humor
7. The ability to listen well
8. The ability to set high expectations for self and others
9. The ability to embrace change and learn from mistakes
10. The ability to lead through example
11. The ability to be a team player, not a boss
12. The ability to take the blame for all that is wrong and pass on the credit for all that is right

———•◦•———

1. Intellect
2. Empathy
3. Vision
4. Charisma
5. Strong public speaking skills
6. Self confidence
7. Most important is an environment where you can be great. After that, financial and personal skills.

—·◆·—

Great integrity, complete honesty and ability to maintain confidence, strong functional skills, good interpersonal skills, and a hide as thick as an elephant's are necessary. Credentials that can be thrown at a lawyer help.

—·◆·—

1. Drive
2. Discretion
3. Stamina
4. Persuasiveness
5. Presence of mind, spirit and appearance
6. Sense of humor
7. Intellect
8. Street smarts
9. Strength of will

—·◆·—

I think risk tolerance is important and the courage to lead the group to making decisions. It's a balance between push, pull, sitting back and jumping when you get the chance.

A corporate-type executive can submerge his own ego needs and convince the attorneys that his ideas are really their ideas.

—·◆·—

1. Interpersonal skills (Some partners resent having a non-lawyer in a position that sets policy.)
2. The ability to build a good support team and delegate to that team
3. A well-rounded background, to deal with all the responsibilities for which the Executive Director is responsible - Finance, HR, Marketing, IS and Facilities, to name the more obvious

—·◆·—

1. Excellent communication skills and judgment
2. Strong ego but one that doesn't require constant stroking

———•◆•———

1. Knowledge of the business
2. Ability to assess business "opportunities" and decline them independently (free from partner pressure)
3. Ability to attract, motivate and retain key staff
4. Lots of energy
5. A beaming personality and acceptable (if not great) performance on the golf course

———•◆•———

1. Business leadership ability
2. Business management experience
3. Good communication and people skills

———•◆•———

Having the right level of knowledge in each of the disciplines we oversee and building a strong professional management team and providing good support to the revenue producers and counsel to the firm's management are the minimum requirements for being a "good" Executive Director. Greatness within a firm comes with building a broad-based reputation for personal excellence and building a relationship of mutual trust and respect with the vast majority of the partners (shareholders) of the firm. When you reach a point where partners generally (not just the Managing Partner or Executive Committee) regard you as a critical part of the firm's success, you probably have achieved greatness within your firm. I don't think it is possible to be "great" outside the context of a specific firm (that is, to be regarded as "great" in the context of the legal community).

———•◆•———

In addition to possessing and applying a substantial technical business knowledge and skills, a great Executive Director should have honesty, integrity, patience, political agility, ability to listen, ability to communicate well, self-motivated, energetic, organized, focused, team builder, leader, optimist, sense of humor, detail oriented, compassionate, quick to grasp new concepts and manager of successful change. I probably missed something. I hope each day that I can show just a few of these traits.

———•◆•———

Willingness to assume risk. Expertise in change management, finance, technology, HR management. Political skills. Ability to multitask under pressure.

———•◆•———

1. The ability to inspire confidence
2. The ability to influence others by effective persuasion
3. The ability to demonstrate consistently good and fair judgment when making numerous decisions, not all of which will be successful or popular

———•◆•———

A great Executive Director is like that guy who's the Chief of Staff on "The West Wing," Leo McGarry: confident, little or no ego needs, takes risks on behalf of the partners, makes the partners feel successful when they are, mentors the partners when they need it, dispenses "tough love," is the soul of integrity, and is well aware of his personal flaws and demons. My role model.

———•◆•———

The same skills that make a great CEO:
1. Strong leader
2. Strategic thinker
3. Consensus builder
4. Ability to build a great team in underlying tiers of management along with added traits related to day-to-day operations such as making positive things happen at all levels of the organization

———•◆•———

In our industry, we as Executive Directors must continually keep in mind what is in the best interest of our partners, balanced with maintaining an effective and efficient support team. We must walk a jagged fence so that both groups, partners and support staff, perceive that we understand their respective value to the organization. Of course, both groups know that the other group couldn't persist without them.

———•◦•———

I believe that an effective Administrator has to love people and must be an inspiring mentor so that he or she can bring out the best in others. An Administrator is only as good as the people surrounding him or her, so attracting and retaining first-rate people in key positions is critical. And working with them so that they attract and retain people at the top of their fields allows them to work most effectively. While respecting the culture and history of the firm, an effective Administrator must embrace change, and must guide others through the change process.

———•◦•———

Most important in my mind: Never forget that every decision must be made in the best interest of the firm, not a partner or group of partners. Even unpopular decisions or positions will be respected if no hidden agenda is perceived or exists. Less important: good communication skills, visiting "remote" offices frequently.

———•◦•———

Management abilities — a law firm is a business! Flexibility, even-keel, personable, quiet strength.

———•◦•———

I would summarize with the statement that CEO-like qualities are what is needed. Big-picture thinking through implementation skills. Strong people skills to be able to work with both lawyers and staff at all levels. Good listening skills. A sense of humor. Good financial skills. A background in organizational behavior and psychology would be helpful.

———•◦•———

Being crazy helps! Seriously, though, I think you have to consider the firm as your own so that the decision making is in the best interests of the firm. Excellent communication skills are essential to the position.

———•◦•———

Leadership skills and vision. Ability to develop an organization that is flexible and able to adapt to the rapidly changing legal environment.

---

1. Leadership abilities, the most important attribute being trust
2. The opportunity to demonstrate that your judgment is as good, or better, than many of those who were "doing what I do" before I started doing it
3. Some gray hair/experience is necessary for most Executive Directors to be successful and with that a broad understanding of the industry. Most lawyers do not have the time to take into account all that is changing in their industry, let alone many of the industries they work with through their client.

ASSOCIATION OF LEGAL ADMINISTRATORS

Career Resources

The Association of Legal Administrators offers many tools to help your career progression as a legal manager. A great place to begin is the "Career Center/Job Bank" section of the ALA Web site: *www.alanet.org*. Here, you will find the ALA Management Connections[SM] job bank, a collection of career-related articles under the name "Career Talk" and links to major newspapers and employment resources.

A PRICE FOR A PEOPLE

A PRICE
FOR A PEOPLE

The Meaning of Christ's Death

TOM WELLS

THE BANNER OF TRUTH TRUST

THE BANNER OF TRUTH TRUST
3 Murrayfield Road, Edinburgh, EH12 6EL
PO Box 621, Carlisle, Pennsylvania 17013, USA

*

© Tom Wells 1992
First published 1992
ISBN 085151 623 8

*

Set in 10½/12 pt Linotron Plantin
Typeset at The Spartan Press Ltd,
Lymington, Hants
and printed and bound in Great Britain by
BPCC Hazells Ltd
Member of BPCC Ltd

*

All Scripture quotations, unless otherwise
marked, are taken from the HOLY BIBLE: NEW
INTERNATIONAL VERSION. Copyright © 1973, 1978, 1984
by International Bible Society. Used by
permission of Hodder and Stoughton and
Zondervan Bible Publishers.

Contents

An Opening Word

My plan in this book is quite simple.

First, I want to look at three words that tell us what the Lord Jesus did, in dying on the cross. They are the words, 'redemption', 'reconciliation' and 'propitiation'. Every Christian knows these words, but what do they mean? Can the ordinary man grasp their meaning? I believe he can.

Second, I want to look into the question that is often put this way, 'For whom did Christ die?'

At one time I had hoped to make this second point the theme of the entire book. There are not many books devoted to what is called 'the extent of the atonement'. There seemed to be room for one more.

But the reason for this lack of books is not hard to find. As soon as you ask, 'For whom did Christ die?' you see that the answer hangs on what the Lord Jesus *did* in dying. What kind of thing is the atonement, anyway? Next thing you know, you find yourself face to face with those three words I mentioned above. So the right thing to do, it seems to me, is to follow the plan I have laid out.

Whenever one sits down to write a book of this sort, he is faced with a problem at the outset, a certain impatience most people seem to have with theology. Often they do not even like the word 'theology'. It seems to grab the Bible they love out of their hands and take it off who knows where, while a man they do not know says to them, 'I'm awfully sorry, of course, but you really can't understand your Bible without my help!'

Well, we all know what to do with that fellow, don't we? If he wants to call himself a theologian, we have no objection. Let him call himself what he pleases. But if he insists on wedging himself between us and the word of God, we will say, 'No, thank you,' and send him on his way.

I have the feeling that this impulse is a good one in many ways. The Bible is meant to be read – devoured, even – by people who make no claim to the name 'theologian'.

It is worth a good deal to know that you can read God's word for yourself and understand its basic message. You can be right with God through faith in Christ, and you can grow as a Christian without much outside help. That is an important truth, and we should be impatient with those who deny it.

But a serious Christian wants to know as much as he can of the word of God, and one thing he soon finds out is that the great truths of the Scriptures are often bound up with some pretty big words. Those words are not there to make him stumble, but to help him. Often the 'big words' have a great deal of truth wound up in them. If a friend comes along to help unravel that truth, he will prove to be a friend indeed.

The Scriptures themselves teach us that we need others to help us in our understanding. Who are the New Testament men we meet with titles like 'apostle', 'prophet', 'evangelist' and 'teacher'? These men play a chief role in the work of the church in the New Testament, yet they are all teachers of one kind or another.

God has given us teachers today, our pastors for instance. We need them. On the one hand we must not fall under the spell of mere men, taking whatever they say as gospel without further thought and prayer. That could be fatal. On the other hand we must never despise those who seek to teach us the word of God. Even when it looks like they are going to give us theology! Compare what you read and hear with the Bible. Prayerfully use your judgment.

Then I hope you will join me on what is, without doubt, one of the most important studies a Christian can make.

I have designed the chapters of this book to be read in one of two ways. You may read it through, while ignoring the appendices. Or you may stop to read each appendix as it comes up. Those who follow the first plan will find, I hope, that they get a simple summary of the truth concerning Christ's atonement. Those who follow the second plan will be digging deeper into some of the controversial points that come up along the way. Either way, may the Lord bless you!

1: *What Kind of Act was the Death of Christ?*

If we ask the question, 'What kind of act was the death of Christ?' one answer is not hard to find. It was an act that aimed to bring men to God. Every Christian, I think, will agree with that answer. You and I may not understand Christ's death in the same way, but this much seems clear to us: Christ died so that men and women and children might come to God.

That raises another question, however. What kinds of things keep a person from coming to God? If there was nothing to keep me from God, Jesus would not have had to die for me. That is clear also, isn't it? There were barriers between me and God. In some way the Lord Jesus' death was meant to deal with those barriers.

Of course one barrier was my unwillingness to come to God. But I am not thinking of that problem alone. If that had been the *only* thing that stood between me and God, Christ's death would not have been necessary. All that I would have had to do was to change my mind, to turn to God. The problem would have been solved, and that would have been that!

I can see from my Bible that the problem between God and myself was far greater than a mere change of mind on my part. It is true that I could not have become a Christian without my mind being changed on a lot of things. You know that as well as I do, if you are a Christian. But Christ's death was meant to do much more than work a change in my mind. Most Christians agree that the death of Christ deals with more than my attitude toward God.

But what are these barriers that keep men from God?

Let's start with some forces that hold men in bondage. The Scriptures tell us that all men have been gripped by powers that they cannot break away from. What are these powers? Let me list them:

1. Men are slaves to sin.
2. Men are slaves to Satan.
3. Men are held for punishment in God's justice system.

These things are not all the same. God may need to address them in different ways. If the death of Christ aims to bring the sinner to God, we will not be surprised if His death touches on these forces that hold men in their grip.

There are other ways to describe the problems between us and God. The Bible calls us God's enemies. If we are to be made friends of God, the death of Christ will have to work that out as well.

Finally there is a barrier within God Himself. There is His wrath that must be taken out of the way if men are to come to God. He is angry with sinners over their sin. The wrath of God is real. If it was not dealt with – if He Himself did not deal with it in some way – no man, woman or child could ever come to Him. But how could God remove His own wrath? The answer lies in the cross, the death of Jesus Christ.

We can answer the question, 'What kind of act was the death of Christ?' in still another way. It was the act that gave meaning to all of His other acts. Since Christ's death is the solution to so many problems, it is plain that His death is the key fact in His earthly life. Did He come 'to seek and save' the lost? Yes, He did. That was His main purpose in coming to us. But His death was the chief means that He used. We may say, then, that He came to die.

Many men have missed this point. Some have seen Christ as a martyr for a good cause, a victim of a turn of events that went against Him. There is no ground for this view in the Scripture. We might even call this an atheistic view; it leaves God utterly out of the picture.

Other good men have looked on the death of Christ as a fitting climax to His unique life on earth, but they have not seen it as the key to all else. For them the incarnation is the thing that saves us. The big thing was that God and man joined together in the person of Christ, who was both God and man. He draws God and man together in Himself and, in that way, brings us to God. This is far from atheism; it is a distinctively Christian stance. But it too falls short.

Where does the Bible put the emphasis? It is true that Jesus Christ is both God and man. It is also true that we could not have been saved if that were not so. But the key point is this: Jesus Christ died and rose again for sinners. Without that, nothing else matters. That is where the New Testament puts the stress.

What kind of act was the death of Christ? It was the key act of His life. It was the act that we must look to, to see the barriers between ourselves and God taken away. And it is the act revealed to us in some of those tough-looking words that I spoke of at the beginning of this book.

It is time now to turn to those words.

2: Redemption, Its Old Testament History, Part One

The idea of the word 'redemption' is not hard to grasp. What do we mean by it? Something like 'deliverance'. We are said to redeem something when we set it free. We could also use the word 'release'. Or 'ransom' might fit.

I want to start with the word 'redemption' because the Bible is a book of redemption. In the Bible, nations, individuals and even things are said to be redeemed. You cannot get away from this idea, no matter where you turn in God's word.

Redemption in the Bible often – some would say 'always' – involves the payment of a price.[1] If a man holds slaves he will not let go of them without being paid in some way. He wants money to free them. A man who has a piece of land that he once bought from his neighbor will not want to give it back without getting something of value in return. Cases like these turned up in ancient societies every day. And they were common in Israel.

[1]There is usually no price mentioned in the Old Testament when God is the redeemer (*but see Isaiah 43:1–4*). Did it cost God to redeem Israel from Egypt and later from Babylon? The answer is not clear, but compare our English idiom, 'There's a price to be paid!' with a verse like Exodus 6:6 where God says, 'I will redeem you with an outstretched arm and with mighty acts of judgment.' In that sense it was 'costly' to God.

In addition, when God speaks of doing the opposite of 'redemption', when He threatens to hand His people over to their enemies, he often describes this as 'selling' them, an idea that suggests the receiving of a price. (*For example, see Deuteronomy 32:30; Judges 2:14, 3:8; Isaiah 52:3.*) A price, then, may always be connected, more or less consciously, with the idea of redemption.

We will start with slaves.

An Israelite could sell himself as a slave to an alien who lived in Israel. Why would he do that? To pay off his debts, perhaps. Would that be the end of him? No. God's law saw to it that he would not be simply left in bondage and forgotten. At any time a blood relative could redeem him. His foreign master would have to give him up.

The price of his freedom would be based on the number of years left until the Year of Jubilee.[2] Let's use U.S. dollars and say that a slave's work was worth $300 a year. If there were still five years until the Year of Jubilee, it would cost 5 times $300 to redeem him. That would mean that his relative would have to spend $1500 to set him free.

You can see here what is meant by redemption. The slave's relative paid a price to get him his freedom. When the price was paid, the slave was ransomed or released. He was redeemed. Often, then, redemption meant 'freedom by the payment of a price.' We will see more of that fuller meaning when we come to the New Testament.

A 'price' is part of other redemptions in the Old Testament, as well. You may remember that just before God brought Israel out of Egypt He destroyed all the firstborn Egyptian sons. At the same time He claimed all of Israel's firstborn sons for Himself. When the Lord took something for Himself that was alive, it was usually sacrificed to Him, put to death. But He did not want to kill these sons of Israel. Instead, He redeemed them. Here is how He did it:

> The Lord also said to Moses, 'I have taken the Levites from among the Israelites in place of the first male offspring of every Israelite woman. The Levites are

---

[2]The Year of Jubilee was a merciful provision of the Lord for freeing Israelites who were forced into slavery. Every fiftieth year all male Hebrew slaves were set free from alien masters in the land. You can read about the Year of Jubilee in Leviticus 25:8–55.

mine, for all the firstborn are mine. When I struck down all the firstborn of Egypt, I set apart for myself every firstborn in Israel, whether man or animal. They are to be mine. I am the Lord.' (*Numbers 3:11–13*)

Here is a simple exchange: a Levite for a firstborn son. The Levite, a member of Levi's tribe, became a helper to the priests. In that way, he was a special servant of God, God's own possession (*cf. Titus 2:14*).

You might say that the Levite was the 'money' by which a son of Israel was redeemed. Since the Levite spent his time serving the Lord at the Tent of Meeting, the firstborn son was free to do his own work and to live his own life.

Can you see that the Levite was like money? A later text makes this plain. God is speaking:

To redeem the 273 firstborn Israelites who exceed the number of the Levites, collect five shekels for each one . . . Give the money for the redemption of the additional Israelites to Aaron and his sons. (*Numbers 3:46–48*)

There was a problem: there were more firstborn sons than there were Levites. How could those sons be redeemed? The answer: with money. A price had to be paid. If it could not be paid with a Levite it had to be paid with shekels. Here again we have an exchange, but it is not one man for another. In this case money replaced the Levite.

Earlier we saw that redemption could mean 'freedom by the payment of a price.' We see that here as well, but we see more. The price might be another person, a substitute. That too will be important when we turn to redemption in the New Testament.

Let us look at one more law about redemption:

If a bull gores a man or a woman to death, the bull must be stoned to death, and its meat must not be eaten. But the owner of the bull will not be held responsible. If, however, the bull has had the habit of goring and the owner has been warned but has not kept it penned up and it kills a man or woman, the bull must be stoned and the owner also must be put to death. However, if payment is demanded of him, he may redeem his life by paying whatever is demanded. (*Exodus 21:28–30*)

This case borders on murder, so I think I want to add the law that God laid down for the redemption of those who kill others in cold blood:

Do not accept a ransom for the life of a murderer, who deserves to die. He must surely be put to death. (*Numbers 35:31*)

What do we learn about redemption from these two passages?

It is clear, isn't it, that there was to be no ransom paid to free a murderer? That is the first thing.

But something else is here. The man who let his bull run loose, after he had been warned, was also a kind of murderer. That is why he might suffer the death penalty. He was responsible for the death of another; it was his fault. Yet he might be set free from the penalty by paying a ransom or a fine to the relative(s) of the dead man or woman. So a murderer of sorts could be redeemed, after all.

There is no contradiction here because we can see that the two cases are not quite the same. One man – the man in Numbers 35 – killed in cold blood, what we call 'premeditated murder.' The other case was different. No planning went into it. Still it was worthy of death. The owner of the bull could not plead innocence. He had been warned and he rejected the warning.

The thing to see here is this: redemption may operate where there has been sin. In the case of the outright murderer you could think about redemption; it was conceivable, but unlawful. God would not let you do it.

But in the other case the owner of the bull was freed from one of the consequences of his sin. Sin and redemption meet together in this part of the law of God. We have here a hint that will be worked out in the New Testament. The answer to sin may be 'freedom by the payment of a price.'

3: *Redemption, Its Old Testament History, Part Two*

Redemption in the Old Testament, as we have seen, is deliverance. The payment of a price often went with it. Slaves were redeemed, as were firstborn male sons. Even a murderer of sorts went free when he paid a ransom. We see that redemption played a major role in the life of Israel.

Here is something else: redemption was often a family matter. Most of the time the 'redeemer' was a close kinsman of the man who had to be redeemed. That was no accident. A man in need of redemption did not simply look around until he found someone who might help him. Not at all! His family was responsible to help in ways that may seem strange to us.

Therein, as the saying goes, lies a tale, one of the great true stories of God's word. It is the story of the book of Ruth.

A man from Israel, along with his wife and two sons, left there during a famine and moved to the nearby country of Moab. It was not a happy move – before long he died. His wife, Naomi, stayed with the boys and found Moabite wives for them, but the sons did not live long and eventually Naomi was the only one left of the family that had come to Moab ten years earlier.

When she heard that the famine in Israel was over she decided to return home. One daughter-in-law, Ruth, went with her. Ruth's devotion to Naomi fairly sings in the words she uses to tell her mother-in-law that she will not forsake her:

Don't urge me to leave you or to turn back from you.
Where you go I will go, and where you stay I will stay.
Your people will be my people and your God my God.
Where you die I will die, and there I will be buried. May
the Lord deal with me, be it ever so severely, if anything
but death separates you and me. (*Ruth 1:16–17*)

Ruth's speech, now about three thousand years old, can
never dim as a witness to the character of selfless love. We
feel its power yet, as Naomi must have felt it then.

The two women returned to the town of Bethlehem to
live. In that culture it was bitter for Naomi to come back as
an old woman stripped of all the male members of her
household. She had no one but Ruth to support her and
there was little that Ruth could do to make a living for them.
Since it was barley harvest Ruth went to the fields to pick up
grain that had been dropped or missed by the reapers. The
work was hard and normally it produced very little. If Ruth
had not been the devoted woman that she was – loving both
Naomi and the Lord – she might have wondered what
possessed her to come to Israel!

Here the story takes the turn that is important to the subject of redemption. In God's goodness, Ruth soon found
herself gleaning in the fields of a man named Boaz. She had
not planned it that way; she had no idea who Boaz was.
Boaz, however, was a relative of Naomi's husband and he
was well off, just the opposite of poor Naomi and Ruth.

In Boaz we meet a kinsman-redeemer. I know the name
sounds awkward but I have a good reason for using it. Its
two parts nicely match the meaning of a Hebrew word that
shows up in this story quite a few times. Let me explain.

God's law provided for the poor to be able to get back
land that they were forced to sell because of their poverty.
The one who bought the land back for them (the
'redeemer') would be a brother or other close relative
('kinsman'). Hence the name 'kinsman-redeemer'.

After the harvest, Naomi and Ruth may have had no means of feeding themselves. But they owned a field.[1] They could sell it to raise the money to live and that is what they decided to do. They were free to sell it to any man in Israel, but it made sense to offer it to a kinsman-redeemer. Why? Because there was a good chance that he would be called on to buy it back later anyway. By selling to him directly they would keep the land in their family and he might be more willing than a stranger to give a good price.

In the story of Ruth, the sale of the land was tied to something else, marriage to Ruth. We can understand why a widow might want to marry, but there was more to this condition than that. Ruth's first husband, Mahlon, would have been the heir to the field that Naomi and Ruth were selling. In His Law, God made clear that He wanted the land to pass down from father to son. But that posed a problem. What if a man left no sons? After all, Mahlon had died childless. In that case the Lord commanded the man's brother to step in. He must take the dead man's widow as his wife and produce an heir that would be considered the dead man's son.

But what if the dead man had no living brothers? In that case the letter of the law was silent. There was no further command.

In Boaz we meet a man who sought to carry out the spirit of God's law. He was ready to marry Ruth and raise up an heir for Mahlon. There was just one thing that held him back. Another man was a closer relative. Boaz had to see what that man would do. When the closer relative

---

[1] Strictly speaking no one owned a field in Israel. The land belonged to the Lord who had given the use of it to the tribes of Israel. He did not, however, allow them to dispose of it permanently. In the Year of Jubilee it returned to the tribe and clan that held it at first. Naomi and Ruth, as widows, had the use of the land (by custom, apparently) until they died. Since 'use' was all that anyone really had in Israel, their disposing of it was treated as a sale by a male owner would have been treated.

refused to take Ruth as his wife, Boaz redeemed the field and married Ruth. The story ends with Naomi receiving congratulations from the women of Bethlehem on the birth of a grandson, Obed. 'Praise be to the Lord,' they cry, 'who this day has not left you without a kinsman-redeemer. May he become famous throughout Israel!' And Obed did become famous, as the grandfather of King David.

The marriage of Ruth and the birth of an heir interest us, but our main concern is with the redemption of the field and with the deliverance of Ruth and Naomi from poverty. That required a kinsman-redeemer, and Boaz played that part.

Here are three things that were true of every kinsman-redeemer:

1. He had to be a family member.
2. He had to have the ability to redeem. Since redemption was from debt or slavery or death, that meant that he could not be in debt or a slave (or be dead!) himself, and he had to have a surplus from which he could help another.
3. He had to have a willing heart.

Boaz fitted this picture well. He was a close relative. He was wealthy. And he was willing to use his goods to deliver both Ruth and Naomi from their distress.

When we turn to the New Testament and the story of the Lord Jesus we will see God form a new family. Since that family will be made up of needy people, unable to help themselves, it will call for a kinsman-redeemer. And when He comes He will do what a kinsman-redeemer does. He will deliver His people by the payment of a price, the price of His own death. As God is the father-redeemer (*Isaiah 63:16*) of the Old Testament, so the Lord Jesus will be the brother-redeemer (*Hebrews 2:14–17*) of the New Testament.

Redemption is a family matter!

4: *Redemption in the New Testament, Part One*

It is time for us to look closely at the death of the Lord Jesus in connection with this word 'redemption.' To do so, let me remind you that more than 1000 years separated the days of Moses and of Ruth from the days of Christ.

Things change in 1000 years, as you know. Israel was no longer an independent nation when Christ came. It was a Roman land, and it had a culture tinged with Greek influences. Even the Greek language was in common use. That is why we find the New Testament written in Greek, not Hebrew. In fact, the Hebrew language, that is alive in Israel today as I write, was a dead language when Christ came. The Jews spoke what we now call 'Aramaic'.

Why is all this important? Because words reflect the world of the people that use them. We will have to look at the word 'redemption' with these changes in mind. Jews such as Paul were steeped in the Old Testament – so far, so good. But they were men of the Roman and Greek world as well, and that affected the way they spoke and wrote.

We have seen that both men and property could be redeemed in the Old Testament. Men might be redeemed from either slavery or death. A good example was the Exodus from Egypt. The Lord delivered Israel from slavery and He gave them a land and a life of their own in which they would not die at the whim of a foreign slave owner. His act was a pattern for the kinsman-redeemers of Israel. But when they did as He did and delivered their relatives, they did it by paying money. They 'purchased' or 'bought' their kinsmen from slavery and death. In that way, 'redemption' often came to mean 'freedom by the paying of a price.' (Perhaps the idea of 'price' was always in the word. Many scholars think so.)

What do we find in the world of the New Testament? Something very similar.

We know that war has always played a chief role in world history. In the Roman Empire there were slaves everywhere who had been taken in battle. No one cared about most of them. If they had relatives back in the old country, those kinsmen would not know if they were dead or alive. Slaves were slaves, for the most part, and that was that.

But there were exceptions. Suppose you were out fighting and you captured a nobleman. What would you do with him? Back in his land somebody might be willing to pay a good deal to free him. If you thought his freedom was worth more to you than his services were, you might let him be ransomed. You would lose a slave but gain some money. Slaves need to eat, but you can put money in the bank!

This example is a good one because it shows the most common idea that would jump into a man's head in the first century if he heard the Greek word for redemption. To us it may carry other ideas – in the Roman Empire it called to mind freedom from slavery by paying a ransom.

There is another important example from that day. So far the Greek idea of redemption, as I have described it, has had little to do with religion. But the Greek world also knew of freedom for slaves as a religious act. Let's look at that next.

Under Greek law a slave could gain his freedom if he could gather together the price his master would ask for him. That would be hard, of course – more than most slaves could ever do. But he might manage it. Then, with money in hand, he and his owner would go to the temple of a god and the slave would give the money to the temple officials. They in turn would use it – less their fee, no doubt! – to 'buy' him from his master for the temple god.

But this was merely a legal fiction. He would not stay to serve the god. He would be set free. And he would get a document to prove it with a phrase such as 'for freedom' or 'on the condition that he be set free' as part of its text. In that way, no one could claim that he had been bought to do chores around the temple. There might also be a record of his being set free carved into the wall of the temple. In that case, he could return and look at it at any time, and he could use it as proof of his freedom if someone questioned it.

'See,' he could say, 'the god, Apollo, bought me here at his temple so that I could be free.' Students of ancient Greece have found quite a few inscriptions of this kind on temple walls of that day.

We see, then, that the thought-world of the people in both the Old Testament and the New Testament is full of the idea of redemption as 'freedom by paying a price.' If you had lived in first-century Palestine this is what you would have understood when you heard the word 'redemption'.

When we turn to the teaching of the New Testament about the death of Christ, we find 'redemption' words again and again. There are several families of such words. And we find something more. We find the death of Christ treated as the price that He paid to make us His own. By bringing these two things together – redemption and price – we see that 'freedom by paying a price' is a good summary of the gift Christ died to give us.

We must look at this more closely.

In Mark 10:45 we read, 'The Son of Man did not come to be served, but to serve, and to give his life a ransom for many.' Here the Lord Jesus stresses the price of our freedom – it is His death, the giving up of His life. The Old

Testament phrase, 'A life for a life,' comes to mind when we read this. The Lord served God and God's people in many ways, but the greatest way was this, He gave His life as the price of His people's salvation.

We can see the price connected with our redemption in a passage such as Romans 3:24–25. Men 'are justified . . . through the redemption that came by Christ Jesus . . . in his blood.' As so often in the New Testament, the word 'blood' is put here for Christ's sacrificial death. That death was the price of our redemption.

Ephesians 1:7 is another example. 'In [Christ] we have redemption through his blood.' We have been freed and it was done by Christ's blood, His death as a sacrifice for sin.

In 1 Peter 1:18–19 we find the price of our redemption spelled out:

> For you know it was not with perishable things such as silver or gold that you were redeemed . . . but with the precious blood of Christ, a lamb without blemish or defect.

Silver and gold are the things men often use to pay the price for what they want. But there is a greater price, a precious price, the bloody death of Jesus Christ. By it we were redeemed, we were set free.

All of the examples I have given above are from one family of redemption words in Greek. The following verses use words from another family, a family that in everyday Greek was used for buying merchandise. Look for forms of the word 'buy' in these examples.

1 Corinthians 6:19–20 reminds us, 'You are not your own; you were bought at a price.' In 7:22–23 Paul expands on this idea. 'He who was a free man when he was called is Christ's slave. You were bought at a price; do not become slaves of men.' The Lord Jesus has gone into the slave market of this world and bought the believer to be His

own slave. The price is not mentioned in these four verses, but we know what it was. It was His death.

In other places these words for buying or purchasing are used when the price He paid is made clear.

In Galatians 3:13 Paul writes about redemption using one of these words. 'Christ redeemed [bought] us from the curse of the law by becoming a curse for us, for it is written: "Cursed is everyone who is hung on a tree."' Here the price is His being hung on a tree. Every Christian recognizes that as a reference to the Lord's death on the cross.

Finally, look at the song sung to the Lamb, our Lord Jesus, in Revelation 5:9.

> You are worthy to take the scroll
>   and to open its seals,
> because you were slain,
>   and with your blood you purchased men for God
>   from every tribe and language and
>   people and nation.

No one should be able to look at the New Testament without seeing what it teaches: Christ has redeemed His people by dying for them. They enjoy 'freedom by the paying of a price.'

5: *Redemption in the New Testament, Part Two*

So far we have talked about what redemption is. It is freedom by the paying of a price. Christian redemption is the freedom Christ has bought for His people by His death.

But now it is time to answer the question: freedom from what? If Christ has freed us, what has He freed us from?

In chapter 1 I gave you a list of forces that hold men in bondage. Here they are again.

1. Men are slaves to sin.
2. Men are slaves to Satan.
3. Men are held for punishment in God's justice system.

Redemption brings men out of the grip of the powers that hold them tight.

Let's look first at slavery to sin. What is it? And what does the death of Christ have to do with it?

In the New Testament sin is personified as a king or slave owner that determines the course of the unsaved man's life. Kings in those days were often much more powerful than the kings and queens we know today. They did what they pleased; in that way they were much like men who held slaves.

Sin has that kind of sway in a natural man. He thinks of himself as doing what he pleases, but he does what sin drives him to do. He does not notice the difference between his own desires and the desires of sin within him because he is so given over to sin that what pleases sin pleases him. In theory we might distinguish between his desires and sin's desires, but in practice they are the same.

Does this sound too extreme? Is the man without Christ really in this kind of bondage? Paul told the Romans, 'When you were slaves to sin, you were free from the control of righteousness' (6:20). A man or woman can be loyal to only one king at a time. Righteousness was not king; sin was. Yet the Romans were not unusual. Sin reigns in every natural man.

Jesus said the same thing. 'No-one can serve two masters. Either he will hate the one and love the other, or he will be devoted to the one and despise the other' (Matthew 6:24). Where the commands of two 'masters' conflict, a man will show where his true loyalty lies by the way he acts. If his or her master is not God, it will be something else. In the case of those without Christ that master is sin.

Men may not admit this bondage. I can go further – they may not even recognize it. When the Lord told a group of His listeners that 'the truth will set you free,' they took offence. 'We . . . have never been slaves of anyone,' they said. 'How can you say that we shall be set free?' (John 8:32–33). But they were wrong. They were slaves to sin, and Jesus decided that they needed to be told that to their faces, so that is what He did, without mincing words.

Redemption breaks this bondage to sin. Paul said that Jesus Christ 'gave himself for us to redeem us from all wickedness and to purify for himself a people that are his very own, eager to do what is good' (Titus 2:14). He bought us. The price was 'himself'. The freedom in view here is freedom from the practice of sin. Christ bought His people so that they would no longer be bound by sin, but would serve Him as His very own possession, a people eager to do His will.

Does this mean Christ's people never sin? No, it does not mean that. But the reign of sin has been broken.

Think of sin as a king that has been thrown from his throne and now carries on a guerrilla warfare. He no longer controls the territory, but he is still able to make raids upon it. So sin no longer controls the heart of the believer in Christ, but it is still there, causing him to stumble.

Righteousness, however, now rules his heart and sets him back on his feet. His new master will not allow him to lie in his sins, wallowing in filth. He sins, but righteousness characterizes his life. God and Christ have control of his heart. He is redeemed from slavery to sin. Christ's death is the price of his freedom.

We look next at slavery to Satan.

Is the natural man a slave to the will of the devil? Yes, he is. The Lord Jesus made this clear in John 8:42–47. Here is what He said of all who do not have God as their Father:

> If God were your Father, you would love me, for I came from God . . . Why is my language not clear to you? Because you are unable to hear what I say. You belong to your father, the devil, and you want to carry out your father's desire. He was a murderer from the beginning, not holding to the truth, for there is no truth in him. When he lies, he speaks his native language, for he is a liar and the father of lies. Yet because I tell you the truth, you do not believe me! . . . He who belongs to God hears what God says. The reason you do not hear is that you do not belong to God.

All men belong to God or the devil. They are the sons and slaves of one or the other.

How, then, do men and women come to belong to God? By the purchase of Christ. Listen to this hymn of praise to the Lord Jesus:

[31]

> You are worthy to take the scroll
> > and to open its seals,
> because you were slain,
> > and with your blood you purchased men for God
> > from every tribe and language and people and nation.
> > > > *(Revelation 5:9)*

Jesus Christ 'purchased men for God.' No wonder Paul wrote, 'You are not your own; you were bought at a price' (*1 Corinthians 6:19-20*. Compare *7:22-23*.). We are the slaves of God and of Christ and are no longer in bondage to Satan.

There is one further kind of bondage that we are under. We are like men in jail, awaiting punishment for breaking God's laws. God's justice system holds us fast.

A main theme of all of Scripture is that God is our judge, coming at the end of history to see what we have done with His commands. The number of His commands varies with who we are. The Jews had a staggering number of commands from God. He designed them to keep His Old Testament people apart from the rest of the nations of the earth, so that they might keep alive the knowledge of God until Christ should come. The Mosaic Covenant formed a barrier between Israel and the peoples around her.

Gentiles had fewer laws from God, but they too were responsible to God to do what He told them to do. Both Jews and Gentiles failed to keep God's laws. Of both Jews and Gentiles Paul wrote, 'There is no one righteous, not even one,' and again, 'there is no one who does good' (*Romans 3:10-12*). All men are guilty before God, and God's justice demands that there will be punishment for sin.

Christ's death redeems His people by freeing them from the penalty for their sins. 'In [Christ] we have redemption through his blood, the forgiveness of sins' (*Ephesians 1:7*). Here again we see that redemption is freedom by the payment of a price. This freedom is release from the necessity to pay for our own sins. The price is the 'blood', the sacrificial death of our Savior, the Lord Jesus Christ.

We see, then, that though we had three powerful foes that held us in their grip – sin, Satan and the justice system of God – Christ has released us from these foes. We have our freedom, but not by our own power or merit. No, our freedom is a redemption, a purchase of Christ, for which He laid down nothing less than His own life.

6: *Reconciliation*

We come now to the second of those 'big words' that describe the work of Christ, the word 'reconciliation'. The death of Christ is more than redemption, it does more than release us from our foes. The Lord's sacrificial death removes the enmity between God and man, and replaces it with friendship. Christians are not mere slaves to God. We are the friends of God and God is our friend. In fact, we are now members of God's family. An earthly judge may pronounce a prisoner innocent and then never again see that prisoner. But God does much more. He makes those who were slaves to sin into His own sons and daughters!

Let me start with a question: Does the Bible teach that there is enmity, hostility and estrangement between God and man?

From man's side the answer is not hard to find. All through Scripture after the fall we find men in rebellion against God. Paul tells the Colossians, 'Once you were alienated from God and were enemies in your minds' (*1:21*). These Colossians were not unusual. All natural men love sin, and to love sin is to hate God, to be hostile to God, because God and sin are at war with one another. The man who sides with sin takes his stand against God. We are called to love righteousness and to hate iniquity, and the call goes out so forcefully because God finds us in just the opposite state.

'The sinful mind' – the only mind the natural man has – 'is hostile to God,' says Paul (*Romans 8:7*). Man has declared a state of war between himself and his creator. The words of the parable in Luke 19:14 capture the spirit of the natural man toward God and Christ. 'His subjects hated him and sent a delegation after him to say, "We don't want this man to be our king".' God is the ruler of all His creatures, but man is an enemy to the reign of God.

Of course, men and women often hide this enmity from themselves. Mary and John would not be caught dead saying an unkind word against their maker. But that is not the whole story. Those who are not positively *for* God and Christ, are *against* them according to the word of Jesus (*Matthew 12:30* with *John 15:23*). Mary and John assert their hostility by not submitting themselves to the kingship of Christ.

We can say – we must say – that there is hostility between man and God from man's side.

But is there hostility and enmity from God's side as well? The answer to this question must be a cautious Yes. I say 'cautious' because we do not want to cast a shadow over God's love. His love is real and it extends to men and women who feel enmity toward Him. But there is more to be said.

The Bible also speaks of God's wrath, His anger against sinners. Some have tried to soften this truth by speaking of wrath as an impersonal process. They want to make wrath a kind of natural law, like reaping what you sow. But God's wrath against sinners is not impersonal. The psalmist wrote:

> God is a righteous judge,
>   a God who expresses his wrath every day.
> If he does not relent,
>   he will sharpen his sword;
>   he will bend and string his bow.
> He has prepared his deadly weapons;
>   he makes ready his flaming arrows.(*Ps. 7:11–13*)

Without a doubt some of this language is figurative, but it is clearly God who lies behind the acts of judgment awaiting the wicked. It is God 'who expresses his wrath'. It would have to be that way in a world in which God is king.

The New Testament tells us the same thing. In Romans 11:28 Paul describes the way God sees Israel in these days:

> As far as the gospel is concerned, they are enemies . . .
> but as far as election is concerned, they are loved . . .

God has two attitudes toward them. In one sense He loves them; in another sense He is their enemy. Not all hostility is on man's side. I will have more to say about this in the next chapter when we look at the word 'propitiation'.

Since there is enmity between God and man, some way had to be found to make peace between them. God found that way in the death of His Son, the Lord Jesus. Paul says that it was at the cross that God reconciled men to Himself.

> For if, when we were God's enemies, we were reconciled to him through the death of his Son, how much more, having been reconciled, shall we be saved through his life! (*Romans 5:10*)
> God was reconciling the world to himself in Christ, not counting men's sins against them. (*2 Corinthians 5:19*)

The act of Christ at the cross, His death, reconciled the world to God. Or we can put it another way and make it the act of God. God reconciled us to Himself by putting His Son to death. In the words of Isaiah, 'It was the Lord's will to crush him and cause him to suffer' (*53:10*). We may think of reconciliation as being both the work of the Father and the work of the Son.

The word 'reconciliation' stresses the personal bond that God has with His people. We use the word 'redemption' when we think of the things that held us in bondage, things like sin, Satan, and God's legal system. These are the things that we are delivered *from*. But reconciliation reminds us that men once enjoyed fellowship with God and that God made us for such fellowship and friendship. Christ came to make sure that that fellowship and friendship would be restored between man and God. The Lord's attitude toward His people is not mere toleration.

The Bible pictures this friendship by the act of eating. Someone has called the Gospel of Luke 'the Gospel of Jesus at Table.' Often there we find Him dining with others. When His critics mocked Him for eating with tax collectors and sinful people, they did not know that He was mirroring the heart of the Father. (How often the Lord's acts are parables to us!) This was His way of saying, 'Do you know what kind of bond My Father will make between Himself and ordinary men and women? It will be this kind of bond, the kind that leads two friends to sit down and to eat together.'

That's why we read of 'the wedding supper of the Lamb' in the Book of Revelation. Some think of this 'supper' as a single event; others see it as a picture of eternity. But in either case the truth is the same. God and Christ will enjoy the fellowship and friendship of their people in such a way that a shared meal depicts it best.

One thing more. Reconciliation leads us to become members of God's family and that, in turn, makes us His heirs. Friendships come in many degrees, but ideally the closest friendships are within families. We have a proverb that says, 'Blood is thicker than water!' It means that families have a way of sticking together when a crisis comes. In this life, of course, that is not always true. But it shall be true in eternity where we will be part of a family not based on human 'blood', but on the blood of Jesus Christ.

When we received the reconciliation that Christ worked out on the cross, we received the groundwork for all the other good things that God has in store for His people. At one time it was said that 'No eye has seen, no ear has heard . . . what God has prepared for those who love him' (*1 Corinthians 2:9*). That is no longer fully true since Paul goes on to say, 'but God has revealed it to us by his Spirit' (*2:10*). Today we look in God's word and see our inheritance.

But surely we do not see it all. No doubt there is much more than we have yet imagined. But this much is true: none of it would be ours if we had not been reconciled by God through the death of His Son. All of the glory and honor and praise for our friendship with God must go to God and to the Lamb who made peace between God and man by dying for sinners on the cross of Calvary. We did not reconcile ourselves to God. God reconciled us to Himself.

7: *Propitiation*

This chapter brings us to the one word for the death of Christ that is least familiar to us, the word 'propitiation'. If that word does not mean much to you, don't feel alone. I preached for more than 15 years before I could keep its meaning in mind. I would look it up, use it briefly, and promptly forget what it meant!

A propitiation is an act that turns away the wrath of another. 'Appeasement' is a synonym. We use the word when someone is angry with us and we do something to remove his or her anger. We appease him or propitiate him so that his anger toward us is removed.[1]

Just now, as I write this, I have a problem that may demand propitiation if it is not handled quickly. The church in which I am a pastor had to run a sewer line under the driveway of a nearby school. That was some months ago. At the moment their driveway is still torn up and needs to have blacktop replaced. So far there has been no estrangement over this. As far as I can tell, they are not angry with us. But how long will they wait for us to fix their driveway? The matter may already irritate them. How long will it be before it does more than that? Will it shortly require an appeasement, a propitiation? Will we

[1]Some scholars have questioned whether 'propitiation' is a good translation of the Greek words *hilasmos* and *hilasterion*. Since this is not an issue for most people who are likely to read this book, I have not stopped to argue the case for this translation. For those who are interested I suggest chapters IV and V of Leon Morris, *The Apostolic Preaching of the Cross*, Eerdmans, Grand Rapids, 1955, pp. 125–185.

have to pay damages over and above the cost of fixing their driveway to appease their anger? Let's hope not!

The idea that God is angry with men is not a popular idea. But the Bible plainly teaches it. For some people it raises the spectre of a man flying off the handle, losing control of himself in a fit of fury. 'Certainly,' they tell us, 'God is not like that!' And we must listen to them. They are right. God is not like that at all.

But the story about the blacktop shows that people can become very angry without 'flying off the handle.' When they are continually provoked, they may reach a point where their entire persons cry out for justice to be done. Far from being an irrational 'fit', their feeling may be the most reasonable feeling imaginable.

When we speak of God's anger or wrath we are speaking of His feeling toward the presence of injustice and wickedness. He hates these things. Where men and women are married to evil, they feel the weight of God's wrath against them. The Bible could not be plainer than it is on this subject. The Old Testament mentions God's wrath over 500 times. When we turn to the New Testament, we find such things as this: 'The wrath of God is being revealed from heaven', says Paul, 'against all the godlessness and wickedness of men who suppress the truth . . . ' (*Romans 1:18*). Godlessness and wrath go hand in hand. Where there is one, there is the other. Paul goes on to show that God's wrath leads Him to give men over to vile acts that finally destroy them (*1:24-28*).

More than that, God has stored up wrath for the days of judgment at the end of history. The book of Revelation makes this clear. It speaks of 'the great day of their wrath'– the wrath of the Lamb and of Almighty God – and it asks, ' . . . who can stand?' (*Rev. 6:17. Cf. 11:18, 14:10, 16:19 and 19:15*). If men will defy Him, He will justly cast them into 'the lake of fire' (*20:15*). God's wrath is not satisfied by the day-by-day judgments that fall on men. 'Whoever rejects the Son will not see life, for God's wrath *remains* on him' (*John 3:36*).

Is there an answer to God's wrath? Yes, there is. Can He be propitiated, appeased? Yes, He can. Jesus Christ is the 'propitiation' that turns away God's wrath. The Lord Jesus is the one 'whom God displayed as a propitiation in His blood through faith' (*Romans 3:25, NASB*). That is Paul's witness. John says the same thing: 'Jesus Christ the righteous . . . is the propitiation for our sins; and not for ours only, but also for *those of* the whole world' (*1 John 2:1–2, NASB*).[2]

Christ is the answer!

This is plain enough, but it has led some to raise an objection against the whole idea. 'What you've done,' they say, 'is to set the Father against the Son. The Father is angry with men and would destroy them, but in the nick of time the Son steps in to keep Him from doing it. God the Father and His Son are working at cross purposes!'

That, of course, is not what Scripture teaches at all. The answer to the problem lies in this fact: it is God who supplies the sacrifice. 'The Father has sent his Son to be the Savior of the world' (*1 John 4:14*). The propitiation comes from God Himself. 'In this is love, not that we loved God, but that He loved us and sent His Son *to be* the propitiation for our sins' (*1 John 4:10, NASB*). There is no question of any division between Father and Son. But the fact remains: a sacrifice was needed to turn

---

[2] I have quoted these verses from the New American Standard Bible because the New International Version uses the phrases 'sacrifice of atonement' and 'atoning sacrifice' instead of the single word 'propitiation' in these passages, perhaps because the word 'propitiation' is not widely understood. The NIV margin in both places offers a fuller explanation. At Romans 3:25 it describes the Lord Jesus as 'the one who would turn aside [God's] wrath.' At 1 John 2:2 it says, 'He is the one who turns aside God's wrath.' In both cases the idea of propitiation is clearly set forth.

aside God's wrath. God sent that sacrifice, His Son Jesus Christ. In that act, as always, Father and Son were one.

There is mystery here, of course. Taking all that Scripture says we must believe that God both loved men and was angry with them at the same time. He discharged His anger, then, by sending Christ to die, and that was an act of His love. But Christ was not forced to die for sinners. It was an act of love on His part as well. 'No one takes [my life] from me,' He said, 'but I lay it down of my own accord' (*John 10:18*). Nor did He die unwillingly. Above all else He longed to do His Father's will (*See Hebrews 10:7*).

Let's see, finally, how propitiation and reconciliation fit together. Simply put, they are cause and effect. Christ's death turns aside God's wrath. The result? We are reconciled to God! The effect of Christ's work is to make peace between God and His adopted people (reconciliation). The work itself is the work of propitiation.

The Old Testament sacrifices pictured the work of Christ. The priest would take a lamb, for example, and slay it to take away the sins of the people. Why do that? Because God was angry with the people for not keeping His law. The system of sacrifices pictured how God one day would turn aside His own wrath, reconciling His people and Himself. The Israelites

> . . . were not faithful to his covenant.
> Yet he was merciful;
>   he atoned for their iniquities and did not destroy them.
> Time after time he restrained his anger
>   and did not stir up his full wrath. (*Psalm 78:37–38*)

The hard hearts of Israel stood in bold contrast to God's mercy. But that mercy was not without cost to God. 'He atoned for their iniquities.' The Psalmist does not tell us how God did that. But whatever He did was done with His eye on a greater propitiation than any that Israel received in Old Testament times. The writer of Hebrews reminds us that 'it is impossible for the blood of bulls and goats to take away sins' (*Heb. 10:4*). Men and women and children needed much more than that. And they received much more in Jesus Christ, the propitiation for our sins.

We need to pause and worship God for the truth contained in these three words: redemption, reconciliation, propitiation. They are not empty words. They are words that gather up in themselves much of the rich truth found in the death of Jesus Christ.

At great cost to Himself God saved us from sin, from Satan and from our bondage to His own justice system. Looking at the death of Christ from that angle, we call it redemption. Surely we must worship God for that great truth!

With infinite love and kindness God made peace between Himself and poor sinners and adopted us into His family. Seen in that way, we call Christ's death our reconciliation. Here too is a call to adore God!

When we had nothing to give to remove God's anger toward us, God Himself through Christ took it all away. The death of Christ was every believer's propitiation. Wrath – then no wrath! No wonder Paul said, 'God forbid that I should glory, save in the cross of our Lord Jesus Christ!' (*Galatians 6:14, AV*). Can we say less?

The death of Christ for sinners is a fact. No one who has read this far is likely to dispute that. Worship, however, is the work of a changed heart. I dare not leave this chapter, then, without asking you this question: Is all that I have written so far merely academic to you?

If your answer is 'yes', let me urge you to turn from your sin and trust this great Savior of whom I have written.

Trust Him to save you both from the power and the consequences of your sin. Lay down your arms and He will receive you. Then worshipping God for the death of Christ will seem the most natural thing in the world!

8: *For Whom did Christ Die?*

In the earlier chapters I tried to show you what kind of death Christ died. To do that I used three words from Scripture, 'redemption,' 'reconciliation' and 'propitiation'. Why did I choose those words? Because they seem to lie at the heart of what God has told us about the death of Christ. Those three words teach us what a great thing Christ did in dying for sinners. They call us to worship and adore God.

But there is a problem with what I have said. You may not have thought of it, but you will see it when I explain what I mean.

If what I have said is true, then it would seem that we were redeemed and reconciled to God before we were born! If the death of Christ was the time of our redemption then it looks as if we were saved centuries before we existed! Is that possible? And if it is, why do we speak of being reconciled to God and redeemed and saved at some later time in our earthly life? After all, many of us point to a date when our Christian lives began, when we were born again. Is that wrong? When were we redeemed? When were we reconciled to God? When did God turn His wrath away from us? Was it when Christ died or when we came to trust Him?

To get to the answer to these questions, look with me at Romans 8:29–30:

For those God foreknew he also predestined to be

conformed to the image of his Son, that he might be
the firstborn among many brothers. And those he
predestined, he also called; those he called, he also
justified; those he justified, he also glorified.

These verses have been called 'Paul's Golden Chain of
Salvation,' because they list many of the things that
make up our salvation in Christ.

Now here's the important point. Paul lists all these
things in the past tense, as if they were all finished
in the life of every believer. But we know that is not
the case. All believers have been called and justified,
for example, but how many have been glorified? Not a
single one! To be glorified is to be made perfect in
every way, including having a new body. But even believers who have passed into the Lord's presence do
not yet have their resurrected bodies. So not a single
Christian has been glorified. Yet Paul speaks as if all
Christians have been glorified – 'those he justified, he
also glorified'!

Now which is it? Were we glorified in the past, or
will we be glorified in the future?

You can see, can't you, that this is the same kind of
problem we have with redemption? In the case of redemption we ask, did it happen centuries ago, or does it
happen each time a man is born again? In the case of
glorification we ask, has it happened to everyone who
has been justified, or will it happen in the future?

The answer is the same in both cases. Let me show
you!

Imagine an ancient king about to erect an impressive
building on his capitol grounds. First he sees that it is
planned carefully. Planning takes time. But soon the
day comes when he calls his chief artisan to himself,
hands him the plans, and tells him to go ahead with the
work.

What will the artisan say? Listen!

''Tis done, Your Majesty!'

What?

''Tis done, Your Majesty!'

'But wait!' we cry, 'It is not done!' Although all the courtiers may hear the words, ''Tis done!', he hasn't started yet!

When we recover from our surprise and ask ourselves what the artisan's words mean, all becomes clear. The king's will is law. For him to order the building to be erected makes it certain. That building is as good as finished!

In the same way each step in Paul's Golden Chain makes the following steps certain. Has a man been foreknown by God? If so, he is predestined to be like the Lord Jesus. Has he been predestined? Then he shall be called! Has he been called? Then he will surely be justified! Has he been justified? Then his glorification is as good as done! Why? Because the king's will is law. And this king is an absolute monarch indeed! Nothing and no one can keep Him from carrying out His will.

God stood at the cross of His Son and said, 'Here is the redemption of my people. Here I am reconciled to them. Here my wrath is taken away!' Of course most of His people had not yet been born, but from God's perspective the death of His Son made their redemption and reconciliation certain. That death made it certain that His people would never feel His wrath. Looking back to that moment each of His people can say, 'God did not appoint us to suffer wrath but to receive salvation through our Lord Jesus Christ' (*I Thessalonians 5:9*).

Once the *price* of redemption was paid, the redemption was as good as done. You could write over the salvation of all of God's people, 'It is finished!' In a sense we were saved at the cross – there our salvation was made certain.

[47]

In another sense we were saved when we believed – then our salvation became real to us. In the fullest sense we will be saved when we are glorified – all of salvation will be ours forever![1]

When I began this book, I told you that I meant to look at something else as well, the question, 'For whom did Christ die?' Let me say just a word about the meaning of that question before I begin to try to answer it.

When I ask, 'For whom did Christ die?' I mean, 'For whom was His death a redemption and a reconciliation and a propitiation?' There may be side benefits from the death of our Savior that come to all men. I do not mean to deny that. But I am raising the question, 'Was what is called "the atonement" offered for all men, or was it offered *only* for those who would eventually be saved?'

I feel safe in saying that many Christians have never asked this question in all their lives. That may be true of you – I don't know. But the question really is important. Why? Because so many Christians have said, 'Yes, Christ did atone for the sins of each and every man who ever lived!' They have said it emphatically, but often they have not thought through what that answer means.

It implies one of two things. Either

1. All men will be saved by Christ's death, or
2. Christ redeemed and reconciled and turned the wrath of God away from men who will nevertheless be lost forever. In other words, His redemption will not redeem them, His reconciliation will not reconcile them to God, and His propitiation will not turn God's wrath away from them.

Those are the only two choices. There are no others.

Will all men finally be saved? I would like to think so, wouldn't you? But Scripture will not let us believe that. No, some men will be saved and others will be lost forever.

[1]For a fuller discussion of the time of redemption, see Appendix 2, p. 127.

But the other option cannot be true either. It is nonsense to say that Christ redeemed men who will remain unredeemed through all eternity. Nor can we say that Christ reconciled men to God who will remain unreconciled to God forever. In the same way, we cannot say that Christ turned the wrath of God away from men who will feel the wrath of God forever. To say such things is to play with words.

But what if someone says, 'Christ did all these things for all men, but they must accept what He did for them'? Is that the answer to the problem we've been looking at? Will that help? Let's see.

It is true, of course, that men and women must receive what Christ did for them. That is a plain teaching of the Bible. Indeed, we must emphasize that fact! But that fact will not help us here.

Here we must see *what it was He did*.

The Bible does not teach that Christ's death created the opportunity for men to be redeemed. It describes His death as 'redemption'. Remember what redemption is. It is 'freedom by the payment of a price.' Freedom! So Christ's death actually secured freedom for those for whom He died. Freedom from what? Freedom from sin, slavery to Satan and their consequences.

Again the Bible does not teach that Christ's death created the opportunity for men to be reconciled to God. It describes His death as 'reconciliation'. And what is reconciliation? It is friendship – friendship in this case between God and man. So Christ's death actually secured friendship with God for those for whom He died.

Finally the Bible does not teach that Christ's death created the opportunity for men to have God's wrath turned away from them. It describes His death as 'propitiation'. And what is propitiation? It is the turning away of God's wrath. So Christ's death actually secured –

made certain – that no wrath would fall on those for whom He died.

Christ's death did not 'create opportunities,' it established certainties. Everyone for whom the Lord Jesus died is sure to be reconciled to God. The answer to the question, 'For whom did Christ die?' is clear then. He died for His people, all those – and only those – whom He would bring into God's family forever.

No wonder God's children adore Him!

9: *Didn't Christ Die for the World?*

*Question: If Christ died only for those who will be saved,
where did we get the idea that He died for each
and every man and woman who ever lived?*

Answer: We're sure we got it from the Bible!

Let me make one thing clear at the beginning of this
chapter: I'm not poking fun at, or impugning the motives
of anyone. I believe those who give the answer above. It is
the very answer I would have given not too many years
ago.

But I think I was wrong then. Let me tell you why.

At first glance it looks as if this whole question could be
settled by looking at one or two New Testament texts. For
example, look at 1 John 2:2: Jesus Christ 'is the atoning
sacrifice [propitiation] for our sins, and not for ours only
but also for the sins of the whole world.' That verse
certainly seems to say that Christ made a general sacrifice,
as effective for one man as for another.

And what about John 3:16? Listen! 'For God so loved
the world that he gave his one and only Son, that whoever
believes in him shall not perish but have eternal life.' Isn't
it clear that God gave His Son to die because He loved the
world?

I could cite other texts that say the same thing. If a man
believes the Word of God, why wouldn't he be content
with these plain statements? Isn't it wrong and pre-
sumptuous to look beyond the plain statements of Scripture for our doctrine?

Those of us who believe that Christ died only for His own people agree with all evangelicals in this: all Christian doctrine must be drawn from God's Word and from nowhere else.

Why then do we disagree? We have already seen the answer in the last chapter: if Christ's death is a redemption and a reconciliation with God and the means of turning God's wrath away from sinners – and it is all of these things! – then if He did it for everyone, everyone would be saved.

When Christ is said to do these things for 'all' or for 'the whole world' we must either reduce the redemption words, making them say much less than they say, or reduce the universal terms such as 'all' and 'the whole world.' You can't say, 'We won't do either!' unless you are prepared to say that Christ redeemed and reconciled and turned the wrath of God away from all men at the cross. But that is just to say that all men will be saved! As I said before, we would like to believe that, but the Bible will not let us do so.

Now someone may say, 'All you're doing is tampering with Scripture. Can't you see that?' That is a serious charge, but I'm glad to be able to show you from the Bible itself that it isn't so.

Here is a point you may have never noticed before: *the Scripture normally reduces the value of universal terms, terms like 'all', 'every', and 'world'.*

I must emphasize the word '*normally*'! Does that surprise you? You need not take my word for it. Page after page in your Bible will confirm it. I hope to give you enough examples so that you will see that what I'm saying is true. But after I'm done, you will be able to turn up literally hundreds more if you want to take the time to do it.

Let me start with Acts 2:17 (*AV*) where God says, 'I will

pour out my Spirit on all flesh.' 'All flesh' looks quite comprehensive. But is it?

Does this include the flesh of animals and birds? No – not their flesh. It's talking about human beings, isn't it? The NIV says 'on all people.' So 'all flesh' in this case excludes the whole animal kingdom!

But we're not done. Does 'all flesh' (or, 'all people,' if you prefer) mean 'each and every man who ever lived'? Clearly not. Many of them were already dead when the Lord gave this promise. Does it mean 'all who were alive when the promise was given'? No, it doesn't mean that either.

What does it mean, then? It means 'some men and women,' or, as we say in English, 'all kinds of people,' meaning some from many different groups. God promised that He would pour out His Spirit on men and women from many different countries and cultures. And that is what He has done! It may seem strange, but when He said, 'all flesh,' He meant 'some men and women'!

Now what you must see is this: Acts 2:17 is not at all a special case. Let me repeat what I wrote before: Scripture *normally* reduces the value of universal terms.

Here's another example. Paul says in 1 Timothy 6:10 (*AV*), 'The love of money is the root of all evil.' Is it true that every evil in the world is rooted in the love of money? Satan's first sin is at the root of all the sins that have come after it. Was the love of money the root of Satan's fall? Surely not!

Among humans the sin of Adam and Eve lies at the root of all other sins. Did they fall through the love of money? No. Money, if it had existed at that time, would have been meaningless to them, since there would have been no one to buy from, and nothing to buy! Everything was theirs, except a single tree in the middle of the garden.

How does the NIV translate 1 Timothy 6:10? 'The love of money is a root of all kinds of evil.' 'All kinds'? What does that mean? It means: 'Quite a few evils can be traced to the love of money.' Do you see how Scripture used the universal phrase 'all evil' to mean 'some evils'?

I don't want to weary you with examples, but I must give enough to leave my point beyond doubt.

Here's another: 'But when he, the Spirit of truth, comes, he will guide you into all truth' (*John 16:13*). Ask yourself this question: 'How much truth would the Spirit give to those disciples of Christ?' The answer is 'all truth!' Does that mean as much truth as God knows? Hardly! It means the tiniest part of what God knows. The idea is clear: 'When the Spirit comes, He will teach you everything you need to know.' And that promise was fulfilled to the apostles.

In John 3, John's disciples say of Jesus, 'He is baptizing, and everyone is going to him' (*3:26*). Later John the Baptist says of Jesus, 'No one accepts his testimony' (*3:32*). Yet he immediately adds, 'The man who has accepted it has certified that God is truthful' (*3:33*). Taken literally these three verses appear to contradict each other. Did 'everyone' respond to our Lord's ministry (*v.26*), or did 'no one' receive what He said (*v.32*)? And if 'no one' accepted His testimony, who was it that 'accepted it [and] certified that God is truthful' (*v.33*)?

But I doubt that you ever felt a contradiction in reading this. Why not? *Because we normally reduce universal words without even noticing what we are doing.*

'Everyone' in 3:26 means large numbers, from the perspective of John's disciples. They were impressed with the following that Jesus had. 'No one' in 3:32 means very few compared to the number that should have responded to Christ, as John the Baptist saw it. In 3:33, then, there were men who had accepted Christ's testimony, but there should have been many more.

We will find that the word 'world' is used in much the same way. Let me give you some instances.

In John 6:33, speaking of Himself Jesus says, 'For the bread of God is he who comes down from heaven and gives life to the world.' At first glance this text might seem to teach that all men will be saved. 'What can "world" mean,' someone might ask, 'but "each and every man who ever lived"?' If Christ gave life to each and every man, none would be lost.

It is clear here, however, that the phrase 'the world' stands for those who would believe on Him. Christ gives life to His people, and to no others. Yet here they are called 'the world', perhaps because they come from 'every tribe and language and people and nation' (*Revelation 5:9*).

We find much the same thing in Romans 11:11–12,15. Let me put these verses before you.

> Again I ask, Did [Israel] stumble so as to fall beyond recovery? Not at all! Rather, because of their transgression, salvation has come to the Gentiles to make Israel envious. But if their transgression means riches for the world, and their loss means riches for the Gentiles, how much greater riches will their fullness bring! . . .
> For if their rejection is the reconciliation of the world, what will their acceptance be but life from the dead?

Twice in these verses the word 'world' appears.

First, Paul speaks of 'riches for the world.' What does he mean? In verse 11 Israel's transgression brings salvation to Gentiles. This salvation of Gentiles is what he calls 'riches for the world' and 'riches for the Gentiles' in verse 12. It's clear, then, that Paul uses the word 'world' as a synonym for 'saved Gentiles.'

If there were any doubt about Paul's meaning here, verse 15 makes it doubly plain. The rejection of the Jews, Paul tells us, 'is the reconciliation of the world.' Here the word 'world' excludes unbelieving Jews, and takes in either (1) all who are saved, God's elect, or (2) simply saved Gentiles. In each case 'the world' means those who are saved. 'The world' is a group smaller than each and every man who ever lived.

In starting this chapter I mentioned two verses that have seemed to some to settle the whole question. Let's glance at them again.

I John 2:2 says: Jesus Christ 'is the atoning sacrifice [propitiation] for our sins, and not for ours only but also for the sins of the whole world.' The question is: If Christ died for the sins of the whole world, how could He have died for some sinners and not for all?

In the light of what we have seen this verse can be understood in this way: 'Christ is the propitiation for the sins of all of us who have believed, and for all who will ever believe.' In the words of another writer, if we reject Him 'no sacrifice for sins is left, but only a fearful expectation of judgment' (*Hebrews 10:26–27*). The ancient religions claimed to have sacrifices of their own that would appease the gods. But their claims were worthless.

It seems obvious to Christians today that there could be but one sacrifice for sins to which all men must come if they are to find forgiveness. But that would not have been obvious to first-century Gentiles.

First-century Jews had another problem that John may be alluding to in this verse. Many Jews fully expected that a provision for sin would be for them and them alone. They held that God was not interested in Gentiles unless they first became Jews.

Against this attitude Christ taught that God loved the world, not just the Jews. The point was not that God loved each and every man – though in a sense that is true – but that He loved Greeks and Romans and Syrians and all other nations as really as He loved the Jewish nation. The question was about national groups, not about individuals. John, writing as a Jew, may be saying, 'Christ is the propitiation for our sins (the sins of Jews), and not only for ours but also for the sins of Gentiles.' It seems to me, however, that the first explanation I gave above is the simplest and most natural.

In controversial passages, how we understand universal words depends on how we have been taught to understand them. We may not even know that there has been controversy about them! If you have been taught from childhood that 'the world' in John 3:16 means 'each and every person who shall ever live,' that's the way you will understand it. Many have been taught that all their lives. Any other understanding seems strange and even heretical to them.

But John 3:16 may mean 'God loved mankind as a mass,' without reflecting on individuals, much as a man may say, 'I love Englishmen,' or 'I love Americans.' Perhaps it means, 'God loved Gentiles as well as Jews.' If you had been taught to understand it that way since childhood, that is the way you would understand it.

What does this prove? It proves this: we must get our doctrine of the atonement from the words that describe it – words like 'redemption', 'reconciliation' and 'propitiation' – and not from the universal terms that are used of those who benefit from it.

The descriptive words are not ambiguous as universal terms normally are. When we look at the words that describe what Christ did in dying, we find out that Christ's death is a far greater thing than we thought it was. It does

[57]

not merely make redemption and reconciliation and propitiation possible. It makes them certain to all for whom Christ died.[1]

[1]Those who would like to pursue the use of universal terms further may look at Appendix 1, p. 117.

10: *A Family Matter*

Ask almost anybody who has only a nodding acquaintance with the Bible, and he will tell you that God loves all men equally. That 'fact' is a given: the Lord's love is indiscriminating. He loves each man just as He loves every other man.

The older 'liberals' were sure that this was so. They built their doctrine of the Fatherhood of God on this foundation. After all, every father strives to love his children equally, if he is a good father. Would our Father in heaven do less?

But like so many other fads, this one has largely passed away. Anyone who opens his Bible can see, if he will, that God has a special love for His own people. We see that love in a verse like Hebrews 12:6: 'The Lord disciplines those he loves, and punishes everyone he accepts as a son.' This verse distinguishes between sons whom the Lord loves, and others. The Lord Jesus told His disciples, 'The Father himself loves you because you have loved me' (*John 16:27*). Presumably the Father would have loved those disciples less (or in another way? or not at all?) if they had not loved the Lord Jesus. God, then, does not love all men equally.

That fact – and it really is a fact – raises another question. When did God start to love His people with a special love? Was it when they came to Christ, or did He have a special love for them forever?

To be fair to all the Scripture teaches I think we will have to say that God has had a love for all men from eternity past, including a special love to His own people, a love that increased when they actually came to Christ, as we have seen in John 16:27.

Does God have a general love, common to all men? That seems to be the teaching of Jesus in Matthew 5:43–45:

> You have heard that it was said, 'Love your neighbor and hate your enemy.' But I tell you: Love your enemies and pray for those who persecute you, that you may be sons of your Father in heaven. He causes his sun to rise on the evil and the good, and sends rain on the righteous and the unrighteous.

Jesus' argument amounts to this: if you want to be like your Father in heaven, you will have to love your enemies. You must not restrict your love to 'the righteous,' whoever they may be. You must love the unrighteous as well, for that is what your Father does.

How can we know that God loves unrighteous men? We can know by seeing that He sends them both rain and sunshine. To send rain and sunshine is to show love. The natural inference from this is that God loves all men in some sense and that the presence of sunshine and rain are evidences of that fact.

This love of God shown in rain and sunshine brings us to a definition of love. You will need to know what I am talking about, when I speak of love. Here is what I mean: *love is an affection that leads one person to seek the benefit or promote the interest of another person.*[1] The love of God, then, is His affection for men that leads Him to seek their benefit. If we can identify a case in which God is seeking the benefit of any man or any class of men, we will have found an instance of His love.

[1] Every scholar will see that this definition simplifies complicated data and ignores nuances between various words that can be translated 'love'. At the same time it seems to me to gather together the basic ideas found in God's love for us and the love we are commanded to have for others. Love is not simply activity, but love is always active where activity is called for.

I want you to think back with me now to the time when God created man and woman. In simplest terms, what God did was this: He made the wonderful relationship that we call 'the family.' But here is the important thing to grasp: this family was God's family as well as a human family. 'God created man in his own image' (*Genesis 1:27*), and Adam was not a mere creature but Adam was 'the son of God' (*Luke 3:38*).

Disaster, however, lurked around the corner.

We do not know how long Adam lived before he sinned. What we do know is this: Adam's sin did not completely destroy his own family – he kept his wife, Eve, and produced children 'in his own image' (*Genesis 5:3–4*) – but his sin did destroy his relationship to God. At this point Adam became dead toward God (*cf. Genesis 2:17*). God was left without a human family, without children to joyfully serve and love their Father.

If God was to have another human family He would have to make another Adam. And that is what He did.

But in one way I am getting ahead of my story. What I have told you is true, but it is not the whole truth. The whole truth is this: God had planned for this second 'Adam' and His new family all along. Even before God made Adam and Eve, He had taken man's fall into consideration. He had no need to find a remedy when His first family turned their backs on Him. Not at all! In fact, His plan looked beyond the fall to the creation of a family that would be brighter and better and more glorious than Adam's family was even before they sinned.

Planning to have a family is often an act of special love; it was so in God's case as well. His plan started with a second 'Adam', who 'was chosen before the creation of the world' (*1 Peter 1:20*). And who was He? He was the Son who once said to His Father, 'You loved me before the creation of the world' (*John 17:24*). He was the Lord Jesus

Christ, of whom God said, 'This is my Son, whom I love; with him I am well pleased' (*Matthew 3:17*). Adam headed up the old family; God's beloved Son would head up the new.

And from the beginning God had thoughts of love toward His new family, the family of the saved. Paul had this fact in mind when he wrote to one part of that family,

> We ought always to thank God for you, brothers loved by the Lord, because from the beginning God chose you to be saved through the sanctifying work of the Spirit and through belief in the truth. (*2 Thessalonians 2:13*)

In what better way could God seek the benefit of anyone, than to choose him to be part of that family? No wonder Paul calls the Thessalonians 'brothers loved by the Lord'!

Here, however, comes in an important difference. Adam built his family by natural birth. God had a different plan for the Lord Jesus. *Jesus would gather God's new family out of Adam's old family by dying*.

Only the all-wise God could have formed a family around the 'foolishness' of a cross!

To help us understand how the Lord Jesus could gather God's family by dying, let us look at an Old Testament model, the kinsman-redeemer. Do you remember his qualifications? There were three: (1) He had to be a family member, (2) he had to have the ability to redeem, and (3) he had to have a willing heart. He would not redeem anyone, unless he met these three conditions.

These three things were true of our Lord Jesus when He came to save men and women.

What interests us, right now, is Christ as a family member. Of course, He became a member of the human family, the human race. We must always insist on that. We must never think of our Lord as God dressed up like a man. He was God and He became man as well.

But He was a member of that *new* family too. The writer to the Hebrews made this plain at length:

Both the one who makes men holy [that is, Jesus] and those who are made holy are of the same family. So Jesus is not ashamed to call them brothers. He says,
   'I will declare your name to my brothers;
      in the presence of the congregation
      I will sing your praises' . . .
And again he says,
   'Here am I, and the children God has given me.'
(*2:11–13*)

Nothing could be plainer than this: Jesus Christ and the men He will bring to God's presence are brothers in a new way. Those whom He will save are the children of God, whom God has given to Christ.

The writer to the Hebrews has more to say about this family and its children:

Since the children have flesh and blood, he too shared in their humanity . . . For surely it is not angels he helps, but Abraham's descendants. For this reason he had to be made like his brothers in every way, in order that he might become a merciful and faithful high priest in service to God, and that he might make atonement for the sins of the people. (*2:14, 16–17*)

Jesus Christ became a man. Why? Hebrews does *not* suggest that it was in order to be like all other men. No, it was a family matter – not primarily the human family, but the family of the redeemed. Look at their names in the passage above: children, Abraham's descendants, brothers and the people [of God].

In the last chapter of his book, the writer repeats this point by saying, 'So Jesus also suffered outside the city gate to make the people holy through his own blood' (*13:12*).

The Lord Jesus became a man so that He might die for His family, the people of God. His death was the price of their liberty. He was willing to pay that price because He is the kinsman-redeemer of His people.

11: *Christ Died for the Church*

To most of us in the West the word 'family' suggests a small number of people.

But a family may be very large.

Think of Abraham's family. How large was it? Eventually it took in millions of people. That is true whether you think of his family as the people of Israel, or as the Arabs, or as the church of Jesus Christ.

And then there is a much larger family than Abraham's, the family of Adam. It takes in us all.

A nation or a people is often an extended family. The Bible speaks of the children of God sometimes as a family, as a people or as a nation. The words are interchangeable. In no case did God intend these words to suggest a small group. His new family is made up of 'a great multitude that no one could count' (*Revelation 7:9*).

From this point on, I will use all three names for the group Christ came to save. And I will add one more name, 'the church.' But keep in mind that it will always be this same family that I am talking about – the family God loved before the foundation of the world.

The Scripture teaches us that Jesus Christ died for His church. Consider these verses:

Husbands, love your wives, just as Christ loved the church and gave himself up for her. (*Ephesians 5:25*)
Be shepherds of the church of God, which he bought with his own blood. (*Acts 20:28*)

No one denies that, of course. It is written so plainly that all men can read it for themselves.

But you will meet men who argue this way: 'We grant that the Lord Jesus died for His church, we do not deny that. And here's why: since He died for each and every man who ever lived, that takes in the church and all other groups as well. So the fact that He died for His church didn't keep Him from dying for all other men too.'

And you can see what they mean. If I say, 'I bought a new home for each of my children,' that doesn't mean that I didn't buy a new home for their friends as well. It simply leaves the question open. If I had been rich enough, I might have bought a new home for dozens of men and women.

But here is the point: if I had bought a new home for all those other people, *then they would have new homes*. They wouldn't be left with nothing!

The culprit in this discussion is the phrase 'died for.' Replace it with one of the biblical words that describe Christ's death, that tell us what He did in dying, and the problem goes away. There is nothing wrong with the phrase 'died for,' but we must remember to give it the full value that the Bible gives it. Christ's death is a redemption, a reconciliation and a turning away of God's wrath. When we give it that value, we see that it makes men right with God. Christ died for those He benefited, and for no others.

We can see this if we look at the verses I've just cited. What did Christ do for His church? According to Ephesians 5:25 He 'gave himself up for her.' All agree that that means He died for her. And that in turn means that He redeemed her and reconciled her to God and turned God's wrath away from her, *in the act of dying*.

Do you see how the question, 'For whom did Christ die?' comes down to the same thing over and over again? It comes down to the question, what was Christ doing when He died? Was He redeeming, etc., or was He only making these things possible?

Were we 'bought at a price' (*1 Corinthians 6:20; 7:23*) or was a price simply paid? We were bought! Remember that redemption is not the payment of the price. It is freedom, liberty, emancipation. We would not have these things without the price of Jesus' death. We must never forget that awful payment, but we must always remember that it is the freedom that constitutes redemption.

Acts 20:28 makes this plainer, if possible. It speaks of 'the church of God, which he bought with his own blood.' Were we bought, or was a price simply paid? The price is important, immensely so – 'his own blood.' But the point is not simply the payment of the price. The central fact is this: God acquired the church by the payment. The church became His by the price that was paid. Why? Because that price was also a redemption. It freed us from the things to which we were in bondage.[1]

The Book of Revelation gives us a glimpse of the church celebrating the redemption that Christ performed in His death. Here are John's words:

> I saw a Lamb, looking as if it had been slain, standing in the center of the throne, encircled by four living creatures and the elders. (*5:6*)

The Lamb advances and takes a sealed scroll from the hand of God. This brings a song to the lips of those who are watching:

> 'You are worthy to take the scroll
>   and to open its seals,
> because you were slain,

---

[1] For the sense in which all this was done for us *at the time Christ died*, review pp. 51–54. Those who would like to pursue this subject more deeply should see Appendix 2, pp. 127–133.

> and with your blood you purchased men for God
> from every tribe and language and
>   people and nation.
> You have made them to be a kingdom and
>   priests to serve our God,
> and they will reign on the earth.' (5:9–10)

A great doxology, called 'a new song' (5:9), is based on the death of Christ.

Let's look at two of its parts.

The new song describes two effects of the death of Christ. Its first effect was to separate some men, God's elect, from the great mass of men. This mass was found in the tribes and languages and peoples and nations of the earth. But Christ's death has reached into this mass of men and bought some men and women out of it.[2]

The second effect is that Christ has formed them into a new family called here 'a kingdom and priests to serve our God.' In the Old Testament there was a family of priests, the family of Aaron. Now the church has been made such a family.

In saying this, John, the writer, had his eye on a definite passage from Exodus. In that passage God commanded Israel to be a nation of priests. Here are His words:

> You yourselves have seen what I did to Egypt, and how I carried you on eagles' wings and brought you to myself. Now if you obey me fully and keep my covenant, then out of all nations you will be my treasured possession. Although the whole earth is mine, you will be for me a kingdom of priests and a holy nation. (19:4–6)

In the Old Testament this passage spoke of the people of Israel as the prospective nation of priests.

---

[2]For a discussion of the Greek word translated 'purchased' or 'bought' here, see Appendix 3, p. 134.

But it had a condition attached, '*if* you obey me fully and keep my covenant,' and Israel did not do that.

Did that surprise the Lord? No. All along He had intended that the church play that role after national Israel failed. And so the day came when Jesus said to the unbelieving Jewish leaders: 'I tell you that the kingdom of God will be taken away from you and given to a people who will produce its fruit' (*Matthew 21:43*).

The priestly family or nation or people is the church that Christ bought from out of the larger mass of men. It is the nation of men and women that God loved with His special love before the foundation of the world.

12: *Christ's Death for 'Many'*

You have no doubt noticed that in several places in the Bible the Lord's death is said to be for 'many'. I want to examine some of those texts now.

We look first at Hebrews 9:28. There we read, 'Christ was sacrificed once to take away the sins of many people.' If it is true that Christ died for some men and not for all, using the word 'many' would be a reasonable way to set forth that fact. So we are not surprised to find this statement.

Again we read in Mark 10:45, 'For the Son of Man did not come to be served, but to serve, and to give his life a ransom for many.' Here Jesus is speaking and He is showing the scope of His sacrifice – it is 'for many.' In saying that, Jesus would seem to be implying a contrast, 'for many' and not 'for all.'

If we knew no more than this about the death of Christ, however, we could not be sure what Jesus meant. It is possible to use the word 'many' in at least one other way besides contrasting it with 'all'. We also use the word 'many' to contrast it with 'one'.

We might understand Jesus to mean, 'I am but one man, yet I will die for many.' In that case, the 'many' could be all the men in the world. He is one solitary figure, but He will die for all who ever lived and they are 'many'.

Let's suppose for a moment that the contrast in each of these passages is of this type, 'one' versus 'many'. Even then the 'many' do not have to be all men. And it seems clear that they are not.

The 'many' in Hebrews 9:28 could hardly be all men since in v. 26 Jesus' sacrifice is said to 'do away with sin.' The writer says Christ 'has appeared once for all at the end of the ages to do away with sin by the sacrifice of himself.'[1]

Can this be the sin of all men? No, it cannot – for the sin of many men is not done away with, but will meet them at the judgment. The 'many' whose sin is cancelled and who receive forgiveness can only be God's elect, and no others.

It is true that some men, in order to escape the force of this fact, have argued that all men's sins have been done away with by Christ. Some of them have gone on to say that all men will be saved by what Christ has done. But others have said simply that what men do with Christ is the thing that controls men's destinies, that sin is out of the picture and does not condemn any man. Faith in Christ is the only testing point. Donald M. Lake, for example, writes: 'What is it that condemns a man? Is it his sins, large or small, numerous or few, that condemns a man and sends him into a Christless eternity? The answer of the New Testament is an absolute "No!" . . . What condemns a man is not sins. Why? Because Christ's redemptive and atoning work is complete and satisfying.'[2]

This solution certainly would solve the problem if it were true. But it is not. The 17th-century theologian John Owen made the telling point: either Christ died for

[1] The word translated 'do away with' refers to a legal annulment in Hebrews 7:18. Adolf Deissmann and others have shown this to be its common (only?) use in contemporary papyri. G. Adolf Deissmann, *Bible Studies*, Edinburgh, T. & T. Clark, 2nd Edition, 1903, pp. 228f. See also James H. Moulton & George Milligan, *The Vocabulary Of The Greek Testament*, London, Hodder & Stoughton, 1914, under the word *athetesis*.

[2] In Clark H. Pinnock, ed., *Grace Unlimited*, Minneapolis, Bethany Fellowship, 1975, p. 47. Notice that unlike others who deny that Christ died only for His elect, Lake tries to give the atonement its full effective power. I show above why I think this line of argument fails.

unbelief or He did not. If He did, and He has taken away all sins, then why would any men be lost? Wouldn't their unbelief have been atoned for?

But if He did not die for unbelief, how could anyone be saved, since we were all unbelievers by nature and practice.[3]

No, this solution will not do. You can see how weak it is by watching Lake abandon it almost as soon as he adopts it. On the page following the quotation given above he writes:

> Sin may have made the cross necessary, but the cross has now made sin irrelevant as far as man's relationship to God is concerned. *This is, perhaps, a little too strong*, but the fact is, that man's problem now is *not so much sin or sins*, but his reaction to what God has done in Christ. (*Italics mine.*)

An argument that has to be largely given up almost immediately can't be thought to be of much weight, even by its author.

But why give it up at all? Because Scripture flatly states that men die *for their sins*. After giving us an impressive list of sins, Paul in Ephesians 5:6 writes:

> Let no one deceive you with empty words, for because of such things God's wrath comes on those who are disobedient.

Again he writes to the Colossians:

> Put to death, therefore, whatever belongs to your earthly nature: sexual immorality, impurity, lust, evil desires and greed, which is idolatry. Because of these, the wrath of God is coming. (*3:5–6*)

[3]Robert P. Lightner, *The Death Christ Died*, Schaumburg, Illinois, Regular Baptist Press, 1967, pp. 100ff, tries to answer Owen. I discuss the point he makes about the necessity of faith in Appendix 2, pp. 127–133.

Paul leaves no doubt about one fact: men suffer the wrath of God *because of their sins*.

Mark 10:45 has another problem for those who believe that Christ died for every man and woman who ever lived. It is one of the clearest texts on the substitution of Christ for His people. I want to give more space to the subject of what is called 'substitutionary atonement' later, but if in fact the Lord Jesus substituted for others when He died, it is clear that they will not then bear their own guilt. That is basic to the whole idea of substitution. A substitute is a man who takes the place of another.[4]

The point I want to make now about Mark 10:45 is this. It seems likely that the 'many' there looks back to the 'many' of Isaiah 53:11–12. That passage reads:

> After the suffering of his soul, he will see the light of life and be satisfied; by his knowledge my righteous servant will justify many, and he will bear their iniquities.
> Therefore I will give him a portion among the great, and he will divide the spoils with the strong, because he poured out his life unto death, and was numbered with the transgressors. For he bore the sin of many, and made intercession for the transgressors.

Christ would 'justify many' because 'he bore the sin of many.'

Isaiah 53, of course, is the foremost Old Testament prophecy of the death of Christ. But though we know it well, we may not have thought much about the standpoint from which it was written.

In this part of his book Isaiah is speaking for a later remnant of God's people. He speaks as one who is part of the Messiah's (Christ's) future community of redeemed men and women.

[4]The Greek word, *anti*, translated 'for' in the phrase 'to give his life as a ransom for many,' is the clearest of the Greek prepositions in conveying the idea of substitution. But, again, I want to take this up in more depth later on.

When he writes, 'We all, like sheep, have gone astray' (*v. 6*), he speaks as one of those who can say, 'by his wounds we are healed' (*v. 4*). It is true, of course, that all the men and women in the world have gone astray, but Isaiah speaks for the godly remnant. It is for this same group that he speaks when he says, 'The Lord has laid on him the iniquity of us all' (*v. 6*). He does not mean, 'The Lord has laid on Christ the iniquity of each man who ever lived.' He speaks for his community. 'For the transgression of my people he was stricken' (*v. 8*).

Isaiah has changed standpoints, however, when we come to vv. 11–12. Now he speaks for God. It is God who says, 'My righteous servant will justify many, and he will bear their iniquities' (*v. 11*). It is the Lord who will give his servant 'a portion among the great' because 'he bore the sins of many' (*v. 12*).

While Isaiah speaks for God here, it seems most likely that the same remnant is in view. Who are the 'many' who will be justified? The righteous servant's community. Who are the 'many' whose sins he bore? The answer is the same. Those whom He will justify are those whose sins He bore. That is clear from verse 11. Nowhere here is there any thought of His dying for all men.

Now if this is the background of Mark 10:45, the question about whether the 'many' there is 'all the world' is settled. Christ is the ransom for His people. No others are included. Even if 'many' means 'all,' it will mean 'all who are part of His community.' No others are mentioned.

In the Dead Sea Scrolls scholars have found that 'the many' is a title for the Qumran community. Perhaps that illustrates the usage of the Lord Jesus. The many He died to ransom are His community, the church of the living God.

These are His 'offspring' (*Isaiah 53:10*). Of these He

says, 'Here am I, and the children God has given me' (*Hebrews 2:13*).[5]

[5]For a fuller discussion of the word 'many' you may want to turn to Appendix 4, pp. 137–145 and Appendix 5, pp. 146–151.

13: *Who Died With Christ?*

We may answer the question, 'For whom did Christ die?' by asking another, the question at the head of this chapter: 'Who died with Christ?'

You may wonder what kind of question that is! One answer is, two thieves died with Christ, one on His right and the other on His left. But that does not touch the point I want to make in this chapter.

Listen to Paul in 2 Corinthians 5:14–15:

> For Christ's love compels us, because we are convinced that one died for all, and therefore all died. And he died for all, that those who live should no longer live for themselves but for him who died for them and was raised again.

Paul believed that others died when Christ died. Who were they?

Does Paul mean that in some sense each and every man and woman died when Christ died? After all, he says 'all died.' That is one possibility but let us consider it.

One way to answer the question is to review the ways people die. What kinds of death do men go through?

First, physical death. Did all die *physically* when Christ died? No – physical death does not come on men because of the death of Christ. Men die physically because of sin.

How about spiritual death? Do men die *spiritually* through the death of Christ? No – men are dead spiritually until they are born again. Christ's death did not make you and me dead spiritually. We were born that way.

Again, did men die *eternally* when Christ died? No – Christ came to deliver us from eternal death. To die eternally means that we have not benefited by Christ's death for sinners.

None of these kinds of death can be the death that men share with the Lord Jesus. What's left, then?

The Bible calls this death that Christ and men share, 'death to sin.' Concerning Christ, Paul says, 'The death he died, he died to sin' (*Romans 6:10*). He also says, concerning us who believe, 'We died to sin; how can we live in it any longer?' (*Romans 6:2*). So there it is: the death that is common to Christ and men and women is death to sin.

Let's take a closer look at this. According to Paul, 'One died for all, and therefore all died' (*2 Corinthians 5:14*). We are ready now to see whom Paul includes in this 'all'. does he mean each and every person who has ever lived? Many have thought so, and they have argued that position at length. But their argument usually comes down to this: let 'all' mean 'all men' in the sense of 'all men without exception', because that is the self-evident meaning of 'all'.

But are they right? Is that true? No. We have already seen good reason to deny that. In every case we must take 'all men' to mean 'all the men under discussion.' Sometimes we find that takes in all men who ever lived, but that is not its usual use.

One writer has added this argument:

The real assurance for me that Christ died *for me* is this alone, that he died for absolutely *all*. If he omitted any, then, knowing what a fearful sinner I am, I must come to the judgment that he surely passed by me also.

I'm sure that many Christians will feel some force in that

appeal, but the writer is not explaining Paul's words in context when he says this.

Of course, we must *know* that Christ died for us. But the way to know that is to believe in Him. He died for all who would ever believe in Him. If you are a believer, then you may be sure that He died for *you*. The Scriptures do not call on you to believe in His death first of all. They command you to believe *in Him*, the person Jesus Christ. Our faith is in Him first, and then in what He did (and does!).

But let's return to the text at hand.

Paul's point is this: when Christ died, His people died to sin. Once more we see what we have seen again and again: Paul speaks of the result of Christ's death as having taken place right there at the cross, when He was crucified.

Where were we men redeemed? At the cross! Where were we reconciled to God? At the cross! Where was the wrath of God turned away from us? At the cross! And now we can add another question and answer. Where was it that we died to sin? At the cross!

You'll remember the importance of this: it shows beyond doubt that Paul says all these things only about God's elect. If all, meaning each and every man who ever lived, were redeemed at the cross, then all would be saved. None could be lost. And we can say the same thing about reconciliation and propitiation. If they were done at the cross, then whoever they were done for must be reconciled to God and must escape God's wrath.

Now we can say the same thing about death to sin. If that happened *at the cross* to every man who will ever live then there will be no men who have not died to sin. In other words, there will be no men who will be lost. But we know that some men will be lost, so it is clear that they did not die to sin when Christ died.

Paul's 'all' means 'all of us,' that is, 'all for whom Christ died.' Every one of them, without exception, died to sin when Christ died.

In placing all the blessings of redemption at the cross, God tells us as plainly as He can say it: Christ died for His people, to purchase 'men for God from every tribe and language and people and nation' (*Revelation 5:9*). His death separates His own from the rest of mankind in the world. They are, individually and together, 'a new creation' (*2 Corinthians 5:17*).

It's time for me to raise a further question about what Paul says here. I have asked it before, but we will feel it sharply again in connection with my death to sin. *How can Paul say that I died [to sin] when I did not yet exist?* He can say it because the death of Christ for me, and for all His people, rendered our death to sin certain. His death to sin was *virtually* my death to sin. My death to sin would follow His death as surely as night follows day.

Let me take you to one more passage where Paul speaks of our dying to sin with Christ. Here is part of Romans 6:

> We died to sin; how can we live in it any longer? Or don't you know that all of us who were baptized into Christ Jesus were baptized into his death? We were therefore buried with him through baptism into death, in order that, just as Christ was raised from the dead through the glory of the Father, we too may live a new life. (*vv. 2–4*)
> If we have been united with him in his death, we will certainly be united with him in his resurrection. For we know that our old self was crucified with him so that the body of sin might be rendered powerless, that we should no longer be slaves to sin . . . (*vv. 5–6*)
> Now if we died with Christ, we believe that we will also live with him. (*v. 8*)

Paul wanted all men to know that Christians could not live a life of sin, because they were dead to sin with Christ.

Let me tell you why I think this passage is important. The emphasis here is on another time when the Christian is said to have died to sin. That leads me to make this point: the New Testament recognizes what we may call 'moments of salvation.'[1]

Let me show you what I mean by asking the question, 'When did God's elect die to sin?' There seem to be no less than five answers to that question. Let me list them:

(1) We died to sin when God chose us. 'He chose us in him before the foundation of the world to be holy and blameless in his sight' (*Ephesians 1:4; cf. Romans 8:29*). His choice rendered our holiness certain, so it was virtually done then.

(2) We died to sin with Jesus Christ on the cross. We have already seen that truth in 2 Corinthians 5:14.

(3) We died to sin when we were born again. 'We know that we have come to know him if we obey his commands' (*1 John 2:3*). This is the beginning of the outworking of our death to sin. Here it is really, though imperfectly, happening.

(4) We died to sin when we were baptized. There we symbolically died to sin. Our baptism pictured our leaving our old life of sin and entering on a new life of righteousness.

(5) We will die to sin in all its capacity to harm us and to offend God when we die physically. Then we will be morally done with sin forever. Even then we will know one effect of sin – we will not have our new bodies until the resurrection.

Paul addresses all the 'moments' in his letters. But he is especially looking at (2) and (3) here.

Paul's interest in Romans 6 is primarily moral. He is fighting a perversion of the gospel that says, 'It's perfectly

---

[1]There is a helpful discussion of some of these 'moments' in C.E.B. Cranfield, *A Critical And Exegetical Commentary On The Epistle To The Romans*, Edinburgh, T. & T. Clark, 1975, vol. 1, pp. 298ff.

all right to sin, because sin gives God the chance to display His grace! The more sin, the more grace!'

To this Paul replies, 'Absolutely not!'

Why does he say that? Because 'we died to sin; how can we live in it any longer?' (*v. 2*). The tense of the word 'died' often suggests something that happened once for all time.

Now when was that? Paul's answer is, at our baptism. Does water, then, in Paul's view, make us Christians? Can water put our sins to death? No. The application of a physical thing like water, regardless of how it is applied, can never work a moral change in us. Every Christian who takes his Bible seriously should see that.

If we did not know that, we could learn it from Paul himself. Didn't he insist on this when he told the Galatians that the knife of circumcision could do nothing to change the heart? 'Neither circumcision nor uncircumcision means anything; what counts is a new creation' (*6:15*).

I have no doubt that Paul is really looking at our rebirth. He cites baptism with its symbolism because men and women in the New Testament were baptized when they were converted. Baptism does in a figure what the work of the Spirit does in fact – it begins the death of sin in the life of the believer.

Here, then, are the great facts in the history of the salvation of each of God's elect. Each of these facts has particular men and women in view:

(1) God chose His people in eternity past, with the goal of parting them from their sins. He 'predestined them to be conformed to the likeness of his Son' (*Romans 8:29*). He had particular individuals in mind. Not one of them would be lost.

(2) God sent His Son to die for those He had chosen to part from their sins. 'He will save his people from their sins,' the angel told Joseph (*Matthew 1:21*). His people

died with Christ, when He died. Particular individuals died to sin. Not one of them would be lost.

(3) God calls His people to Himself and brings them to the new birth. 'Those he predestined, he also called' (*Romans 8:30*). They are converted as particular individuals, one at a time. Not one of them will be lost.

(4) At death (and beyond) God finishes the good work that He started at conversion. 'He who began a good work in you will carry it on to completion until the day of Jesus Christ' (*Philippians 1:6*). He will take these same particular individuals to Himself for ever. Not one of them will be lost.

That is the story of those whom God redeems. His redemption is a *particular redemption*.[2] It would be a pity to break this chain of events that focus on particular individuals, but please note one thing more. I am not arguing that Christ died only for His elect because the chain is attractive. The opposite is true. The chain is attractive because of the truth that Christ's people died to sin when He died.

That fact makes the chain *particular* throughout.

[2]For a brief discussion of terminology used by those of us who believe that Christ died for His elect alone, see Appendix 6, pp. 152–155.

14: *Christ Our Substitute*

Do you have a favorite parable? For many, though they don't think of it as a parable, Christ's description of His relation to His sheep is a well-loved passage from the Gospel of John. It has such statements as these:

> I am the gate; whoever enters through me will be saved. He will come in and go out, and find pasture. (*10:9*)
> I am the good shepherd. The good shepherd lays down his life for the sheep. (*10:11*)
> I am the good shepherd; I know my sheep and my sheep know me – just as the Father knows me and I know the Father – and I lay down my life for the sheep. I have other sheep that are not of this sheep pen. I must bring them also. They too will listen to my voice, and there shall be one flock and one shepherd. (*10:14–16*)

Some time after saying these things, the Lord Jesus found Himself in conflict with His enemies. He added these words about Himself and His sheep:

> You do not believe because you are not my sheep. My sheep listen to my voice: I know them, and they follow me. I give them eternal life, and they shall never perish; no one can snatch them out of my hand. (*10:26–28*)

It is clear from all this that Jesus loved to think of Himself and His people under the figure of shepherd and sheep. It is no surprise that His people love these figures as well.

But the thing that interests us here is this: throughout this passage Jesus describes His care for His sheep, even to the point of dying for them. He doesn't describe Himself as dying for other men's sheep. He dies for His own sheep. The sheep for whom He dies were a group larger than the small band of followers that heard Him say these things.

'I have other sheep that are not of this sheep pen,' He said, thinking perhaps of the vast number of Gentiles who would yet be saved. They too would come home to the Father by His death for His sheep.

For whom would He die? He would die for *His sheep*.

Now some may say, 'The fact that He died for His own sheep' – which is the obvious meaning of the story – 'does not tell us whether He also died for other sheep as well.' And they are right.

But there is more here than the simple fact that Christ died for His sheep. There is the kind of death He died, a death in which one person, the shepherd, substitutes Himself for others, the sheep.

Let me show you what I mean.

In the parable the sheep are under attack from a wolf (*10:12*). The attack means that either the sheep will die while the shepherd flees, or the shepherd will die in fighting off the wolf. This 'good shepherd' will not take flight, so He will have to die. He will die *in their stead*. He will die *in their place*. They would have died, but their death fell on Him.

In teaching this way, the Lord Jesus showed us that His atonement is what is called a 'substitutionary atonement,' a death in which one man dies in the place of another man or other men.

But no death can be substitutionary if both the substitute and the men for whom he dies experience death. A man may die in the hope of helping others, but he is not their *substitute* if they die the death he had hoped to save them from.

Of course we would not want to rest substitutionary

atonement simply on a parable. This story illustrates it, but the truth of substitution is found elsewhere in the New Testament. Earlier we looked at Mark 10:45. Let's return there now.

In a context in which His disciples are striving for recognition, Jesus tells them that they need to be servants. Then He gives His reason: 'For even the Son of Man did not come to be served, but to serve, and to give his life as a ransom for many.'

It seems clear here that Jesus has a substitution or exchange in view. His life for the lives of many! The phrase, 'A life for a life!' springs to mind. Here is the highest service He can perform.

We see the idea of substitution here without going into the Greek language. But there is also evidence from the word translated 'for', in the phrase 'a ransom for many.' The Greek word is *anti* meaning 'in the stead of' or 'in the place of'. We might translate, 'a ransom given in the place of many.' This is a clear assertion of substitution. The Greek confirms the impression that one would receive here in any language.[1]

More than that, the word 'ransom' itself suggests substitution when it is a man who is the ransom for another man. Think of the case of the Levites. They were taken 'in place of the first male offspring of every

---

[1] Some have held that *anti* means no more than 'in behalf of' here. The two ideas are, of course, very close. The standard Greek lexicon by Arndt and Gingrich cites Genesis 44:33 as a case in point, but I cannot see how the idea of substitution is absent there. And I am not alone. The NIV renders the Hebrew: 'Let your servant remain here as my lord's slave *in place of* the boy, and let the boy return with his brothers' (*italics mine*). This seems as plain a case of substitution as one could find anywhere. To illustrate a further meaning for *anti* they also cite Hebrews 12:16 where Esau is said to have given up his birthright in exchange for a single meal. But can anyone doubt that this too is a plain case of substitution *as to its idea*? He substituted something almost worthless, a single meal, for his rights as chief heir.

Israelite woman' (*Numbers 3:12*). The Greek translators of Numbers introduced the Greek word for 'ransom' into this verse in their version. And that is clearly the idea. The Levites, in substituting for the firstborn males in Israel, were their ransom. Mark 10:45 could hardly teach substitution more plainly than it does.

But Mark is not alone.

Look in with me at the discussion of the Sanhedrin described in John 11.

> 'What are we accomplishing?' they asked. 'Here is this man performing many miraculous signs. If we let him go on like this, everyone will believe in him, and then the Romans will come and take away both our place and our nation.' (*vv. 47–48*)
> Then one of them, named Caiaphas, who was high priest that year, spoke up, 'You know nothing at all! You do not realize that it is better for you that one man die for the people than that the whole nation perish.' (*vv. 49–50*)

What have we here? A plain case of substitution in the mind of the high priest! 'We will put this Jesus *in the place of* the rest of us,' is what he is saying. A life for a life – and then some!

Now I am not suggesting that we get our doctrine of Christ's death from an unbelieving high priest. Not for a moment. But there is more to this than first meets the eye.

John 11 has more to say. This time John himself is speaking to us:

> He did not say this on his own, but as high priest that year he prophesied that Jesus would die for the Jewish nation, and not only for that nation but also for the scattered children of God, to bring them together and to make them one. (*vv. 51–52*)

John's words throw a new light on this scene.

[86]

Normally we might safely ignore the words of Israel's high priest for Christian doctrine. But this was a special situation. Caiaphas was prophesying here. He didn't know it, of course. If he had, he would have been startled. Unconsciously, however, he was showing the truth of Proverbs 16:1 – 'To man belong the plans of the heart, but from the Lord comes the reply of the tongue.'

The high priest had a plan in his heart, a plan to kill Jesus. And he said just what he wanted to say to further his plan. All the same, his words were also a word from the Lord, in this case a prophetic word! (I say 'in this case' because Proverbs doesn't confine the Lord's control to prophecy. What men say is *always* under the Lord's control. Even Caiaphas' plan was also God's plan. This wicked man was one of those who did what God's 'power and will had decided beforehand should happen' (*Acts 4:28*).

What a great God we have!

But back to the point I was making. John sees in the high priest's *words* about substitution the *word* of God. And John sees in the high priest's *plan* of substitution a part of the larger *plan* of God.

John changes only one of the high priest's points. He does not correct it, but he adds to it. This substitution – this 'swap' between Christ and others – would be more far-reaching than Caiaphas planned. It would take in Gentiles as well!

But someone may say, 'If this is substitution, it is substitution for more than God's elect. It takes in the whole nation of Israel! Yet we know that not every Israelite will be saved. So either this is not substitution *or* the substitute may die for men who will indeed die the same death!'

That would be a powerful indictment against what I have been saying, if it were true.

But John's addition to what Caiaphas said points us to how we must take the word 'nation'. Let me show you what I mean.

John tells us, 'Jesus would die . . . not only for that nation but also for the scattered children of God, to bring them together and to make them one.'

Look at how John treats the Gentiles. He does not treat them as a mass. He treats them selectively and calls them 'the scattered children of God.' Then he gives us God's purpose in Christ's death: 'to bring them together and to make them one.' His meaning seems clear. In speaking of the nation of Israel he has in view the children of God who were not scattered when he wrote. Now, he says, God intends to take the scattered children of God and bring them together with the unscattered children of God, so that together they will be one.

The 'nation', then, in John's mind is the elect of Israel, and the 'scattered children' are the elect among the Gentiles. Jesus Christ is their substitute. He dies in their place. No others are in view here because the purpose of his death is the purpose of forming all for whom He dies into the one body of Christ (*cf. 10:16; 17:21*). That means that we have a real substitution here, and that none will later die the same death that Jesus has suffered in their place.

We might take the time to look up other texts that show vicarious or substitutionary atonement. But it is not really necessary; three cases are as good as ten, *if* those three cases are valid as I trust I have shown these to be.

But let me make this sharp point once more: a man may die in the hope of helping others, but he is not their substitute if they die the death he had hoped to save them from.

To say that Christ's death was substitutionary is to say that no one for whom Christ died can ever be lost.

To say that Christ's death was substitutionary is to say that Christ died only for His people, His nation, His family or His sheep.

15: *A Look at Some 'Hard' Texts*

We are nearing the end, but I still have a few things I want to do. The first one is this: I want to look at some texts that are thought by many to be inconsistent with the idea that Christ died for His people only. Of course, all through the book I have dealt with texts of that kind, but here I want to take up a few that we have not glanced at earlier.

We will look first at 2 Peter 2:1. Perhaps this verse, more than any other, is thought to be fatal to *particular redemption*. Peter writes:

> But there were also false prophets among the people, just as there will be false teachers among you. They will secretly introduce destructive heresies, *even denying the sovereign Lord who bought them* – bringing swift destruction on themselves.

I have italicized the words at the heart of the dispute. They raise the important question: Are there in fact false teachers whom the sovereign Lord bought? And they answer it with a resounding Yes!

Doesn't this text settle the question once for all? If God or Christ has bought false teachers, how can anyone say that Christ died only for God's elect?

It seems to me that the answer to this problem is bound up with a simple oversight on the part of many. They forget that to buy something means to obtain possession of it, when 'redemption' words are being used. They want to make 'buy' mean 'pay' or 'put down a price,' but that's not what it means.[1] If we keep that fact in mind we will see that this verse cannot mean that Christ died for men whom He will never make His own. And once we understand that, we will be able to look more sympathetically at other understandings of this verse.

According to 2 Peter 2:1, then, God or Christ acquired some men who proved false. To be brief we will assume that Christ is the one being spoken of.

How has Christ acquired these men? Here are three possible answers:

(1) He acquired them by saving them. That is clearly not the case here.

(2) He acquired them by their profession. They claimed to be Christians. They said in effect, 'We belong to Christ,' though in their hearts they denied Him.

(3) He acquired them by changing their lives, by freeing them from many of their sins. To redeem a man is to free him from something. According to verses 20–22 of this chapter, there are such people who were freed from many vices by professing faith in Christ. But they were not really saved. They were like sows that are washed outwardly, but that still love the mud.[2]

Let us consider these last two options more closely.

Jesus spoke of false prophets as wolves. 'Watch out for false prophets,' He said. 'They come to you in sheep's clothing, but inwardly they are ferocious wolves' (*Matthew 7:15*).

Why did He use the phrase 'sheep's clothing'? Because

[1] I have discussed *agorazo*, the word used for buying here, at length in Appendix 3, pp. 134–136, so I leave it to the reader to look at the evidence there.

[2] A fourth possible way Christ acquired these false teachers is given in Gary Long, *Definite Atonement*, Nutley, N.J., Presbyterian and Reformed, 1977, pp. 76ff. His entire Appendix 1 is devoted to 2 Peter 2:1. I have not included what Long calls 'the sovereign creation view' because of the complexity of the evidence for it. But it deserves careful attention and is, in fact, Long's own preference. It is, however, closely related to (2) and (3) above.

they would be hard to discern. They would look like they belonged to Him. People who saw them casually would say, 'There is one of Christ's sheep.'

Of course these false prophets would encourage this. They would say, 'We are teachers sent by Christ.' We might say that Christ would have them on His hands whether He wanted them or not! Even in the judgment day they might plead that they were His. Jesus made this point a few verses later when He said, 'Many will say to me on that day, "Lord, Lord, did we not prophesy in your name, and in your name drive out demons and perform many miracles?"'

But Jesus added this: 'Then I will tell them plainly, "I never knew you. Away from me, you evildoers!"' (*Matthew 7:22–23*).

So the Lord Jesus acquires some men, including false teachers, by their profession of faith, as in (2) above.

But there is more to say. Why are men able to maintain a false profession for long periods of time? It is because they often clean themselves up when they profess faith. If they are not conscious hypocrites at the outset, Christ's word has an effect on them. 'My Savior,' they say, 'wants me to do such and such.' And often they run off to do it.

In a real sense, then, Christ has cleaned up their lives. He has freed them from the bondage of some of their filth by His teaching in His word. In Peter's words, 'They have escaped the corruption of the world by knowing our Lord and Savior Jesus Christ' (*2 Peter 2:20*).

So the Lord Jesus acquires some men, including false teachers, by changing their way of living through His word, as in (3) above.

And one thing more is true. It is likely that these two ways of acquiring followers will be found together. That is the way it was in Israel. Peter says that the false teachers among Christians are like the false prophets of days gone by. God had redeemed Israel from Egypt. It was a real redemption, an emancipation from bondage. But though they were really redeemed, many of their hearts were not changed.

What did they do? Often they kept up their profession of faith in the Lord. And they kept up the works connected with Old Testament worship. They offered their sacrifices. They visited the temple. They conformed outwardly, but their hearts were far from God.

It is clear from the New Testament that the same kind of thing happened in the early church. Men kept up their profession of faith. They even left their grosser sins. They prayed their prayers and went to the gatherings of God's people. They conformed outwardly, but their hearts were far from God. Christ had bought, i.e., acquired them, but they were false.

Whatever else 2 Peter 2:1 may mean, it must entail Christ acquiring these people. It is not enough to say, 'He put down a price for them.' Without the element of acquisition, any understanding of this verse is false.

Here is a second 'hard' verse, Hebrews 2:9:

> But we see Jesus, who was made a little lower than the angels, now crowned with glory and honor because he suffered death, so that by the grace of God he might taste death for everyone.

The argument from this verse might go this way: since Christ tasted death for *everyone*, there is *no one* for whom He did not taste death. That would mean that He died for all the men and women who ever lived. Is that what this verse teaches? Let's see.

To begin with, I want to point out that 'everyone' is one of those universal terms that we have already said so much about. We must take universal terms seriously, of course. But we must remember how ambiguous they are.

We have seen that the context must show us their meaning.[3]

When we look at what comes before this verse, we will see who 'everyone' is here. The writer is talking about the future world and reminds his readers that God has promised to put that world under man (*2:6–8a*). Then he adds:

> In putting everything under him, God left nothing that is not subject to him. Yet at present we do not see everything subject to him. But we see Jesus, who was made a little lower than the angels, now crowned with glory and honor because he suffered death, so that by the grace of God he might taste death for everyone.

Whom does he mean by 'everyone'? His argument will show us.

If men are to rule the world to come they will have to be redeemed. One day God will put all things under man. That has not happened yet, except in their representative, Jesus Christ. He has 'all authority in heaven and on earth' (*Matthew 28:18*). But they have little authority.

Still, their day is coming, but it could never come if Christ had not died for *every one of them*. As I have shown earlier, the men and women who will rule the world to come are not all men absolutely.[4] They are the sons of God (*2:10*), the brothers of Christ (*2:11*) and the people of God (*2:17*). It is their sins He has borne and borne away. Hebrews 2:9 teaches no more, then, than we have seen elsewhere. Christ died for His elect people.

[3]I have discussed the context that *follows* this verse already, on pp. 63—64. I suggest that you look at that discussion again.

[4]Robert Lightner seems to miss this point. He speaks of 'the universality of the subjection in verse 8' (op. cit., p. 71). He means that Psalm 8, from which Hebrews quotes, is talking about men in general subjecting the world to themselves. But Hebrews interprets Psalm 8 to be speaking of the future. When that contemplated future subjection comes, it will be subjection to God's elect, or subjection to a mankind made up only of the redeemed.

Here's one more verse, I Timothy 4:10:

We have put our hope in the living God, who is the Savior of all men, and especially of those who believe.

While this verse does not speak of the death of Christ, it often comes into the discussion because it speaks of God as 'the Savior of all men.' What is Paul teaching here? Does he mean to say that Christ died for each and every person who ever lived?

There is no need to think so. The standard Greek dictionary gives 'preserver' as one meaning of the word translated 'Savior' here. And God does preserve or save all men from many dangers besides the misery of hell. Paul does not need to mean more than that here.

In fact, in Acts 27:34, Paul himself speaks of such salvation or preservation. 'Now,' he says to his shipmates who had been fasting in the storm, 'I urge you to take some food. You need it to survive.' The last sentence is literally, 'This is for your salvation.' He is not discussing eternal salvation with these men. He simply means that they need to eat to preserve their strength for the rest of their ordeal, so that they may be saved alive.

God is indeed the Savior or Preserver of all men in many kinds of difficulties. But above all He saves believers, preserving them, not simply in time but also in eternity.

16: *How Does This Affect Our Preaching?*

If you have come with me this far, you may have asked yourself this: 'How does all this affect the way we present the gospel?' Or, more briefly, 'Is this preachable?'

There could hardly be a more important question.

Whatever the truth is, the early church carried it like a firebrand across the Roman world. No one ever doubted that they had something to say! The gospel of Christ is no uncertain sound, no powerless message.

But what is that message? Where shall we find it? In the Bible, of course, but where in the Bible? It seems to me that the place to look is the Book of Acts. Let me tell you why.

When we come to Acts we come to the activity of the church as we know it today. The preaching there is our model. Someone may ask, 'Aren't the four Gospels also our models?' In general the answer is, Yes. But the four Gospels are also transition writings, writings that bridge the time between the old and new covenants. Most Christians agree that once we come into the Book of Acts the preaching we find is standard for our day.

What do we find in Acts? In particular, how are unsaved men addressed? Some things we come across will be familiar enough. But some things may seem startling. There is one caution you must keep in mind: the sermons we find are summaries. You can read most of them in a minute or two! That means that Luke gives us what he deems to be most important.

The first thing that strikes you when you survey the sermons in Acts is how they vary. One important difference is the audience. When they were Jews, as they often were, a great deal was assumed. Both Peter and Paul knew that the Jews were looking for a coming king, the Messiah. Often, then, they spent their time telling their countrymen that the king had come, Jesus of Nazareth. And they had a common method with the Jews; they cited Old Testament passages that showed the Lord Jesus to be the very king the Jews should have been expecting.

But suppose they were preaching to Gentiles, what then? Well, Gentiles fell into two classes. There were those who were interested in Judaism. Often they knew a good deal of the Old Testament. The Apostles' approach to these people was much like their approach to their fellow Jews.

But what of other Gentiles? That was a different story. Paul's message on Mars' Hill in Athens is our fullest example. With pagans he assumed nothing! He started at square one, the fact of the Creator God.

Already we have learned something of great significance. There is no cut-and-dried way to present the gospel. There is no canned approach. It depends on whom you are talking to.

How does this compare with preaching in the Gospels? Jesus approached men and women in a variety of ways. I think it is safe to say that He treated no two people alike.

Let's return to Mars' Hill.

What did Paul do next? He attacked their idolatry and called for their repentance! The call to repentance is something that all preaching must have. 'I have not come to call the righteous, but sinners to repentance,' said Jesus (*Luke 5:32*). 'Repent and be baptized, every one of you, in the name of Jesus Christ so that your sins may be forgiven,' said Peter to his Jewish audience at Pentecost (*Acts 2:38*).

In each case, sin was the issue and repentance was the answer. Every man must turn from his sin and turn to God![1]

Here is a second critical lesson: we do not preach the gospel unless we tell men they must repent.

And here's a third, arising from the second: in the Bible, evangelism is *confrontational*. Man's power and self-sufficiency must be challenged.

When I call the preaching confrontational I am speaking of its content, of course. I don't mean that the preachers were abrasive in their attitudes or in the delivery of the message. That would be far from true, and far from the spirit of Christ. Let's have a portion of Paul's sermon on Mars' Hill before us, so that you can see what I mean:

> Therefore [Paul says] since we are God's offspring, we should not think that the divine being is like gold or silver or stone – an image made by man's design and skill. In the past God overlooked such ignorance, but now he commands all people everywhere to repent. For he has set a day when he will judge the world with justice by the man he has appointed. He has given proof of this to all men by raising him from the dead. (*Acts 17:29–31*)

Here Paul is confronting the sinful ignorance of his hearers.

How does he do it? By telling them that God will not tolerate serving idols, that they must repent of such service. And he adds a threat. God will judge the world some day, and He will not overlook this matter of idolatry.

Is this a fair sample of what preaching should be today?

I think it is, as far as it goes. Paul, of course, was cut off at this point. The crowd didn't listen any further. He had just introduced the Lord Jesus when they had had

[1]For a brief discussion of repentance and faith and their relationship, you may see Appendix 7, pp. 156–158.

enough. But the rest of the preaching in Acts shows us what must be said about Jesus.

We will review what we have seen for a moment. In a single sentence: *while we cannot adopt a canned formula when preaching Christ, we must confront men with their sins and with God's demand for repentance.* These things are basic.

But how was this followed up? Is this the point at which they said, 'God loves you and Christ died for you'? No. As far as the record goes, they never told anyone, 'God loves you.' In fact, the word 'love' does not occur in the Book of Acts. Neither do any of its synonyms, except in the quotation from the Old Testament, 'I will give you the holy and sure blessings [mercies, AV] promised to David' (*Acts 13:34*).

What does this mean? Don't we have to convey the love of God to men if they are to be saved? 'Surely,' someone may say, 'men need to be loved, don't they?' And of course the answer to that question is Yes. I do not doubt that for a moment.

Our problem, however, is to be sure we know as much as possible about what the Scripture teaches on this subject before we decide what our message ought to be. So bear with me.

But someone may say, 'Now we know why you wanted to use Acts as your model. That way you could skip all the places in the Gospels where Christ told men that God loved them!'

Let me briefly summarize what we find about God's love in the Gospels. I think you will be surprised, as I was.

1. Neither God nor Christ is said to love anyone in Matthew.
2. Christ is said to have loved the rich ruler in Mark.
3. Neither God nor Christ is said to love anyone in Luke.

4. John's Gospel, on the other hand, is rich in references to the love of God and Christ. Whom do they love? Nine times they are said to love one another. Nineteen times they are said to love believers. Once God is said to love the world, and once Christ is said to love His friends. I separated 'friends' from believers because some have held that 'friends' includes men who would never be saved.

If the word 'world' in John 3:16 does not mean all men individually, then we are hard pressed to find any reference in which God or Christ are joined to lost men by the word 'love'.

Even if we allow the three exceptions we have found, in none of them is it clear that a man was *told* that God loves him. Christ's love for the rich young ruler is a comment from the writer (*Mark 10:21*). Christ's love for His friends was told to the Apostles (*John 15:13*). That God loved the world may have been said to Nicodemus though we cannot be sure that His address to this ruler of the Jews continued as far as John 3:16. Even *if* it was spoken to him (which is doubtful), and even *if* it meant that God loves each and every man individually (which is also in doubt), we see from later mention of Nicodemus that he was one of God's elect.

Furthermore, the Epistles and the Book of Revelation yield the same kinds of results.

Where does all this get us? It tells us that we may have supposed something that isn't so. We may have assumed that in the preaching in the New Testament there was a great deal more said to sinners about God's love for them than is actually the case. But be careful! Don't draw any conclusions just yet. Instead, return with me to the Book of Acts.

I have to ask another question: Were lost men told that Christ died for them in the Book of Acts? This answer is also surprising: no one was told that Christ died for him or her in Acts.

Wasn't the death of Christ preached? Yes, but notice how.

There are two chief reasons why Christ's death is preached in Acts: firstly, because it had been reversed by His resurrection; and, secondly, to convict the Jews of their sin in putting Christ to death. Take Peter's message at Pentecost. What does it say about Christ's death? Listen:

> This man [says Peter] was handed over to you by God's set purpose and foreknowledge; and you, with the help of wicked men, put him to death by nailing him to the cross. But God raised him from the dead . . . (*2:23–24*)

That is all Peter says about Christ's death directly. He adds a good deal about His not decaying in the grave, but being raised again. Then he draws this conclusion based on His resurrection and ascension:

> Therefore let all Israel be assured of this: God has made this Jesus, whom you crucified, both Lord and Christ. (*2:36*)

That conclusion is important, as I hope to show shortly.

In the next sermon, Peter preaches to those who gathered after the healing of the man crippled from his birth. Here Peter says more about the death of Christ. He notes that it was in keeping with prophecy, but there is nothing on the question of for whom He died. When questioned later about the healing, Peter describes it as being 'by the name of Jesus Christ of Nazareth, whom you crucified but whom God raised from the dead' (*4:10*).

This is a recurring pattern in Acts. No sooner is the death of Christ mentioned than Peter adds, 'God raised Him from the dead.' The resurrection gets the emphasis.

So much is this the case that on Mars' Hill Paul seems to pass over the death entirely and goes directly to Christ's resurrection.

All this raises another question: what does Acts say about the atonement? The answer is, Almost nothing. We would love to know what Philip told the Ethiopian eunuch on the great text from Isaiah 53, but the record is silent (*8:32–35*). We have a couple of phrases on the subject in 10:36, 'peace through him,' and 10:43, 'forgiveness of sins through his name.' These blessings, of course, come through the cross, but so far as the record tells us Peter did not explain their relation to Christ's death.

Paul preaches in Acts 13:16–41 in the synagogue at Antioch of Pisidia. Again he mentions the death of Christ and he tells his hearers of the forgiveness of sins, but he does not discuss the atonement.

In Acts 17:2–3 we read:

> As his custom was, Paul went into the synagogue [in Thessalonica], and on three Sabbath days he reasoned with them from the Scriptures, explaining and proving that the Christ had to suffer and rise from the dead. 'This Jesus I am proclaiming to you is the Christ,' he said.

How I wish we could have been there to hear what he said about the atonement! But the record tells us nothing. Here we see the same themes we have found elsewhere. The Old Testament spoke of a Messiah or Christ. Jesus *is* that Christ. And He died and rose again.

Five more times in Acts Paul preaches.[2] These accounts, too, are silent on the atonement with one exception. Listen to Paul as he speaks to the Ephesian elders:

[2]The records are found in 17:22–31 (which I have already covered); 20: 17–35 (which I am about to discuss); 22:1–21; 24:10–21 and 26:2–29. Acts 28:23ff. tells us of another of Paul's sermons, but does not tell us what he said about Christ.

I have declared to both Jews and Greeks that they must turn to God in repentance and have faith in our Lord Jesus. (*20:21*)

Guard yourselves and all the flock of which the Holy Spirit has made you overseers. Be shepherds of the church of God, *which he bought with his own blood*. (*20:28*)

I think you will find that the words I have italicized above are the only explanation of the atonement in the entire Book of Acts. And what do they say? They say that Christ purchased the church by His death. That is no help at all to those who want to say to lost men, 'Christ died for you.'

The conclusion is clear; so far as the record shows, no sermon in the Book of Acts contained the words, 'God loves you and Christ died for you.'

With these things in mind we can begin to answer the question: what was – and what is – the gospel message?

17: *What Is the Gospel Message?*

When we tell some Christians that 'God loves you and Christ died for you' is not the message of the New Testament, they are likely to feel at sea.

'Isn't this what all the churches preach?' they may ask. Or, 'Haven't churches always told men this?'

The simple answer to those questions is, No.

Besides, most Christians agree that what the church has or has not done is not the acid test. So we need not examine church history in this case. We only need to follow the Bible. What does it say?

But someone else may ask another question: 'Doesn't the Bible give us the gospel in 1 Corinthians 15:3–4?' We must have that passage before us as we talk about it. Here it is:

> For what I received [Paul says] I passed on to you as of first importance: that Christ died for our sins according to the Scriptures, that he was buried, [and] that he was raised on the third day according to the Scriptures.

Is this the gospel? It certainly is a brief summary of the truth concerning Christ, and in fact Paul calls it 'the gospel I preached to you' in verse 1 of the same chapter.

How does this brief summary fit into what we have found so far? Let me see if I can throw some light on that question.

To understand the gospel message you must under-stand the standpoint from which Christ and His Apostles spoke. They thought in terms of two bodies or societies. The first was the world. All men were born into the world and its system because of Adam's fall. None were excluded except our Lord.

The second society is called various names, as we have seen. We may call it the family of God, or God's people, or the new nation, or Christ's body or the church. The name is not of first importance. The main thing is to see that these two societies, whatever we call them, are distinct.

One of these societies can say of itself, 'God loved us and Christ died for us.' And we find members of that society saying those very things over and over in the New Testament.

When persecution strikes them, they say, 'God loves us!' They say it in different ways. For instance:

> Who shall separate us from the love of Christ? Shall trouble or hardship or persecution . . . or sword? (*Romans 8:35*)

And they answer their own question with a hearty, 'No, in all these things we are more than conquerors through him who loved us' (*Romans 8:37*).

They would have been very surprised to hear their opponents say to them, 'Yes, but God loves us in the same way He loves you!'

'No!' they would have replied, 'God is for *us*!' And they would have added:

> If God is for us, who can be against us? He who did not spare his own Son, but gave him up for us all – how will he not also, along with him, graciously give us all things? (*Romans 8:31–32*)[1]

---

[1] The presence of the word 'all' in the phrase 'for us all' is not intended to take in all men. The group in view is the group that can say, 'Abraham is the father of us all' (*Romans 4:16*).

Wouldn't they have been startled to hear their persecutors say, 'But God is for us, too. He delivered Christ for us, too. He will give us all things, too!'?

'No,' they would have cried, 'God's good things are for those who love Him, that is, for those whom He foreknew and predestined and called and justified (*Romans 8:29–30*). We are the ones who may say, "God is for us."'

But, of course, they would not have stopped there, and they did not. They went on to preach to all men the good news that if they would turn from their sins (repent) and turn to Christ (believe) they would be delivered from the world and be brought into God's family. All of their sins would be forgiven – absolutely every one of them! Then they could join God's people in praising the One 'who loves us and has freed us from our sins by his blood, and has made us to be a kingdom and priests to serve his God and Father' (*Revelation 1:5–6*).

Outsiders can never say of the special love that redeems, 'God loves us and Christ died for us!' Insiders, on the other hand, can never cease saying it.

Turn from your sin, hate it, detest it and repent of it! Turn to Christ as Savior and Lord! He will forgive you your sins. Here is the message for a lost world.

When a member of that world does what God commands, he enters a new world, a new creation. Then he can join the other blood-washed pilgrims in singing, 'With your blood you have purchased [us] for God from every tribe and language and people and nation' (*Revelation 5:9*).

Until then, he has no song.

Is this really the message? Yes, it is.

But how about the love of God? Doesn't God's love come into our preaching at all? Yes, it does. It comes in, it seems to me, in two ways. Let me share them with you.

First, think with me about forgiveness. To say to a man,

'God will forgive you,' should prompt him to see the love of God in the preaching. But here is the important point: whether or not the sinner sees the offer of forgiveness as love depends on how he feels about his own sin. If he feels the wickedness and unreasonableness of his sin, he will see the love of God in the offer to forgive it.

Someone may say, however, 'Why beat around the bush? Why not just come out and say, "God loves you!" Wouldn't that be best?'

I don't think so. Let me tell you why. We have already seen that this does not appear to be what the preachers in the New Testament did. This is important. That should give us pause.

But why didn't they do that? Looking around me here in America suggests one reason. It is contained in the common proverb, Familiarity breeds contempt.

Our Lord Jesus once said, 'Do not give dogs what is sacred; do not throw your pearls to pigs. If you do they may trample them under their feet . . . ' (*Matthew 7:6*). I suspect that command applies here. The offer of free forgiveness is a parable to all men of the love of God. Any man who hears of full pardon in Christ ought to see amazing love. The more he knows of his own sin, the greater will seem the love of God to him. The parable will be to him an open book.

But what of the other kind of man, the man who cares nothing about his wickedness?

That kind of man is all too common. He has been told repeatedly, 'God loves you.' And he is sure it's true. What practical effect does it have on his life? In thousands of cases it is the excuse he uses for ignoring or denying the laws of God. For that reason alone we would be wise to follow the pattern we find in the New Testament preaching.

But there is a second way the love of God enters into our preaching.

While the New Testament does not show us men telling sinners, 'God loves you,' it does something else closely related to that. It shows us the Lord Jesus and His followers demonstrating the love of God in the way they preached and worked.

Let me use the Lord Himself as an example. In Matthew 9:36 we read:

> When [Jesus] saw the crowds, he had compassion on them, because they were harassed and helpless, like sheep without a shepherd.

Immediately that compassion turned to action. He told His disciples to ask the Father for workers for the harvest. And He did more. He sent those same followers to preach His good news.

Let me insert a personal word here. At this point, more than at any other in this study, I have had to take stock of my own preaching. Why? Because I did not realize how great a bearing the compassion of Christ has on *how* I am to preach.

If it is true that the love of God was not often spelled out to sinners in New Testament preaching, something else is also true. The love of God was constantly shown in the attitude of the preachers. They did not ordinarily thunder at sinners. If they had done so, sinners would have concluded that God was like the preacher, full of threats and possessed with little compassion.

Is that how the Lord Jesus came across? No. He welcomed sinners and ate with them. That was the scandal of His ministry (*see Luke 15:1–2*). And it was not just repentant sinners that He met, all sinners found a welcome except those who by repeated exposure to the truth had utterly hardened their hearts. At them He could thunder, . . . and He did! (But see how He wooed even them in the latter half of the parable of the prodigal son in Luke 15.)

And what about the apostle Paul? Listen to him:

> As apostles of Christ we could have been a burden to
> you, but we were gentle among you, like a mother
> caring for her little children. We loved you so much that
> we were delighted to share with you not only the gospel
> of God but our lives as well, because you had become
> dear to us. Surely you remember, brothers, our toil and
> hardship; we worked night and day in order not to be a
> burden to anyone while we preached the gospel of God
> to you. (*1 Thessalonians 2:7–9*)

There is the spirit of the preacher of the gospel!

Must we tell men that God loves them? The truth is
embodied in the fact that we are ambassadors for Christ.
He intends that men *see* Himself in us. If we preach with
compassion, they will see it and know that it is Christ's
pity for sinners that they are experiencing.

Earlier I pointed out in the Book of Acts a couple of
things that I want to return to now.

The first was this: the Apostles usually used the death of
Christ as a prelude to talking about His resurrection and
ascension.

The other thing was this: Peter, at Pentecost, wound up
his message by saying, 'Be assured of this: God has made
this Jesus, whom you crucified, both Lord and Christ'
(*Acts 2:36*).

These two things belong together. Let me show you
what I mean.

The emphasis on Christ's resurrection and ascension is
there to show us the Lordship of Jesus Christ. We may be
interested in His death, and in its place that is a proper and
necessary interest. But the preachers in Acts were especially interested in His exalted position. Why this
difference between their preaching and so much that is
heard today?

Because they took seriously the gulf between the world and the church. They saw the world as a camp of rebels. They were rebels against their rightful Lord. And what do you say to rebels? You say, 'LAY DOWN YOUR ARMS!'

Perhaps their rightful Lord loves them. Perhaps he has made wonderful provision for them. But as their Lord he demands their allegiance.

'Lay down your arms' is another way of saying, 'Repent!' And that is what they said. And they said it again, and they said it again.

The resurrection of Jesus Christ proved that He was Lord. As Lord, He is Judge. God 'has set a day,' Paul tells the Athenians, 'when He will judge the world with justice by the man he has appointed. He has given proof of this to all men by raising Him from the dead' (*Acts 17:31*).

Do you see? We dare not teach men in a way that lets them sleep easy in their sins. Men do not need to be told that the greatest blessings of life, the love of God and the sacrifice of Christ, belong to them as much as to those who have made peace with God. That is not what they need, and that is not what the early church gave them. Rather men heard, 'Awake from the dead, before it is everlastingly too late. Lay down your arms and bow before the Lord of the earth!' Or, in the words of the psalmist, 'Kiss the Son, lest he be angry and you be destroyed in your way' (*Psalm 2:12*).

And then what? Then they told them of peace and forgiveness. Then they told them that Christ died for the sins of His people, and that they could become a part of that people, that nation, that society, by faith in Him.

'Christ died for *our* sins,' Paul wrote to the Corinthians. Does 'our sins' mean 'your sins' and 'my sins'? 'Maybe,' Paul would have said, 'but I cannot tell until I see whether you turn from your sin (repent) and turn to Jesus Christ as Savior and Lord (believe).'

Let me close this chapter on the gospel message with two final points.

The first is this: the Bible sets a Person before us, Jesus Christ. It is not an atonement that we are to believe in, but a Person, our Lord Jesus. And this Person is Savior and Lord and Judge and many other things. We cannot divide Him; we must take Him whole. There is much, of course, that we do not know about Him; but what we know we must embrace from the heart.

The other thing I want to say is this: the gospel as I have outlined it is not salvation by the merit of works. Someone may object: 'If men must repent, and if repentance is forsaking sin, then we are saved by what we do!'

But only by the wildest stretch of imagination could a rebel suppose that he merited forgiveness by laying down his arms! Later he may have good works that he hopes will impress the king with his loyalty. But not now! Now there is but one thing to do – lay down his arms!

It is only by overlooking the fact that men are rebels against God, that anyone could suppose that repentance earns salvation. And we encourage that oversight in ourselves every time we say to the lost, 'God loves you and Christ died for you.' If we are to stand on biblical ground we must stand where the Bible stands. The natural man is a hater of God, a rebel by instinct, at enmity with his Maker. Before we console him, we must tell him that. We must confront him, just as the Apostles did.

No, we are not saved by our works. All of our works are faulty; they could never save us. Even our repentance and faith will be so far from perfection that they could not save us in a billion years.

But salvation is from *sin*. That includes forgiveness, but it is more than that. If we do not want to be saved from the power of our sin, we do not want salvation. And a man who does not want salvation will not receive it.

Repentance, then, is a desire to be done with sin. It is not a promise that I will never sin again. That would be arrogance, not repentance. That would grossly underestimate the power of sin. A penitent man has no confidence in himself. But I repeat: a man who does not want deliverance from sin does not want salvation. And a man who does not want salvation will not receive it.

And one thing more. God does not wait for our works. Our forgiveness is *virtually* complete when we come to Christ. It would be too much to say that our future sins are forgiven before they are committed. I will not say that.

Yet future forgiveness is guaranteed in the salvation God gives us when we come. Unless we are hypocrites, ready to desert our king at the least alarm, all our sins and iniquities are never again held against us. That is good news! It is true of all who have left the world and joined the people of God.

Hallelujah! what a Savior!

18: *A Final Word*

Writing this book has been a learning experience for me. Let me show you some of the ways that has been true.

1. As I have twice remarked, I had no idea how little the Bible says *directly* about the Lord's love for men in general. Before I wrote this book I could have imagined someone asking me, 'What do you do with texts like "God so loved the world," and with texts like the one that speaks of Jesus' love for the rich young ruler?' If I had been asked that question, I think I would have shared an important assumption with the person who asked it. Both he and I would have thought that he was asking about two texts out of a much larger sampling that he might have cited. I now know that that is false. When you've cited those two texts you are very nearly done.

Of course, not every text that teaches God's love for men includes the word 'love'. We also read of God's compassion and kindness, for example. Paul speaks of a general love from God toward men when he speaks to the idol worshipers in Lystra:

> [God] has shown kindness by giving you rain from heaven and crops in their seasons; he provides you with plenty of food and fills your hearts with joy. (*Acts 14:17*)

But he certainly does not speak here (or elsewhere, as far as I can see) of His special love to men generally.

Elsewhere he tells us that Christ loved His bride, 'the church and gave himself up for her' (*Ephesians 5:25*). He leaves it to our good sense to figure out if He loves other 'brides' in the way He loves His own.

Jesus makes a similar point in Revelation 3:9:

> I will make those who are of the synagogue of Satan, who claim to be Jews though they are not, but are liars – I will make them come and fall down at your feet and acknowledge that I have loved you.

Again, we are left to surmise that Christ does not love 'those who are of the synagogue of Satan' in the same way.

2. I have also been surprised to see how much is said to have been done *at the cross*, i.e., at the time our Lord was crucified. I knew that redemption, reconciliation and propitiation were said to be done there, but that was not nearly all. I have cited some of these things and could have cited more.

For example, Ephesians 2:14–16 tells us that Jews and Gentiles were made one at the cross. This could not have been said of all Jews and Gentiles. But it was so certain that elect Jews and Gentiles would be made one by Christ's death, that it was *as good as* accomplished there.

Again, Paul tells us in 2 Timothy 1:10 that Christ 'destroyed death.' We tend to glide over a text like that, but think about it for a moment. What can it mean except that Christ destroyed death in the case of His own people, whether you call them elect or believers or Christians? He did not abolish the death of others.[1] But He slew death for some! Who were they? They were His own.

3. One last thing has struck me, the emphases on acquisition and freedom in the words for redemption. It is true, generally speaking, that redemption is freedom by

---

[1]This text is probably the source of the best known book ever written on this subject, *The Death of Death in the Death of Christ*, by John Owen. It appears in volume 10 of his *Works* and is also in print separately, published by the Banner of Truth Trust. The latter edition also has an important introduction by J. I. Packer.

the payment of a price or acquisition by the payment of a price. But a good deal depends on where you put the stress in those definitions.

The Christians around me, I think, tend to stress the payment of the price. Quite unconsciously, I feel sure, that tends to reinforce the idea that Christ died for each man who ever lived. After all, the price He paid, the death of His own person, had infinite value. It is an easy jump from that great value to the notion that His death was for all men in the broadest sense.

But that jump is not so easy when you see that the stress in redemption words is on the first part of the definitions, on the freedom and on the acquiring.[2]

If Christ freed men *at the cross*, and acquired men *there* – if the *Bible* speaks in this way, and it does – then definite men must have been in mind. That clearly makes His redemption, etc., *particular* and not general.

Finally, let me address you personally. I hope I have not left the idea in your mind that the subject of this book is a mere *academic* matter. This question is not something to be tossed about in one's mind as a mental exercise. God forbid that you think of it like that!

No, my friend, you must learn whether Christ died for *you*. If He didn't die for your sins then you will suffer and die for them – forever.

But I have good news for you. God has not told you to sit and wonder whether Christ died for you. He has not told you to try to search out whether or not you are one of God's elect.

---

[2]So much is this the case with two of these Greek words (*apolutrosis* and *lutrosis*), that J. Armitage Robinson has written in his commentary on Ephesians, p. 148, [In these two words in the New Testament] 'the idea of emancipation is dominant, and that of payment seems wholly to have disappeared.' We need not agree with him entirely, but the fact that he seriously argues in this way shows where the emphasis lies in the judgment of a widely respected scholar.

What has He told you?

God has told you to turn from your sin and to trust in Jesus Christ to make you right with God.

Will you lay down your arms (repent)?

Will you turn to God through Christ (believe)?

If you will not do these things, then you could receive no benefit from the death of Christ even if He had died for a million worlds like ours.

If, on the other hand, you *will* turn from your love of sin and cast yourself on Christ's mercy, He will receive you.

Then you may be sure that you are one of those for whom Christ died!

May the Lord help you!

Appendix 1: *The Use of Universal Terms*

Almost every page of the Bible – literally – will supply instances of universal terms used in a restricted sense. If you have not noticed this, it will help you to do so when you are interpreting both the Old and New Testaments. You will soon find that such terms are *normally* restricted.

Let me cite several reasons why this is so:

First, though we are not usually conscious of it, the figure of speech called synecdoche is very common in both English and Greek. *Synecdoche* is the figure in which a part is put for the whole or the whole is put for a part.

We may say, for instance, 'Mr Jones now has a pulpit,' when we mean that Mr Jones is now the pastor of a church. A pulpit, of course, is part of a church building. In this case a part is put for the whole.

Again someone may say, 'Get your lazy bones over here!' when they mean simply, 'Come here!' Your bones, of course, are a part of yourself.

The Greek of Acts 27:37 says literally, 'And all the souls in the ship were two-hundred and seventy-six.' But 'souls' here represents entire persons. The New American Standard Bible reads: 'And all of us in the ship were two hundred and seventy-six persons.' The New International Version captures the same idea with the words, 'Altogether there were 276 of us on board.' Both versions recognize that the part – soul – was put for the whole – person.

Our chief interest in synecdoche is in the form where

the whole is put for the part. Here's an example that you can perhaps identify with. Where I live we say, 'Cincinnati won today, but Chicago lost.' In the summertime that means, 'The Cincinnati baseball team won a game today, while the Chicago baseball team lost.' In the winter you can insert the word 'football' where I have written 'baseball'. In both cases we describe a part of the city, its baseball or football team, by speaking of the whole city, Cincinnati or Chicago.

The most common biblical examples of synecdoche in this sense – the whole put for a part – are found in the uses of words like 'earth' and 'world'. Psalm 9:8 says: 'He will judge the earth in righteousness; he will govern the peoples with justice.' In the first half of the verse 'the earth' is put for a part of it, its people.

Something similar is in Psalm 67:7, where we read, 'God will bless us, and all the ends of the earth will fear him.' Here 'the ends of the earth' stands for the scattered peoples of the earth.

In Psalm 33:8 we read, 'Let all the earth fear the Lord.' The parallel phrase in the second half of the verse shows what the psalmist means: 'Let all the people of the world revere him.' 'The earth' stands for a part of the earth, 'the people of the world.' You will find other instances in Psalm 66:1, 4; Isaiah 13:11; Habakkuk 2:20 and many other places in the Old Testament.

When we come to the New Testament we find much the same thing, especially with the word 'world'. All scholars recognize that the phrase 'the world' is often put for just a portion of its inhabitants, the wicked. In John 17:14, speaking of His disciples, Jesus says, 'I have given them your word and the world has hated them.' Here the world stands for unsaved men. In John 17:25 the Lord Jesus says to His Father, 'The world does not know you,' meaning 'unconverted men do not know you.'

Even the phrase 'the whole world' can mean just the wicked part of mankind. 1 John 5:19 shows this: 'We know that we are children of God, and that the whole world is under the control of the evil one.' Here John contrasts a part of mankind, the children of God, with another part that he calls 'the whole world.'

These verses show that the figure, synecdoche, is also found in the New Testament. They illustrate the use of the whole – 'the world' or even 'the whole world' – for a part of mankind. In these verses, that *part* is wicked, but in principle there can be no objection to the same figure being used for the righteous part of men. In chapter 9 I showed that there are instances where 'world' means 'the godly' or 'believers' or 'saved Gentiles' (*see pp. 51ff.*). I tried to cite the instances that cannot be doubted, but there are others. Let me discuss a few of them here.

In the main body of the text I cited John 6:33 as an example of 'world' used for 'believers'. Jesus there speaks of Himself as the one who 'gives life to the world.' But, of course, He only gives life to believers, so that 'the world' there means 'believers'. It is only reasonable to think that it is the same 'world' that he has in view when a few verses later (*6:51*) He speaks of 'my flesh, which I will give for the life of the world.' That will mean, then, that His sacrifice is for those who would believe in Him.

Another important text is 2 Corinthians 5:19. There Paul tells us, 'God was reconciling the world to himself in Christ, not counting men's sins against them.' If we had merely the first half of that statement to guide us we would be justified in asking, 'Was Christ reconciling each and every man who ever lived to God?' Surely the answer would be, 'No.' Yet it does say 'world' and we know that 'the world' *can* mean each and every person.

But the second half of the statement shows clearly who 'the world' is. It is 'the world' that does not have their sins counted against them. And who is that? It is all the men and women who are or shall be justified. Elsewhere Paul makes this as plain as it could be.

To the man who does not work but trusts God who justifies the wicked, his faith is credited as righteousness. David says the same thing when he speaks of the blessedness of the man to whom God credits righteousness apart from works:

'Blessed are they whose transgressions are forgiven,
    whose sins are covered.
Blessed is the man whose sin the Lord will never count
    against him.' (*Romans 4:5–8*)

Those who do not have their sins counted against them are those whom God justifies by faith in Christ. So 'the world' in 2 Corinthians 5:19 turns out to be that portion of the world we call 'believers.'

Let me leave synecdoche and turn to another thing that affects the way the New Testament uses universal terms. I am thinking now of the frequent use of the word 'all' to mean 'all sorts', or 'all kinds.' I have illustrated this use already on pp. 51ff., but now I want to say more about it.

The classical Greek language had at least two words that meant 'all sorts' or 'all kinds.'[1] But by the time of the New Testament they had largely passed out of use, though they both appear rarely in the Greek translation of the Old Testament. The effect of their dropping out was that the simple word for 'all' took their place.

But there is a great difference between 'all' when meant universally, and 'all kinds', which as we have seen usually means 'many kinds.' Remember that 'the love of money is the root of all evil' really means 'the love of money is the root of many kinds of evil.' There are, of course, many

[1]The words are *pantodapos* and *pantoios*. They are cited and discussed along with the simple Greek word *pas* (=‘all’) in Colin Brown, *Dictionary of Old Testament Theology*, Grand Rapids, Zondervan, 1978, vol. 3, p. 197.

more kinds of evil that we cannot trace to the love of money.

This use of 'all' for 'all kinds' also confuses the issue about the death of Christ.

For instance, we have 1 Timothy 2:4 and 2:6 that speak of God 'who wants all men to be saved and to come to a knowledge of the truth,' and of Christ 'who gave himself as a ransom for all men.' In both cases 'all men' might mean 'each and every man who ever lived.'

But that understanding is not at all necessary. Since 'all' often means 'all kinds', in both cases 'all men' can mean 'men of all kinds, all classes, or all conditions.' That is a perfectly normal way to take the phrase 'all men.'

But some people will hardly admit that. Take the book, *Elect In The Son*.[2] It was written in part to prove that Christ's ransom was not for some men only, but for each one who ever lived. At least twelve times in this book the author cites 1 Timothy 2:4 or 2:6. These citations include words like these:

> Calvin's argument that by 'all men' Paul meant only 'all classes of men' is without foundation and was only a device by which he sought to evade a simple, categorical affirmation of the Apostle which spells shipwreck for Calvin's whole system of theology. (*p.95*)
> Calvin's theology to the contrary notwithstanding, the Holy Scriptures affirm that God desires all men to be saved (*1 Tim. 2:4*), . . . (*p.97*)

At the very least, Mr Shank does not like the way John Calvin understands these two verses. He also tells us that Calvin was bent on forcing these verses into his system.

But is that fair? Let's see.

[2]Robert Shank, *Elect In The Son*, Springfield, Missouri, Westcott Publishers, 1970.

With all these citations from 1 Timothy, accompanied by such strong language, we might suppose that Shank had expounded these verses in context and shown that they had to speak of 'each and every man.' Had he done that, he would have been justified in expecting us to remember his earlier exposition.

But did he do that? No, he didn't; he seems to have done the opposite. In the only place where he discusses the context, he understands 'all men' in exactly the way John Calvin does.

Paul's statements about God desiring 'all men to be saved' are part of a discussion of prayer in which Paul says, 'I urge, then, first of all, that requests, prayers, intercession and thanksgiving be made for everyone – for kings and all those in authority . . .' (*1 Timothy 2:1–2*). Those two verses certainly seem to be looking at all classes of men, rather than at all men individually.

But how does Shank understand them (*p. 91*)? Listen!

Have we gone to our knees and buried our faces in our hands and wept before God for all men? – for the mighty and the lowly, the rich and the poor, the well fed and the hungry, the wicked and the 'good,' the responsible and the lawless, men in the Kremlin and men in Washington, the black, the white, the red, the yellow . . . all men. [The ellipsis here is Shank's.]
When once we truly have prayed for all men, . . . we may understand something more of the mercies of 'God our Savior, who desires all men to be saved and to come to the knowledge of the truth' (*1 Tim. 2:4 RSV*). [The second ellipsis is mine, and does not affect the sense.]

Here we have Shank's most extensive exposition of the context of 1 Timothy 2:4 and 2:6.

What do we find? Nothing could be plainer than this: when Shank wrote this passage he – unconsciously, no doubt – adopted the same understanding as John

Calvin, that Paul is speaking of classes of men in the context.

The evidence is twofold. First, in asking whether we have ever prayed 'for all men,' Shank goes on to list classes of men and not individuals. He does not ask, 'Have we prayed for Mary and John and Bill and Sally?' No, he asks about classes of men.

Second, he promises that once we have prayed for 'all men,' 'we may understand something more of the mercies of God.' What can this mean, unless it envisions us as praying for all classes of men? If the promise will only be fulfilled to those who pray for 'each and every man who ever lived,' we may be sure that the promise is not given to us![3]

Despite all the hard words against both John Calvin's understanding and motive, when Shank is not for the moment thinking controversially, when he is pleading for our prayers (and rightfully so!), he sees clearly enough that 'all men' in 1 Timothy 2:1 means 'men of all sorts.' Is it twisting Scripture, then, to suppose that in the immediate context (*vv.4 and 6*) it very likely means the same thing?

But there is more evidence that 1 Timothy 2:4 is looking at 'all classes of men' in the sense of 'many different kinds of people.' It is found in that phrase 'who wants all men . . . to come to the knowledge of the truth.' The fact is, God does not now, nor has He ever, provided a way for all men to hear the gospel. Even though He has commanded us to take it to as many men and women and children as we can reach, His providence never made it possible for His people to carry out that mandate.

There is more than human failure here. It will not do to say, 'The church has failed!' That is true, of course, and

---

[3]Even 'all classes' is beyond us, unless it means only 'many classes of men'! Anything more than that would require virtual omniscience.

we must never forget it. But as an answer to the problem we are talking about it is no answer at all.

I say that for two reasons. First, God knows all things. In eternity past, before man yet existed, God knew that the church would fail. If it was His serious purpose to have all men hear the gospel, He could have planned for that to be done in spite of the church's foreseen failure. But it is obvious that He did not do so. He included the church's failure within His plans, but He made no provision for each one to hear.

Second, even if the church had been utterly faithful to her Lord, she could not have taken the gospel to lands that she did not know existed. No matter how zealous the church was, she could not have, for instance, brought the gospel to North and South America before they were discovered.[4]

Taking everything into consideration, then, it seems best to understand Paul in this way: 'God wants all kinds of men to be saved' and to that end 'Christ gave Himself as a ransom for all kinds of men.' That makes good sense out of the Greek text and it accords with the rest of the New Testament on the subject. It is also in keeping with Paul's commission from the Lord. Speaking on Christ's behalf, Ananias told Paul, 'You will be his witness to all men of what you have seen and heard' (*Acts 22:15*). Paul did not witness to every man who ever lived or to every man who was his contemporary. But he did witness to 'all kinds of men' including kings and other men in authority.

Finally let me say one more thing about universal terms. Occasionally you meet someone who thinks that the meaning of these terms was a settled matter until the

---

[4]Some have looked at the phrase 'God wants all men . . . to come to a knowledge of the truth', and have found in the word 'wants' something less than the purpose of God, a desire of sorts that might apply to all men individually. This does not seem to me to fit the context as well, but the idea is not impossible in itself.

reformers of the sixteenth century came along. When they hear one of us speak of the 'world for whom Christ died,' for example, they feel that only recent controversy could have caused men to use such terminology.

It may be useful, then, to see what some writers of the early centuries understood by a word like 'world'. Here are some quotations from before the time of Pelagius and Augustine, the men who first clashed on these questions extensively.

The Martyrdom of Polycarp is usually dated between 150 and 180 A.D. In it the church at Smyrna speaks of our Lord as one who 'suffered for the salvation of the whole world of those being saved.'[5] Here Christ is spoken of as having a world of His own that He is bringing to Himself.

Origen, who died about 254 A.D., having cited 2 Corinthians 5:19, wrote: 'Of the world of the church this is written.' Just after that he cites John 1:29 where Christ is said to be the Lamb of God, that takes away the sin of the world,' as illustrating the same truth. (Gill, p. 246)

In the same work on the Gospel of John he writes, 'Let the church be called "the world," because it is enlightened by the Savior,' citing Matthew 5:14; John 1:29; 1 John 2:2 and 1 Timothy 4:10 to be understood in the same way. (Gill, p. 246)

Cyril of Jerusalem (died, 386) speaks of 'the world of men who believe in Him that was crucified.' (Gill, p. 256)

Last of all, the famous Ambrose of Milan (died, 397) writes: 'The people of God hath its own fulness. In the elect and foreknown, distinguished from the *generality of*

---

[5] J. Stevenson, *A New Eusebius*, London, 1974, SPCK, p. 23, translates this (less literally in my judgment): 'who . . . suffered for the salvation of them that are being saved, throughout the whole world.' You may find the Greek text in both John Gill, *The Cause Of God And Truth*, Grand Rapids, 1980, Baker, p. 243, and John Owen, *The Works Of John Owen*, London, 1967, Banner of Truth, vol X, p. 422. The rest of my examples will be from these volumes of Gill or Owen and be marked accordingly.

all, there is accounted a certain *special universality*; so that the whole world seems to be delivered from the whole world, and all men to be taken out of all men.' (Owen, p. 423)

Here, what I have called 'the new nation' or 'the family,' Ambrose calls 'the whole world.' Those who are inclined at first to be doubtful about this language must remember that one day there will be an entire 'world' that is under the domain of Christ, the new heavens and the new earth. Its people will be the world of the redeemed. As God both saved the world of mankind and destroyed them at the flood, so now Christ by His Spirit is saving the world of a new mankind while preparing the world's destruction.

Appendix 2: *The Time of Redemption*

Some of the confusion about the identity of the people for whom Christ made atonement seems to me to arise from a conceptual problem: How could I have been redeemed and reconciled to God and have had God's wrath turned away from me before I was born and before I was born again?

The thing seems impossible. And even if it is not impossible in itself, it is clear that there was a time when I was unredeemed and unreconciled to God. There was a time when 'like the rest, we were by nature objects of wrath' (*Ephesians 2:3*).

If it were not for this problem the words that describe the death of Christ should have settled the issue long ago. Even though universal terms like 'all' and 'the whole world' come in for most of the discussion, this other problem, I am convinced, also keeps up the disagreement.

Scholars on all sides realize the restrictions that often accompany universal terms. It is a commonplace of theology, for example, to say, 'All' may mean 'all without exception' *or* 'all without distinction.' Some, perhaps, have not noticed that the restricted use is the rule, the common use. But that can be easily shown, and when it is, the conceptual problem still looms so large that there seems to be no way around it.

In chapter eight I have tried to show the solution in simple terms. Here I want to go into greater detail.

First let me point out that the problem is not peculiar to

the subject of the extent of the atonement. Here are some questions that will bring other examples to light:

(1) When are or were Christians saved?
(2) When are believers adopted into God's family?
(3) When did Christ die for sinners?
(4) When were demonic powers disarmed?

This is just a sampling of the questions that we could ask.

Let us take the first question, when are Christians saved? Someone may answer, 'At the moment they believe!' And that is a biblical answer. The promise is: 'Believe in the Lord Jesus, and you will be saved' (*Acts 16:31*). In answer to such faith exercised by a sinful woman, the Lord Jesus said, 'Your sins are forgiven . . . Your faith has saved you; go in peace' (*Luke 7:48,50*). We might also cite Ephesians 2:8 that speaks of salvation in the past tense: 'For it is by grace you have been saved, through faith.' Every believer in Christ is already saved.

But is that true? Yes, but – Consider these verses!

Watch your life and doctrine closely. Persevere in them, because if you do, you will save both yourself and your hearers. (*1 Timothy 4:16*)
So Christ was sacrificed once to take away the sins of many people; and he will appear a second time, not to bear sin, but to bring salvation to those who are waiting for him (*Hebrews 9:28*).
All men will hate you because of me, but he who stands firm to the end will be saved. (*Mark 13:13*)

These verses treat salvation as a thing of the future!

There is no contradiction here. Let me show you why.

The New Testament looks forward to the glorious day when the Lord Jesus will come to bring fiery judgment and wrath on this earth. That coming to judgment is called 'the blessed hope' of the Christian (*Titus 2:13*). How can that be? Paul's answer, looking toward that day, is this: 'God did not appoint us to suffer wrath but to receive salvation through our Lord Jesus Christ' (*1 Thessalonians 5:9*).

He makes the same point to the Romans: 'Since we have now been justified by his blood, how much more shall we be saved from God's wrath through him!' (*5:9*). So, salvation is really future!

But it is treated as present because it is *certain* to all who believe. Let a man believe in Christ and his salvation from the coming wrath is as certain as the faithfulness of God! Hence, in a real sense, he is already saved.

The situation is much the same with adoption or sonship. In this case sonship is already true of the Christian and that fact ensures that it will be finally true in the fullest sense (*cf. Romans 8:22–23 with 8:14–16 and with Galatians 4:4–7*). Sonship, then, is spoken of as both present and future. The revealed purpose of God makes future sonship certain.

But let me come to the questions that are related to Christ's atonement.

When did Christ die for sinners? The answer seems straightforward: Christ died for sinners in the 1st century A.D. during the term of Pontius Pilate, governor of Judea. No Christian will want to argue with that answer.

Many expositors, however, following the understanding of the translators of the AV and the NIV, find Christ spoken of as 'the Lamb that was slain from the creation of the world' (*Revelation 13:8*). If that is the correct translation – and it is the most obvious way to understand the Greek – what can it mean?

No doubt it looks at God's purpose to offer His Son. Peter speaks of 'a lamb without blemish or defect,' and says of Him, 'He was chosen before the creation of the world, but was revealed in these last days for your sake' (*1*

Peter 1:19–20). The purpose of God rendered the sacrifice of Christ so certain that it was *as if* it had been carried out when God purposed it, before He made the world.

Let us look at the last question I proposed above, 'When were demonic powers disarmed?' The answer: 'Having disarmed the powers and authorities, he made a public spectacle of them, triumphing over them by the cross' (*Colossians 2:15*). What a grand truth: In dying Christ disarmed our foes; the war is won!

Is that true? Yes, but –

Paul does not always speak that way. 'Our struggle,' he writes to the Ephesians, 'is not against flesh and blood, but against the rulers, against the authorities, against the powers of this dark world and against the spiritual forces of evil in the heavenly realms. Therefore put on the full armor of God . . . ' (*6:12–13*).

Is it time to take our armor off, because Christ has disarmed our spiritual foes? Or is it time to put our armor on, because we are under their attack? Which is it?

Right now it is time to put (keep) our armor on, but that is not the whole truth. We must also remember that the ultimate defeat of the foe was rendered certain by the death of Christ. The purpose of God in the death of Christ to disarm our foes is so certain that it is *as if* it had been carried out when Christ died. He triumphed at the cross!

These last verses, it seems to me, are exactly parallel to our redemption in the death of Christ. As we have seen, the Scriptures speak of redemption and reconciliation and propitiation as taking place when Christ died. And that is the way they speak of our foes being disarmed. In each case the reason is the same. The cross of Christ rendered the salvation of each of His elect certain, just as it guaranteed the destruction of each of His (and our) spiritual foes.

Now if Christ had redeemed all men at the cross, then all men would be saved. We cannot speak of a real redemption at the cross that is for all men, unless we believe that all men will be redeemed. We could speak of the cross as making redemption *possible*, or as making reconciliation *possible*, but that is simply not the way the New Testament speaks.

In calling the death of Christ a redemption and reconciliation and propitiation, the New Testament does not make these things possible for some. It makes them certain for all for whom Christ died.

Finally let me say a word about a misunderstanding of this truth that seems to be harbored by some who do not accept it. They seem to fear that if they were to accept the fact that Christ redeemed and reconciled His elect at the cross, they would be forced to deny that regeneration and faith are necessary for salvation.

'If Christ's death renders salvation certain, then men will be saved whether they are born again and believe or not,' they seem to be saying to me. 'After all, "certain" is "certain" and so nothing else is needed.'

Since this objection has arisen more than once, I want to spend some time on it.

Let's see it in the words of one of its proponents, Robert Lightner:

> Even though those who accept the limited view pay lip service to the need for faith, the fact remains that if their view of the design of the atonement is true, faith is meaningless and without purpose.[1]

Lightner's mentor, Lewis Sperry Chafer, has similar remarks in his *Systematic Theology*.

An objection parallel to this is often heard against the

[1] Robert P. Lightner, *The Death Christ Died*, Schaumburg, Illinois, Regular Baptist Press, 1967, p. 124.

doctrine of election: 'If the elect are going to be saved, it is unnecessary to preach the gospel to them.'

The answer seems to be the same in both cases: the purpose of God renders the salvation of His people certain, but it tells us nothing about how He will reach the goal of actually bringing them to Himself.

In the same way, each step in the process may be said to render their salvation certain, without at all making the following steps unnecessary. If all this sounds a little heavy, it will seem simpler when we look at the actual case in point.

Let us go back to Paul's Golden Chain and at the appropriate place insert the death of Christ. Here are the links as found in Romans 8:29–30: foreknowledge, predestination, calling, justification and glorification.

Now, where shall we place the death of Christ? For us today it would have to fall between predestination and calling. The result looks like this: foreknowledge, predestination, death of Christ, calling, justification and glorification.

Let me ask some questions. Does God's foreknowledge render salvation certain? Yes, it does. Does God's foreknowledge make His predestination – the next link in the chain – unnecessary? Surely not. One might make up a theoretical scenario in which God jumped from election to glorification, but that was not God's purpose as Paul explains it.

We move to the next link. Does God's predestination render salvation certain? Yes, it does.

But someone may say, 'It was already certain!' And so it was! But God purposed that it would not be accomplished without His predestination. So predestination was necessary in order for men to be saved *and* predestination made their salvation certain.

We move further. Does predestination make the death

of Christ – the next link in the chain – unnecessary? Not at all. Again, in an imaginary scenario it might. But not in the plan of God that Paul gives us. In God's real plan the death of Christ is necessary.

So let's take the following steps all together. Does the death of Christ render calling and justification and glorification unnecessary? Not in the least! Yet they would never have come to pass if Christ had not died. On the other hand, since He died they are rendered certain!

And we must add one more thing. Somewhere in that chain faith must come in, because that is God's way of bringing men to justification. The death of Christ does not make faith unnecessary. In God's real plan – not one we might concoct if we were in His place – the death of Christ makes faith certain. Had Christ not died, the rest of the links, including justification, would never have taken place. But Christ *did* die and, therefore, God's plan could move forward.

If we put in the chain all the items we have talked about, it will look like this: foreknowledge, predestination, death of Christ, preaching of the gospel, calling, faith, justification and glorification. Each is necessary; each renders the following links certain. Yet none can be left out.

We who believe that Christ was a sacrifice for His people's sins, *and theirs alone*, do not simply pay 'lip service' to the necessity of faith. We believe that the entire plan of God would fail without it!

But then we also believe that God's purposes can never fail. They are as immutable as God Himself!

Appendix 3: *The Greek Word for Purchase*

The New Testament uses several words to indicate the idea of buying or purchasing. My object in this appendix is to show that the word used several times in connection with the death of Christ does not mean simply to put down a price but actually to gain possession of something.

A related object will be to examine how this idea is treated by several writers who do not believe in Christ's death for His elect alone.

The word under discussion is, in Greek, *agorazo*. According to the standard New Testament Greek lexicon, Arndt and Gingrich, its meanings are 'buy' and 'purchase'. Both of these words in English mean, of course, 'to acquire ownership by paying a price.' You can confirm this by consulting any standard English dictionary. But that is hardly necessary, since no one, as far as I am aware, disputes this definition.

But in some discussions of *agorazo*, this simple fact soon gets overlooked. Lewis Sperry Chafer, for example, says concerning *agorazo* in its connection with the buying of slaves, 'Its technical meaning implies only the *purchase* of the slave, but does not necessarily convey the thought of his *release* from slavery.' And again, 'There is, then, a redemption which *pays the price*, but does not of necessity *release* the slave . . .'[1]

[1]Lewis Sperry Chafer, *Systematic Theology*, Dallas Seminary Press, Dallas, 1948, vol. 3, p. 192. Italics are Chafer's.

There seems to me to be some confusion here. The first statement I quoted above is true, but not, I think, in the way Chafer takes it. A man might indeed *purchase* a slave without releasing the slave from bondage. He might purchase the slave for the specific purpose of keeping the slave in bondage to himself, the purchaser. That happened in slave markets all the time. But what remained true in such transactions was this: *the slave was always released from his previous master by such a purchase*.

There are times when the New Testament represents Christians as being precisely in that situation. We were bought out of slavery to sin and Satan, but we are now the slaves of Christ.

But the second quotation from Chafer, above, suggests that this is not the situation he was thinking of as he wrote. That statement suggests something quite different, *the payment of the price without acquiring ownership*. If that is what he means, he has simply departed from the definition of the word. *Agorazo* means 'to buy' or 'to purchase,' not simply to put down a price.

Robert Lightner seems to reflect the same shift of meaning in his discussion of redemption words, including the word *agorazo*.[2]

He starts off with the following excellent statement about *agorazo* and related words: 'Though various words are used in Scripture to convey the idea of redemption, the basic meaning remains the same – freedom by the payment of a price.'

But he immediately begins to reduce the meaning of *agorazo* to the payment of the price, without the main idea of freedom. In commenting on 2 Peter 2:1, he says, 'The purchase price of redemption was paid by the Lord for even the false prophets and teachers . . . ' And again,

[2]Op. cit., pp. 74ff.

concerning the same men, 'They are the very ones for whom Christ paid the purchase price.'

Whatever 2 Peter 2:1 may mean – and it is a problem text for those like myself who believe that Christ died for His own alone – it is evident that Lightner has perhaps unconsciously changed the meaning of *agorazo*. He has given up the idea of purchase, with its attendant notion of acquiring ownership, and has reduced the meaning to the putting down of a price.

Nor is this a slip of the pen. He writes again on p. 77, 'Christ paid the ransom price even for those who deny Him.' And once more on p. 91, 'Christ by His death redeemed or paid the price for sin.' Here he seems to equate redemption with the bare payment of a price.

In light of what we have seen, it is difficult to see how Lightner can also quote with approval on p. 78, the following statement: 'Christ's death constituted an act of purchase in which the sinner is removed from his former bondage to sin by payment of the ransom price.'

If this is so – and it is – Christ's death is something far more glorious than the payment of a price that may leave millions still in bondage to sin. As we have seen throughout this study, Christ's death is emancipation. That shows beyond doubt that His atonement was only for those who actually come to experience liberty.

Appendix 4: *Who Are the 'Many' for Whom Christ Died?*

In a carefully prepared study of the work of Christ I came across the following statement on the meaning of the cross:

> [Jesus] is the ransom provided by God, for He bears death on behalf of the many that they may be redeemed from destruction. He acts as their substitute in doing for them what they could not do for themselves. He performs an act of universal significance, for it has been convincingly shown by J. Jeremias that 'many' is a Hebrew figure of speech for 'all'.[1]

It has not been too many years since a defense of 'substitutionary atonement' was considered by many (at least in America) as anachronistic and suitable only to the 'fundamentalist' mentality. But here was the recognition of the Lord's vicarious work without apology or embarrassment in the writing of a recognized British scholar. And that is cause for rejoicing, especially since it is now no isolated phenomenon.

What caught my eye, however, was the last sentence that I have quoted. I wanted to read the article in which J. Jeremias had convincingly shown 'that "many" is a Hebrew figure of speech for "all".' A footnote directed me

[1] I. Howard Marshall, *The Work of Christ*, Grand Rapids, Zondervan, 1969, p. 42

[137]

to it, and I felt immediately grateful for having had it pointed out to me.[2]

Let me explain why. One common frustration of those of us who believe that Christ atoned for the sins of particular people is that this particularity is often ignored in places where we might reasonably expect a discussion of it. To go no further afield, I might mention the excellent books by Leon Morris on our Lord's atonement. It seems to me that I can recommend these almost without qualification. But then I must add a caveat: the question of the extent of the atonement is largely (entirely?) ignored in these works. That is the case though I have no idea why.

When I turned to the article by Jeremias, however, I suddenly found myself staring at a discussion that limited itself almost entirely to the question: for whom did Christ die? I could hardly believe what I was seeing, but Jeremias opened with a fully satisfactory explanation. His assignment in the article was to discuss the theological significance of the Greek word for 'many', and he found that the main theological question bound up with the word 'many' is the question of 'the circle of men to whom the saving work of Jesus applies' (p. 536). With that understanding as a starting point he launched into his discussion, aiming eventually to show that Christ's death was not 'only for the redeemed community [but] . . . for all without limitation' (p. 543).

I have divided Jeremias' argument into six sections. Let me list them first, and then we will look at them one by one.

1. The Greek word for many (*polloi*) often has a different nuance than the Hebrew word (*rabbim*). The Greek word – when unaffected by Hebrew or Aramaic

[2] J. Jeremias in *Theologisches Wörterbuch zum Neuen Testament*, VI, pp. 536–545. I will quote the English translation, *Theological Dictionary of the New Testament*, Grand Rapids, Eerdmans, 1968, VI, pp. 536–545.

influence – is only used in an *exclusive* sense 'for many (but not all).'[3] On the other hand, the Hebrew word 'in contrast, . . . can have an inclusive sense: "the many who cannot be counted," "the great multitude," "all"' (p. 536).

2. 'This inclusive use is due to the fact that Heb. and Aram. have no word for "all."' Jeremias means that the Hebrew word for 'all' (*kol*) indicates totality or the whole, not the *sum* of the parts.

3. Isaiah 52:13 – 53:12 contains the inclusive sense.

4. Due to Hebrew influence the Greek word for 'many', both with and without the article, is often used *inclusively* in the New Testament.

5. Due to the use in Isaiah and to Hebrew influence the Greek word is used *inclusively* in four critical texts in the New Testament which then teach that Christ died 'for all without limitation' (p. 543).

6. This *inclusive* sense is original in the tradition that lies behind Mark 10:45 and 14:24, and is not an apologetic, editorial reworking.

POINT ONE

The Greek word, Jeremias says, is used as an antonym of a minority. No doubt he is correct. But only usage can tell us whether the Hebrew word is used differently. Jeremias first turns to examples of the Hebrew word as a noun with the article. He finds only two certain examples, but four others seem likely (*1 Kings 18:25; Daniel 12:3 show clear indications of the article. The others are Isaiah 53:11c, 12a; Esther 4:3; Daniel 9:27; 11:33*).

Taking 1 Kings 18:25 as his first example, Jeremias says that when Elijah speaks to the prophets of Baal he means:

[3]'Only' is my word, but it is implied in the next point which would not be a contrast without it. Note: throughout the rest of this article I shall generally use 'Hebrew' to include both Hebrew and Aramaic usage unless there is some reason to distinguish them.

'You are the great host,' that is, 'you are in the majority' (p. 537). The NIV renders this 'there are so many of you.'

But does this illustrate the *inclusive* sense that Jeremias hopes to find? On his own showing he has illustrated just the opposite. If Jeremias understands Elijah correctly, Elijah used the Hebrew word *as an antonym of a minority*. And that, he has told us, is the characteristic sense of the Greek word, *polloi*. This is not an auspicious start.

Daniel 12:3, his other example of 'many' with the article, is inconclusive. It may take in all of those who 'will awake . . . to everlasting life' (*Daniel 12:2*), but it is uncertain.

POINT TWO

What is the evidence that Hebrew has no word for 'all' that indicates *the sum of the parts*? Jeremias points out that '*kol*' is singular while 'all' is plural. But function is the acid test. James Barr, in examining '*kol*', finds that it functions the way 'all' functions in English whether with collectives ('all the sheep and goats'), with plurals ('all the men') or with singulars ('all the house').[4]

POINT THREE

Do the instances in Isaiah 53 illustrate the inclusive use of 'many'? I have agreed with Jeremias that they are inclusive. But note: they are inclusive of the group Isaiah had in view. I have shown why I believe it is the Messiah's remnant community (pp. 73ff.). So Isaiah 53 will not prove that Christ died for all men.

[4]James Barr, *The Semantics of Biblical Language*, Oxford, Oxford University Press, 1961, p. 99. He is discussing there the similar views of T. Boman.

POINTS FOUR & FIVE

Is the Greek word for 'many' used *inclusively* in key texts on the atonement? If so, do they teach that Christ died 'for all without limitation'?

We may grant Jeremias' first contention. When the Lord speaks of giving 'his life as a ransom for many,' He is speaking of giving His life for all of the group He has in mind, His elect. What Jeremias must prove is that the group Christ had in view was larger than His elect. Does he do that? Let us consider it.

He begins by framing a question:

> The question raised by these verses is whether *polloi* ['many' in Greek] is understood exclusively in Greek fashion (many, but not all) or inclusively in the sense that 'many' can have in Semitic (the totality which embraces many individuals).

That is the proper way to put the question, and I have no hesitancy to answer it. Yes, 'many' in Mark 10:45 and elsewhere is used for 'the totality which embraces many individuals.' Put that way, it tells us nothing about what group that 'totality' is. It might be a group as small as the twelve apostles (or smaller) or as large as each man who has ever lived.

But in the next sentence, apparently unconsciously, Jeremias changes the terms of the whole discussion.

> In other words [he says], does the vicarious work of Jesus avail only for the redeemed community or does He die for all without limitation? (p. 543)

Notice the subtle change here.

When he first framed the question, we were to choose between two options for the meaning of 'many': (1) some, but not all of a given group, or (2) the totality of a group. The evidence shows that we should pick (2).

But when Jeremias reframes the same question – note the phrase, 'in other words' – he presents us, not with his original selection but with two things both of which fall in the second category. The problem is this: Jeremias treats 'the redeemed community' as the representative of his first category, thus eliminating it from the discussion!

What is left, then? 'All without limitation.' Presto! Christ has died for each and every man that ever lived!

What's wrong here? Simply this: the redeemed community is a 'totality which embraces many individuals,' to use Jeremias' own phrase.

And what is the effect of this fact? Understanding Christ as having died for His elect community meets the requirement of the way 'many' is used in this and other passages (i.e., (2) above).

Incidentally, I point out in passing that Jeremias himself limits redemption to the community in his phrase 'the redeemed community.' Can the ransom take in more than the ransomed or redeemed? Or is the ransomed a larger group than the redeemed?

But Jeremias is not done. After surveying a number of passages that speak of Christ dying for 'all' or 'the world' he concludes:

> This means that the New Testament, following Semitic usage, took the *polloi* ['many'] in statements concerning the atoning work of Jesus in a comprehensive sense. Jesus died for all, for the reconciliation of the world. (p. 543)

Look at this conclusion carefully.

First, it is really two conclusions made to appear as one. We may agree that 'many' is used in the sense of the totality of some group. But, again, that tells us nothing about how large the group is. The second part, therefore, – the idea that Christ died for each and every man, which is presumably what Jeremias means by 'all' – is a different conclusion entirely.

Second, the idea that Christ died for 'all' is not at all drawn from the conclusion about the use of 'many'. It is drawn entirely from the discussion about 'all' and 'the world.' So far as the discussion of 'many' is concerned Christ could have died for any total group made up of two individuals or more.

POINT SIX

Since not many of my readers are likely to doubt that Mark 10:45 represents Jesus' words accurately, we may agree with Jeremias' point that the inclusive sense is not an editorial reworking by the author of Mark.

But in connection with this last point, as well as earlier in his article, Jeremias tries to show that 'many' in Isaiah 53 means 'all men', apparently without exception. I will not repeat my own understanding of Isaiah 53 (see pp. 73ff., above). I will briefly examine Jeremias' argument, however.

His points, with my comments, are these:

1. The second use of 'many' in Romans 5:19 is equivalent to 'all men' in Romans 5:18b. We may grant this, but it is debatable whether 'all men' in 5:18b means 'each and every man.' It *may* mean all men without exception in 5:18a, but even that is not certain. It may mean all men without distinction, i.e., both Jews and Gentiles. In any case 'all men' in 5:18b must be understood on its own. The grammatical evidence would slightly suggest a difference in the two uses.[5]

[5]Middleton's rule called *Renewed Mention* says: 'when a person or thing recently mentioned is spoken of again, the Article, as is well known, is inserted when the mention is renewed.' See C. F. D. Moule, *An Idiom Book of New Testament Greek*, Cambridge, The University Press, 2nd Edition, 1959, p. 117. The article is *not present* in Romans 5:18b.

2. Paul 'thus ascribes the greatest conceivable breadth to *hoi polloi* [the many]: Christ's obedience affects mankind in the same way as does Adam's disobedience' (p. 542). This statement is ambiguous – is mankind thought of distributively here? – but, in light of the conclusion toward which Jeremias is driving, it must mean 'Christ's obedience affects every man who has ever lived.'

Since this is a conclusion drawn from his first point, it is no more certain than that point is.

We do have a comment by Paul on this passage in the following verse where he says, 'But where sin increased, grace increased all the more' (5:20). Here Paul cannot be speaking quantitatively of the number of men redeemed by Christ, for Christ does not save more than were lost in Adam. Paul speaks here qualitatively, of the greatness of the salvation received by God's people.

Since Paul is not thinking distributively in 5:20, he may not be thinking that way in 5:18–19.

3. Romans 5:19b 'is a rendering of Is[aiah] 53:11c acc. to the Heb[rew] . . . Paul thus takes . . . Is. 53:11c inclusively: the "many" are all men . . . In his reading of Is. 53 Paul thus applied ['many' with, or without the article] without distinction to all mankind' (p. 543).

Again, this conclusion depends on the conclusion to point one, which is doubtful.

More than that, I have shown that the inclusive use can refer to Christ's community.

Still further, to speak of all mankind 'without distinction' retains the ambiguity noted at point two.

4. Finally under this heading we have Jeremias' conclusion to the whole subject. 'As we have seen, ['the many'] in Is. 53 is interpreted inclusively . . . It is taken to refer to the whole community, comprised of many members, which has fallen under the judgment of

God. There is no support for the idea that Jesus interpreted Is. 53 any differently' (p. 545).

There is no reason to dispute this conclusion as long as we retain the right to specify what community it was that had fallen under the judgment of God. Perhaps Jeremias takes it to be the whole human race, but I have shown elsewhere that that is not at all necessary. Taking the godly remnant as the community makes perfectly good sense.

My own conclusions are these:

1. Jeremias is right: 'the many' in both Greek and Hebrew can stand for the totality of a community or group, however small or large.

2. The church of Jesus Christ is such a group and can be referred to as 'the many.'

3. Marshall's conclusion, drawn from Jeremias' study, apparently needs to be modified. His words are: 'He [Christ] performs an act of universal significance, for it has been convincingly shown by J. Jeremias that "many" is a Hebrew figure of speech for "all".'

Jeremias has indeed shown that 'many' may mean 'all of a given group'. But the conclusion that Marshall has drawn that Christ 'performs an act of universal significance' is false *if* it means that Christ died for each and every man and woman. That is the way, I think, most readers would take it.

Perhaps, however, Marshall intended to find some other 'universal significance' in Christ's death. It is due him to point out that elsewhere in his chapter on the death of Christ he nowhere asserts, as far as I can see, that Christ died for every man who ever lived. In keeping with the Bible he speaks of Christ's death for 'many' or 'the many.'

Appendix 5: 'Many' and 'All Men' in Romans 5:12–20

The statements about 'many' and 'all men' in Romans 5:12–20 have caused difficulties for every student of the word of God. If we had nothing but this portion of Scripture we might suppose that Paul was saying simply:

(1) all men have been lost through Adam's sin, and

(2) all men will be saved through Christ's obedience.

In fact, of course, some people have held this very view. They are called universalists because they look for universal, all-encompassing salvation, that will leave no one out. But most Christians have felt that this optimistic reading of Paul is inconsistent with most of what the Bible teaches about the destiny of the lost. So we must seek to understand Paul in another way.

The problem I must discuss is not with (1) above. Most who are reading this book will agree that 'all men have been lost through Adam's sin.' But if it is not true – and it is not – that all who ever lived will be saved, how does Paul use the words 'many' and 'all men', especially in verses 15, 18, 19?

Verse 15 reads:

> But the gift is not like the trespass. For if the many died by the trespass of the one man, how much more did God's grace and the gift that came by the grace of the one man, Jesus Christ, overflow to the many!

The phrase 'the many' appears twice in this verse. Whom do these words refer to? Let us look at the possibilities:

(1) In both cases they refer to all men, *or*

(2) the first case refers to every human in Adam, but the second case refers to all who are in Christ, *or*

(3) in both cases they refer to those who are in Christ. Which is it?

It is very hard to choose between these possibilities. If we take choice (1) and we are not universalists it seems to me we must water down the 'gift that came by the grace of the one man, Jesus Christ.' That gift, according to verse 16, brings justification with it. It is the gift of right-eousness, i.e., of right-standing with God (*5:17*); it is the gift of eternal life (*6:23*).

To whom does such a gift come? It comes to believers alone. To make 'the many' mean 'every man' here reduces the gift to something less than eternal life or justification before God. This understanding makes Paul draw a weakened contrast between Adam and Christ. Adam's sin brought death, but Christ's obedience brings only the *possibility* of life.

Choice (2) seems better. In essence it says: Adam's sin brought death to his group, 'the many,' who included all the human race; Christ's obedience brings life to His group, 'the many,' who include all who shall ever believe in Him.

The advantage of this understanding is that it recog-nizes that Adam and Christ appear in Scripture as the heads of two great races of men. Adam heads the human race and Christ heads the race or family or nation of the redeemed. In this understanding the 'gift' can be given its full force as the gift of eternal life to all of God's people.

The problem with this view is that the exact phrase 'the many' is made to refer to two different groups. The problem is not insuperable. Choice (2) may be correct.

Choice (3) above, however, seems to me to retain the strengths of the other two choices without their difficulties. This understanding says that Paul is speaking of the redeemed in both sides of his comparison. The many who die and the many who are given life are both the same group, God's elect.

In this understanding Paul announces at the beginning of verse 15 that he is now going to emphasize the gift. Since he will do that, the following statement will be about those who receive the gift. What can he say about them, about those whom he calls 'the many'? Two things. First, they all died by Adam's trespass and, second, they all receive the gift of life by Jesus Christ.

In recent years, many commentators have felt that when Paul uses the phrase 'the many,' he is echoing the language of Isaiah 53 where the Servant of the Lord is said to 'justify many' (*v. 11*) and to bear 'the sin of many' (*v. 12*). Due, in part, to Jeremias' article on 'the many' in which he concludes that Isaiah refers to all men, they have concluded that Paul uses the same phrase to mean each member of mankind. But I have tried to show in Appendix 4 that Jeremias drew the wrong conclusions from his own evidence. I have also given on pp. 73ff. my own understanding of Isaiah's standpoint. Isaiah speaks for a future remnant, God's elect. They are 'the many' for whom the Servant dies. 'The many' is the Servant's community, just as at Qumran 'the many' was the community of those who produced the Dead Sea Scrolls.

The same three choices are before us in verse 19 where Paul writes:

> For just as through the disobedience of the one man the many were made sinners, so also through the obedience of the one man the many will be made righteous.

Choice (1), however, could hardly apply here unless,

again, we are universalists. Choices (2) and (3) are both possible, but for the reasons I gave above I prefer (3).

Finally we must look at verse 18 where Paul has 'all men' on both sides of the comparison:

> Consequently, just as the result of one trespass was condemnation for all men, so also the result of one act of righteousness was justification that brings life for all men.

Who are 'all men' here?

The first part of the verse offers little trouble whether we think of all men without exception – the most likely meaning in the minds of many commentators, since Paul seems to be resuming his indictment from verse 12 – or all men without distinction.

But who are the 'all men' in the second clause? Here are the possibilities:

(1) All men absolutely, meaning that all men and women will be justified.

(2) All men absolutely, meaning that provision has been made for each man and woman *to be offered justification*.

(3) All men without distinction, i.e., some of each kind.

(4) All men who belong to Christ.

Each of these has its difficulties.

Choice (1) is universalism, which we feel forced to reject on the grounds of its inconsistency with the rest of Scripture.

Choice (2) retains the parallel use of 'all men', but seems to break the parallel between what Adam has done and what Christ has done. Adam brings condemnation, but Christ brings only the *possibility* of life, not life itself.

Choice (3) breaks the connection with verse 12 unless it too is to be understood of all men without distinction.

Choice (4) breaks the parallel use of 'all men' within the verse.

The meaning is further complicated by the grammar of the verse, which contains no verbs. I very tentatively choose (3) above. My reasons are:

(1) The distinction between Jews and Gentiles was very much in Paul's mind in Romans. Hence he was likely to think in those terms when dealing with the condemnation of mankind. It is true that all men distributively have sinned and been condemned with Adam, but it is striking that Paul deals with these groups individually in developing his indictment against the whole race in chapters 2 and 3.

(2) The assumption that Paul means 'all men without exception' in verse 12 when he says 'all sinned' may need to be reexamined. Barring the case of the Lord Jesus, each and every man *has* sinned, but that does not mean that Paul had to have that fact in view. In 3:23 where the same phrase in Greek occurs ('all have sinned' – NIV), Paul does not appear to have each and every man in mind, though that is the way the verse is often taken. It is preceded by 'There is no difference.' That apparently means 'there is no difference between Jew and Gentile' (*cf. 10:12a*). Hence 'all have sinned' would mean 'both Jews and Gentiles.'

If the way the NIV connects vv. 23 and 24 is correct, making 'all' the subject of the verbs 'sinned' and 'are justified,' a further restriction may be in his mind. The 'all' would then refer only to 'believing Jews and Gentiles.' The grammar here too is difficult, but it seems fairly certain that the classes, Jew and Gentile, are what Paul is thinking of in 3:23. Perhaps, then, he has the same groups in mind in 5:12. In that case both sides of the comparison in 5:18 would refer to Jews and Gentiles when it says 'all men.' No argument could be made for a distributively universal reference to all individuals in verse 18b. That, in turn, means that it does not teach that Christ died for every man who ever lived.

Appendix 6: *Some Thoughts on Terminology*

Through most of the book I have avoided giving the work of Christ a special, all-encompassing name beyond the general name of atonement. The reason is this: there does not seem to be a name that makes clear both what Christ did and for whom He did it.

Historically many have spoken of *particular redemption*. The point has been to say that Christ died with particular people in mind, His elect. Those who have opposed this point of view have argued for *general redemption*. They have meant that Christ died to redeem men generally, that is, all the men and women and children who have ever been born into this world.

Another tag has been *limited atonement*. This name has a couple of perceived advantages. From the point of view of those who agree with it, it fits tidily into the TULIP acrostic:

*T*otal depravity
*U*nconditional election
*L*imited atonement
*I*rresistible grace
*P*erseverance of the saints

These are the so-called Five Points of Calvinism.

Some, on the other hand, who do not agree also like the title *limited atonement* perhaps because it is easier to ridicule. In speaking of Christ's work as somehow 'limited' it is simple to make those who hold to a limited atonement appear to take something away from the death of Christ.

It has often been shown that that is unfair. It is true that some of us limit the extent of the atonement. But we do it because we believe in its power, in keeping with what we perceive to be the teaching of Scripture. We believe that the atonement decribed in the Word of God is so powerful that it renders certain the salvation of all for whom it was offered.

Our opponents disagree. They believe that the death of Christ encompasses all men. But then they must limit its power or be universalists. So both sides have a 'limited' atonement.

Once more, some have opted for the name *definite atonement*. This puts the shoe on the other foot; does anyone want to defend an indefinite atonement?

As you have seen in the text, I have usually avoided this terminology, but I offer these explanations so that readers can make up their minds for themselves.

There is another matter of terminology that is also relevant to this subject. It is tied up with the relation of what Christ did on the cross and what He does in believers.

Historically theologians have spoken of 'impetration' or 'accomplishment' when they have referred to what Christ did on the cross. They have tended to use 'application' to refer to what is done for men when they come to Christ.

The word 'impetration' meant the obtaining of good things by Christ for His people. It is unfamiliar to almost everyone, but it was perhaps useful in its day. I say 'perhaps' for reasons that will become evident shortly.

More recently we have heard of redemption accomplished and applied. This, of course, is the title of the excellent book by John Murray on the subject of salvation.[1]

[1] John Murray, *Redemption Accomplished and Applied*, Banner of Truth Trust, Edinburgh and Carlisle, 1979.

We may ask the question: Should the atonement be divided in these ways? It appears that those who do not believe in particular redemption were the first to use these divisions, so that they might hold to the work of Christ as general in one respect and particular in another. He died for all, in this view, but all do not receive the benefit of what was done for them.

The Remonstrants, men in seventeenth-century Holland who denied that Christ died only for the elect, used this distinction in their Acts of Synod. This may have been its source, though I cannot be sure about that.

The important point to be remembered is that the death of Christ determined the salvation of those for whom He died. So much is this the case, that the re-demption, reconciliation and propitiation are said in Scripture to have happened when Christ died.

This points up the real difference between those who believe in particular redemption (limited atonement) and those who deny it. The first class hold that the power of the death of Christ is such that it will certainly produce salvation in those for whom it is offered. Their opponents hold that that is not so; if it were, all men would be saved.

The issue of terminology does raise another inter-esting side observation, however. It is simply this: the death of Christ was not only a virtual redemption for those who would come after Him, but it was in large measure – barring glorification which is yet future – the actual redemption, reconciliation and propitiation for those who were already believers at the time He died.

This explains, no doubt, the backward reference of a text like Romans 3:25 where God is said to have offered Christ to 'demonstrate his justice, because in his forbear-

ance he had left the sins committed beforehand unpun-
ished.' They were now punished in Christ and the wrath
of God was turned away from believers who had lived
'beforehand'.

Appendix 7: *Repentance and Faith*

Unfortunately, in discussing what men must be commanded to do, it is easier to agree on the words 'repent' and 'believe' than it is to agree on their meanings. I want to give my own understanding for that reason.

It seems to me that 'repent' has both a broader and a narrower sense even when we are talking about the genuine conversion of a man to God. In the broad sense it means 'to change one's mind.' An example from the Old Testament is found in 1 Samuel 15:29: 'He who is the Glory of Israel does not lie or *change his mind*.' The Greek translation, the Septuagint or LXX, uses the word for 'repent' in the phrase I have italicized. This is the word most commonly used in the New Testament for 'repent'.

Elsewhere in the Old Testament, according to the LXX, God is said to repent (*Jeremiah 18:8; Amos 7:3,6 – NIV* 'relent' in both books). The fact that God is said to repent shows that repentance had no *necessary* connection with forsaking sin.

In the New Testament the chief evidence for this broader use of 'repent' or 'repentance' lies in the fact that we often meet it where we would expect men to be called on to 'believe' or to exercise faith. In Acts 2:38, after arguing that Jesus Christ is the promised Messiah, Peter urges his audience to 'repent and be baptized' where we would expect a call to believe in the Lord Jesus. We find the same thing in Acts 3:19. In both cases I take Peter to be telling his audience to change their minds. I will discuss what they were to change their minds *about*, in a moment.

By far the most common use of repentance in the New Testament is what I have called the 'narrow' use, the use in which sin is the thing about which men must change their minds. For example, John the Baptist rebuked the Pharisees and Sadducees by demanding that they 'produce fruit in keeping with repentance,' where their bad fruit, i.e. their sins, are in view. The Lord speaks to the church of Thyatira and says, 'I have given [Jezebel] time to repent of her immorality' (*Revelation 2:21*), where she must change her mind about her sin. The point is such a radical change of mind that she will hate it, and thus forsake it.

The same idea is in Acts 8:18ff., where Simon supposes he can pay Peter for the privilege of being able to bestow the Holy Spirit. 'Repent of this wickedness,' says Peter, 'and pray to the Lord. Perhaps he will forgive you for having such a thought in your heart' (*8:22*). 'Hate this sin,' he says in effect, 'so that you will forsake it.'

Repentance in these instances is a radical change of mind with reference to sin.

Now let me return to the broader sense. In Acts 2:38 and 3:19 I take Peter to be using the word 'repent' generically to take in the two changes of mind that the gospel always calls for. In calling for repentance he is commanding men to turn from their sins (repentance in the narrow sense) and to believe God or to believe in Christ (another change of mind).

We may diagram the idea of repentance in this way:

Repentance (broad sense) = change of mind, including both

  1. repentance (narrow sense) = hatred of sin, and
  2. faith in God or Christ.

We might summarize the demand of the gospel by saying men must turn from their sin and turn to God. Together, this is repentance in the broad sense. Turning from sin is repentance in the narrow sense, and turning to God is faith. Both are necessary.[1]

[1]For my own understanding of what faith is and why repentance in the narrow sense always appears with it, see my *Faith: The Gift of God*, Edinburgh, 1983, and *The Moral Basis of Faith*, Edinburgh, 1986, both published by The Banner of Truth Trust. As I understand them, both faith and repentance are products of regeneration.

Index of Names and Subjects

Index of Scripture References

OLD TESTAMENT

NEW TESTAMENT

Index of Hebrew and Greek Words

SOME OTHER
TITLES BY THE
SAME AUTHOR

COME TO ME!

An Urgent Invitation to Turn to Christ

'Come to me, all you who are weary and burdened, and I will give you rest. Take my yoke upon you and learn from me, for I am gentle and humble in heart, and you will find rest for your souls. For my yoke is easy and my burden is light.'

These are, perhaps, the best known and most frequently heard words which Jesus ever spoke. They are read at church services, funerals and many other occasions. They are often called 'the comfortable words'. But what do they mean? What does it mean to '*come*' to Jesus? Who is he, and why should we '*come*' to him?

In this attractive presentation of the Christian faith, Tom Wells answers these questions. In an engaging style he explains who Jesus Christ is and what it means to 'come' to him. He writes honestly about the barriers which stand in the way of faith, and about the cost involved in being a disciple. But he also shows clearly that there is nothing more important we can ever do than 'come' to Christ.

ISBN 0 85151 471 5
116pp. Paperback

CHRISTIAN: TAKE HEART!

How easily and frequently many Christians become discouraged! Yet, as Tom Wells shows, even more alarming is *the reason* why some Christians are so depressed in their discipleship. The teaching they have received about the Christian life has been sadly mistaken!

Christian: Take Heart! is an antidote to bring healing to the lives of Christians impaired by wrong-headed teaching. But it is also Tom Wells' confession: 'I too have been a thief. I have stolen God's Word from his people'. His exposition of biblical teaching is all the more relevant because it is written out of a background of personal experience of its misinterpretation. The book's chapters on assurance, abiding in Christ, defeat, God's work in our lives, perseverance and security will encourage both healthy thinking and healthy living in the lives of God's people.

ISBN 0 85151 508 8
176pp. Paperback

FAITH: THE GIFT OF GOD

Two men hear the Gospel. They are from similar backgrounds. One turns to faith in Christ; the other turns away from Christ. Why the difference? Faith in the one, unbelief in the other! But how does faith come? Answers vary considerably. Some lay emphasis on God's work; others stress man's action. Many imply that a doctrinal understanding of the problem does not matter.

In this book Tom Wells shows us that it certainly matters. He invites us:

(1) to search into the Scriptures which bear on the matter, and
(2) to look back and examine our own coming to faith in Christ.

Under the blessing of the Holy Spirit this should help our whole understanding of the doctrines of God, man and salvation.

ISBN 0 85151 361 1
156pp. Paperback

A VISION FOR MISSIONS

Foreign missionary endeavour sometimes appears hesitant, even half-hearted before the problems of this age. Poverty and famine, national religious and cultural issues, and above all the weakness of the 'Christian' West, have thrown doubt on the work of missions as it was once understood.

Tom Wells writes with the conviction that Christians must come back to first principles. Human need and world conditions are not the starting point. The Gospel is a call to know and worship God, and the primary conviction of the messenger must be that God is *worthy* to be known. The missionary vision must begin with the vision of God. Only then can the Church truly respond to the command to 'declare his glory among the nations'.

This is a challenging book, and equally relevant to Christians at home or abroad. It treats missionary endeavour not as a separate interest but as basic to Christianity itself. By reference to Brainerd, Carey and Martyn the author also shows the true inspiration which lay behind the missionary movement of the 18th and 19th centuries.

ISBN 0 85151 433 2
160pp. Paperback

For free illustrated catalogue please write to
THE BANNER OF TRUTH TRUST
3 Murrayfield Road, Edinburgh EH12 6EL
PO Box 621, Carlisle, Pennsylvania 17013, USA